REACHING

Reaching

THE JOURNEY TO FULFILLMENT

Morton Kelsey

1817

Harper & Row, Publishers, San Francisco

New York, Grand Rapids, Philadelphia, St. Louis
London, Singapore, Sydney, Tokyo, Toronto

REACHING: *The Journey to Fulfillment.* Copyright © 1989 by Morton Kelsey. All rights reserved. Printed in the United States of America. No part of this book may be used or reproduced in any manner whatsoever without written permission except in the case of brief quotations embodied in critical articles and reviews. For information address Harper & Row, Publishers, Inc., 10 East 53rd Street, New York, NY 10022.

FIRST EDITION

Library of Congress Cataloging-in-Publication Data

Kelsey, Morton T.
   Reaching: The journey to fulfillment / Morton Kelsey.
     p.   cm.
   Bibliography: p.
   ISBN 0-06-064384-6
   1. Spiritual life—Anglican authors. 2. Theodicy. 3. Future
life. 4. Kelsey, Morton T.   I. Title.
BV4501.2.K4268 1989
248.4—dc20   89-45248
                                                      CIP

90 91 92 93 RRD 10 9 8 7 6 5 4 3 2

To our son John Colburn Kelsey
1954–1988
who taught us more about fulfillment
than any person we have known.

Contents

Every book is, in an intimate sense, a circular letter to the friends of the one who wrote it. They alone take his meaning; they find private messages, assurances of love, expressions of gratitude, dropped for them in every corner. The public is but a generous patron who defrays the postage.

ROBERT LOUIS STEVENSON, *TRAVELS WITH A DONKEY*

Preface

This book has taken many years to write. It began as an attempt to understand the journey toward fulfillment. My wife, Barbara, and I have been deeply involved in our separate and joint journeys for nearly forty years. We have found that our different paths diverged and then crossed one another now and then. However, they led to the same destination.

I was halfway through the manuscript when our younger son, John, was crushed by several calamities. We spent much time with him, and it was no time for creative writing. Instead, I rewrote a former book into quite a different one at the suggestion of an editor at Harper & Row, and so *Psychology, Medicine and Christian Healing* was born. Our son recovered and started a new life. We had a year of wonderful trips and times of simply being together.

Suddenly in the summer of 1988 when he was visiting us in Europe, John was stricken with a serious illness, and his condition worsened. He returned home to the Kona coast of the Big Island of Hawaii, where his condition continued to decline. He asked us to come to him immediately. We came the next day from California. We remained as his principal companions and care givers until he died in December 1988.

I was his principal companion during much of the day. Although he slept many hours, we also talked a great deal and came to know each other as we never had before. He asked me what I would have been doing if I had not been there with him. I told him of the book I had planned to complete. He suggested that I get out his typewriter and finish the manuscript; the subject was of great interest to him also. The last six chapters of this book were completed in Kona next to my son's bed, listening to the roaring of the waves outside. As I corrected the typescript, I would lie on his bed with him and read sections of it to him. When I did not keep at my work, he urged me to continue.

Chapters 1 through 5 were written in a reflective mood. The last six chapters were written as we watched our son's health decline. As he had an indomitable belief in the life after death, he had no fear of death, and his medical caretakers were very caring and kept him free from pain. He never complained, and we became closer in those three months than we had ever been before. I had already planned to write on the subjects contained in the last six chapters of the book.

However, I had not planned to deal with the necessity of such trying circumstances, nor in the indispensable need of prayer and religious ritual to sustain us facing the death of a young and gifted son. The importance of our continued work in our journey toward wholeness became patently clear to me in these stress-filled days. I had not faced the problem of evil with this kind of existential confrontation since I was a young man of twenty-one.

I had written on the subject of meditation as a way of dealing with evil, but it was from the viewpoint of dealing with my own darkness—not of dealing with disintegration and death of one I dearly loved. I had also written on the subject of life after death, but not with death staring me in the face. How much our son's faith sustained us during our periods of doubt. I finished the last chapter on utter fulfillment less than two weeks before he died peacefully in his own bed with his family around him and waves still booming against the lava rocks below his bedroom.

So many people have helped me in this writing project that it is impossible to mention all of them, but some deserve special gratitude. Barbara and I had worked and played and disagreed with each other for nearly forty-five years, yet we had never been closer than during these months during which we tried to bring as much healing and comfort as we could to our son. Never before did I realize the full measure of her strength, courage, devotion, and love.

Without the loving and skillful help of Frances Dennis we would never have been able to care for John the last four months. We also had the professional help of Stuart Warren, who was a faithful friend to all three of us and a registered nurse as well.

Our other two children came the moment that we needed them and stayed with John and with us as long as we needed them.

A constant stream of friends came from the mainland to see John and let him know how much he was loved. His friends on the island were supportive and helpful, and both these groups of people gave us renewed confidence in the ultimate power and reality of love.

Both Barbara and I had friends who kept in touch with us and gave us a place to share our pain and grief and supported us in our prayer for courage, patience, strength, love, and faith for ourselves and for an easy birth into a new life for John. Muriel McGlamery, Tom Lischwe, Bill Beargie, Andy Canale, John Vara, Margie Grace, Jack and Linny Sanford, Charlie Potter, and Betty and Robert Buffum kept in weekly contact with us during these months. They shared our burdens and gave us the strength that real friendship gives. They all encouraged me to continue this writing and complete the manuscript.

In several of the biblical passages I made my own translation of the Greek text to render Jesus' meaning more precisely and to avoid sexist language.

In the midst of a very busy life, Cindy Wesley turned my mangled manuscript into a readable typescript.

John Neary edited my manuscript under great pressure of time and helped me say precisely what I wanted to say.

This book began as a reflective meditation on the journey to wholeness. It then became a step-by-step journey through crisis to greater confidence in human dignity, in survival after death, and in the magnificence of the human person as well as a proving ground for the journey to fulfillment.

Kailua-Kona
Advent 1988

CHAPTER 1

Answering a Question

Several years ago a friend asked me a question: "What is the fulfilled life?" The question intrigued me, and I began to ponder what shape the fulfilled life might take. I was busy with other projects, but that question haunted me. I began to jot down notes about the various elements that might make up such a life. Over two years the list of jottings grew to nearly fifty items. Finally my commitments were completed, and I had free time; the nature of the person who has truly realized his or her potential demanded my attention. I could put it off no longer.

Those still young may think that reflecting on this subject at the age of three score and ten, when life is nearly over, is somewhat futile. In fact, though, I find this an excellent time for such reflection, for I have come to believe that unless life goes on beyond the grave, the whole business is futile anyway. What a marvelous time to look back over seventy years of living—forty-four years of marriage to one person and forty-two years of parenting. I began to wonder where I have gone amiss, what I have done that needs to be rectified (when possible), what I will yet become and do, what empty portions of my being yet need to be filled, what additional work yet needs to be accomplished. I don't know what chance I will have to change on the other side of life, but I do know that the future is contained in the present, and that I can still shape that future now.

I continued pondering the question of what my life is meant to be, what potential in me needs yet to be realized, what fulfillment means for us human beings. I then realized that I needed to write my reflections on the subject for myself, and that others might be interested as well. I started to write, but I could get no handle on the subject; I made several starts, but each one came to a dead end. I am well aware I am no paradigm of fulfillment. Indeed, it was my very need for more fulfillment that prompted me to reflect on this issue in the first place. I looked around at

other people that I admired in the present and past, and the only historical person who filled the bill for me was Jesus of Nazareth—and his close
relationship with the Divine was so great that he seemed beyond human
grasp. Some Christian thinking has made him look more like God than
like a human being. I needed a more down-to-earth, concrete symbol of
what fulfillment might mean.

The Redwoods: Symbols of Fulfillment

My wife, Barbara, and I live in a very special place on the wild Pacific
coast, several hours' drive north of San Francisco. Before this rugged
country was logged, magnificent redwood forests covered our valleys and
hills. Our small home is set among towering second-growth trees. The
vitality and vigor of these monarchs of the forest touch me very deeply;
I have read everything I could find about these trees. And while pondering the issue of human fulfillment, I made two trips: first to the virgin
coast-redwood forests that still stand to the north of us, and then to the
high Sierra to visit the giant redwoods, ancient cousins of the trees
among which we live. Barbara and I had not seen these giant trees in
forty years. And while we were in the high Sierra, an image came to me.
I could imagine no better example and symbol of maturing, realizing
potential, and coming to fulfillment than these majestic trees.

The coast sequoias are the tallest living things, and the giant Sierra
trees are the largest living creatures. Both have a life span that makes the
longest living member of the animal kingdom look insignificant. The
towering trees on the coast mature only after three or four hundred years,
and many live well beyond two thousand years. The great trees of the
mountains are adolescent at three hundred years, and mature only at a
thousand—and some have lived well past three thousand years. And
what is more, they begin as a seed so tiny that it takes three to six thousand of them to weigh an ounce. That kind of growth is certainly realized
potential.

In addition, these trees are one of earth's original plants. Fossil remains
of redwoods have been discovered in rocks that are one hundred fifty million years of age. They lived before flowering trees or plants emerged to
grace our earth. Dinosaurs rested and ambled under their shade. But the
dinosaurs disappeared some sixty million years ago, while redwoods
continued to be the dominant trees throughout the Northern Hemi-
sphere of earth, stretching from Western North America through Europe
to China; twenty-five million years ago these great trees blanketed this
entire area. But the world has changed, and now these trees survive in

only three places: in one out-of-the-way valley in mountainous China, and in California—along the coast, and in the high Sierra mountains. Some magnificent zest for life has enabled these long-living and gigantic trees to endure, adapting to new climates and environments. I know of no better examples of fulfilled potential. How can we human beings come to our fulfillment as these awesome trees have?

Many reflective people I have talked with are seeking an answer to the same question. My purpose here is not to argue or convince, but merely to share. The reader should approach this book as a grazing cow approaches a pasture; slowly, the cow walks munching here and there, savoring what is pleasing and tasty. The cow does not get upset or annoyed at what is distasteful or even dangerous; she just passes it by. Anyone who wants reasons or evidence for my reflections, thoughts, and conclusions should examine the books that are listed in the Selected Bibliography.

As I mulled over the fifty items I had jotted down as important in human growth, I began to see that some of them were far more crucial than others, far more important, basic, undergirding. These are my foundation stones; they are to be found in nearly all of the more than twenty books that I have written. Upon these foundations are built the superstructure of my individual, unique existence. But while the foundations of most structures are similar, the buildings differ. Likewise, we human beings share some needs in common—these make us human—but at the same time what we may erect upon these foundations can be very different. Just as one builder constructs an apartment, another a school, another a factory or a temple, a home or a store, and some construct multipurpose buildings, so human talents and lives vary widely. Indeed, each individual's particular combination of skills and preferences is one of the things that make him or her human. Each of us does not have to do the same things or to do all things well.

So I offer no final universal answers, but many suggestions. Some, I hope, will have fairly general application, but others will click only with people who are somewhat like me. Before I go on, however, to examine in depth some of the qualities that I have found fulfilling and have seen to be fulfilling in others, I will point out what I consider some of the foundations of our common humanity. This will help chart the territory that we are exploring together.

Foundations for Fulfillment

One of my first realizations, as I considered this book's topic, was that fulfillment is based not so much on how far I have developed, but on whether I am on the right path and am still following it. Those who think that they have already rounded out and completed their lives have in many ways already died. Only when we realize that we are not totally whole—no matter how old or successful or holy we may be—can we continue to grow. Then we realize that actualizing our potential is a process; it is not a goal that we can finish or complete in the here and now. Too often we have a far too limited view of ourselves and what we can be, and of the Divine and what it can enable us to become. For those who think that they are completed, finished, the hands of the clock have stopped and growth is over. Jesus, it is true, cried out, "It is finished," as he hung on the cross, but he meant only that his human task was completed. He went on to rise again—he returned to broken, defeated disciples and gave birth to a new religion of hope, and he also gave his followers the Holy Spirit to continue the work that he had begun. So even though Jesus' task as a human being was done, completed, finished, his most important transforming power was still waiting to be released among us. Indeed, throughout the Gospels Jesus praised the incomplete and unfinished, the poor in spirit, those who mourn their incompleteness and inadequacy, those who are still hungering and thirsting. Process, continued seeking, eternal growth seem to be essential to satisfy our deepest needs. What does not continue to grow usually dies.

Infinite human potential is another solid base on which our potential wholeness rests. But what is this "potential"? To understand it we need to rediscover our sense of wonder, which we too often neglect (even though we live in a physical universe that possesses awesome complexity, both within the electron and beyond the stars). I walk in a virgin redwood forest, looking hundreds of feet to their towering crests, and I feel in my hand the tiny seed from which they sprang; that is what I mean by potential. Nearly all the great religions of humankind speak of the divine potential dormant in us, and they go on to tell us how this can be released and realized.

We often fail to notice something that we are not prepared to accept; I had read the New Testament dozens of times, but it took a Jewish Jungian psychiatrist to point out to me Jesus' answer to those who accused him of blasphemy for calling himself the Son of God. As they were about to stone him, he said: "Is it not written in your own Law, I said: You are gods?' Those are called gods to whom the word of God was delivered—and Scripture cannot be set aside" (John 10:34–35 NEB). So Jesus claimed that humans have *divine* potential. Indeed one of the great ideas of Greek Orthodox theology is that as we allow the Holy Spirit to live and express itself through us, we can be divinized. Compared with this possibility, even the potential growth of redwoods is small indeed.

No two leaves on any tree are precisely the same; no two redwoods are identical. Even twins, although they emerge from the same cell, are not entirely the same: when cells divide they begin to take on their own individuality. So each human being is unique, with special abilities, goals, directions. My way is never the same as that of any other human being; what is right for another may be totally wrong for me.

Achieving my greatest possible development is a lifelong task. I must know who I truly am and what I am meant to be. Slowly my way unfolds before me, step by step. I crawl before I stand and walk. This process of letting our uniqueness develop and flower is what C. G. Jung calls the way of individuation. Each of us, in other words, has a destiny; I was not called to be Jesus or Moses, John or Andy, or anyone but Morton. I need again and again to check what I know about myself against the inner wisdom, the Spirit of God, if I am to pick my path through the dark forests and the treacherous sands. To become truly what I was meant to be is no easy task.

Once I have grasped the radical, fundamental idea that like every other human I have a uniqueness to express, a place to fill that no one else can fill as well as I, then I am led to pause and ponder, to look back, to reflect. I need to consider all aspects of my inner and outer life. (Isn't it interesting that the word "consider" originally meant to observe the stars?) Without this study, contemplation, meditation, continual attention to what I am and do, I can give myself no direction. I float along unknown currents, motivated by unknown goals, desires, impulses. Without this careful consideration, I live unconsciously, unaware. I am likely to be the pawn of fate rather than a person directing my life toward wholeness and beyond.

Of course, there is little reason to reflect unless we have some freedom to shape what we can do. But we humans do have freedom. It is an often painful freedom, though; I sometimes envy the trees that stand rooted in the ground and have little choice. They are dependent on the rain and fog, the soil, and the warmth and light of the sun. And yet some trees have learned to adapt to totally different climates, as the great redwoods of the Sierra mountains have been able to do. Others, like coast sequoia, migrated to places where the conditions remain congenial for them. Still another ancient member of that family has clung to life in an almost forgotten valley of China. Animals have more freedom but they pay a price for it—the dinosaurs and mammoths, for instance—have disappeared.

And we human beings have even greater freedom; with this freedom, however, we are faced with choices, which bring responsibilities that often seem unbearable. It is much easier to blame others for what we are than to take responsibility for ourselves.

Although we are not totally masters of our fates or captains of our souls, we do have some ability to choose. We can reflect, consider, and decide; we can make changes. Nonetheless, there are people who are so broken that they have lost hope—the very poor, the oppressed, the enslaved, the mentally ill, those who have known little love, those whom life has crushed. Freedom, then, is not an either/or proposition but a many-pointed scale. But the more I reflect, the more possibilities I see, the more I can make better choices and find greater freedom. Looking at the tangled swamp of my life, I find that I need not only my own reflection and the best wisdom of the past and of the wisest people I know, but also the inner voice of the Spirit of wisdom, who continues to dwell in the vestibule of my soul and who will guide me when I turn to her. Often I have found the path of freedom and choice painful and difficult; often I have misunderstood the inner voice, or have not listened, or have acted before I considered and made mistakes. But mistakes go hand in hand with freedom and growth. A friend, the owner of a manufacturing plant, once wrote out a list of rules for successful management. The last suggestion was particularly wise: "Forgive honest mistakes where the person making the mistake is honestly self-critical. If people are not self-critical, they must learn to be, or they can never successfully supervise others or develop to their best abilities." I even have to forgive my own honest mistakes and keep on trying to be as complete as possible.

One way of avoiding all responsibilities, however, is to take the view that the species *homo sapiens* is nothing but a mechanical and accidental material configuration of atoms and subatomic particles. If this is true, then we are fully determined to be what we are by our genes and by our conditioning. Melvin Konner writes in *The Tangled Wing* that individual men and women are nothing but the means by which physical genes reproduce themselves. B. F. Skinner stated again and again that the human physical organism is totally shaped and formed by its conditioning. Freud wrote that we are the result of blind primitive instincts and nothing more. Within these views there is no meaning, no hope, no freedom. All three would laugh at the idea of a soul; in what organ would we find it or in what part of the brain? The only human beings who can be called "responsible" are those who condition us, and they too have little choice. If we believe this, what reason could there be for us to pause, reflect, consider, or try to direct our lives? We are, in that view, nothing but a part of an inevitable physical or psychic chain of events that is slowly winding down to a deathlike inactivity. Hope and meaning, purpose and goals have little place in such deterministic theories of humanity; as far as we can discern, there is little purpose in colliding particles of matter or in blind instinct.

If we are even to think about fulfillment, about directing our lives toward wholeness and individuation, we need another view of reality. There are many others. Most Eastern religions see this physical world as illusion and assert that as we realize this we can begin to shape our souls so that we become free of the chain of karma and reincarnation. Nearly all "primitive" religions speak of powers of light and darkness, and believe that shamans who know these powers can lead us on the way of light and holiness; from this point of view we are both body and spirit, and we need to care for both. Plato believed that human beings possess an eternal dimension, a spiritual as well as physical side. Jesus told his followers to go out and preach, teach, and heal. They were to touch the souls of men and women and bring them to the hope of the kingdom of God; they were to inform and educate the minds of people, to teach them how to live according to the kingdom. They were to heal the bodies and minds of people, because our bodies and minds, as well as our souls, are important and have eternal significance. We are more than a body, Christianity says, but we are still connected to our bodies and these are sacred. (Sadly, much of Christian culture is afraid of the body; it suggests that attention to it may draw us away from God and wholeness. But from a truly Christian viewpoint, it is clear that we cannot ignore our bodies or abuse them and still come to human fulfillment.)

One of my reasons for great gratitude to Carl Jung is that he gave me a sophisticated alternative view of myself and of the world in which I live. His view had a place for a spiritual dimension of reality, for God and eternal life. He and several of his followers opened my eyes to the possibility that the view of Jesus and Christianity was a genuine option for men and women of the twentieth century. I am amazed at the number of the so-called intellectuals who remain caught in a closed system of meaninglessness. The number is shrinking, but it is still frightening. Many of them are teachers and professors in our schools and colleges. Even the University of Notre Dame had a psychology department dominated by Skinner's ideas during much of the time that I was teaching there. But if we are merely conditioned things, we cannot contribute much to our fulfillment; indeed, fulfillment is essentially a meaningless word.

Someone has described folly as a systematic resistance to our own self-interest. If there is a meaning to this world of ours, then our best self-interest requires us to search for that meaning, or we will be out of sync with the universe. We will go against its grain. We will empty ourselves rather than fill ourselves. We will be fools.

At one time I found myself without roots or meaning. Only those who have known that abyss know how hard it is to be honest and still survive. I needed to *experience* real meaning as well as have ideas about it. I found the reality of this Other as I listened to my dreams, the dark speech of the spirit, and as I was deeply quiet and listened in the dark stillness. I found a Presence that was seeking me before I knew enough to listen, and who was always available when I turned inward and paid attention. I discovered Love. I found a reality that wanted my company, one who did not judge, who loved me as I was and who would be with me whenever I invited companionship. This luminous presence had the same qualities that I found in Jesus of Nazareth when I studied his life and teachings with my blinders removed.

When such caring and guidance is available, I would be stupid if I did not avail myself of this very concrete presence of purpose, meaning, and love. I began to frame a regular time for being open and listening. I found some times more fruitful than others. I also found my nightly awakenings were times of enrichment, new insights, support, understanding, and being cared for.

Over twenty years ago I was flying home from a conference that I was leading with Tommy Tyson. I was alone on a small plane. I took out my journal and was reflecting on the time I had just spent trying to lead a group of people into a deeper knowledge of the spiritual way. I realized that I was flying not far from the home of my brother, with whom I had a mere Christmas-card relationship. Then it occurred to me that I was flying not far from the home of my father and his wife, who appeared to me a fairy-tale stepmother. When I landed, furthermore, I was to see my daughter in college, with whom my relationship had been strained since her early teens. Then out of the quiet depth of me welled forth these words: "O Divine Master, grant that I may not so much seek to be consoled as to console; to be understood as to understand; to be loved as to love." I did not know at the time where they came from, but I knew that they spoke to a deep need, an empty part of me. I realized that I had not been living in accordance with these words of Francis of Assisi, especially with my own family.

One realization after another flooded over me. First of all, I realized that the main problem in the parish of which I was rector was that people were like me. They wanted to be loved more than to love. There was no possibility that I could lead them on another path until I changed my own attitude, and I needed to start with my own family. Then, for the first time, I truly saw that emotional maturity only began when I was able to love without expecting anything in return. I had been involved in psychological study and analysis for years, but until that moment on the plane I did not see that I had been copping out, expecting others to love me before I ventured to care for them.

And then the most important insight engulfed me. I realized that the very essence of the way of Jesus of Nazareth was that of loving more than being loved. I realized that these words express the very nature of Jesus and his gospel message, the essential nature of God and of the universe itself. So if I did not try to be more interested in giving love rather than in receiving it, I was out of sync with the ultimate nature of reality. I would not be a true follower of Christ or a really developed human being until I was able to be more concerned with loving, understanding, and consoling others than with receiving love, understanding, and consolation for myself.

I have already alluded to my belief that a life that ends at the grave would be futile. And nearly all the great religions of humankind have taught that life goes on after death, that life continues after life. It amazes me, therefore, that most Western religious leaders avoid discussing an afterlife, or express no belief in the idea. For example, in Harold Kushner's recent book, *When All You've Ever Wanted Isn't Enough*, there is no suggestion that these lives of ours go on beyond the grave. Even though Kushner provides many excellent observations on the fulfilled life, he leaves me at the end of his book with no hope and with empty hands. In fact, though, there is growing nonreligious evidence that human beings *do not* cease at death. The refusal of many thinking people to look at the observable, often cross-cultural data about life beyond death is probably the result of our Western materialism, which simply has no place for any reality that is not physical.

Some people live in terrible pain that does not cease until death. Others are oppressed, tortured, and denied freedom and hope and life, and then die. We were recently in South Africa where 80 percent of the people has no say about their own destiny, and this is true of many other places as well. And then there are those who eke out a miserable existence in poverty and hunger, watching their children die. Unless there is some compensation for these lives, our own enjoyment of a satisfactory life is shallow if not heartless. As I look at the potential of the human soul, I realize that it is a mockery to think that it can be fulfilled within three score and ten years, or four score. If there is no life beyond the grave, then the life on this side of it is a bad joke indeed.

Complex Patterns

To what can we compare the fulfilled life? What does "kingdom living" look like? Such a life is certainly made up of many different parts that produce a coherent whole.

Such a life is like a mosaic with tens of thousands of pieces of stone fragments. In themselves, these pieces are meaningless colored stones, but together they can present a picture that takes our breath away. I recently saw an artist creating a monumental mosaic. It looked like nothing until she showed us a painting of what it would be; it was amazing to see what a magnificent whole these individual fragments would ultimately create.

The full life is like a tapestry, woven with hundreds of different colored threads. Remove only a few threads and the picture is marred or destroyed. When it is intact, however, the undamaged tapestry weaves together many different kinds of strands to tell a story. It can be a work of priceless art.

More prosaically, the fulfilled life is a jigsaw puzzle in which all the pieces found their place. Sometimes we understand the picture only when the last few pieces are in place.

Wholeness may also be like a deeply satisfying bread. The cook has blended many different ingredients in the right order; he or she has allowed it to rise, and then has baked it to a crisp brown.

The completed life has the mystery of a many-faceted jewel, perfectly cut. It sparkles and flashes with different colors. Sometimes it seems on fire.

Or we can return to our original picture of fulfillment—the magnificent, giant redwood. So many different elements and processes go together to enable these trees to become monarchs among living things.

The fulfilled life is almost infinitely complex. In the pages that follow, I will try to take up one element after another of what that life looks like to me. I will look at some of the most important facets of the gem, some of the important threads of the tapestry, some of the bits of stone making up the mosaic, some of the important pieces of the jigsaw puzzle, some of the most significant processes of the giant tree. Reality, however, is seldom put together in neat, logical, understandable patterns; the various elements, therefore, will overlap and sometimes seem repetitious. Some of the essential ingredients may not even appear until the end, as in a complicated recipe.

I wish I could express many different ideas at the same time, but that would be chaos. So I start with one component of the fulfilled life—the seeking, searching, zestful drive that is a quality of nearly all vital living beings.

CHAPTER 2

Seeking, Searching, Desiring

The tree has often been seen as an image or symbol of human life. It is rooted in the earth, and it stretches its branches high into the sky. On a recent visit to the giant sequoias, I stood awed before the largest known redwood, the largest living creature. This tree is thirty-five hundred years old; most of recorded human history has taken place within its lifetime. It is nearly three hundred feet high, a hundred feet around, and over thirty feet in diameter—and *it is still growing*. Each year this gigantic symbol of tenacious life adds five hundred more board feet to its girth, the equivalent of a tree fifty feet in height and a foot in diameter. This is certainly continuing fulfillment.

What zest for life this tree has! Its rootlets are capped so that they can push out into the hard soil to search for water and nutrients. These roots reach out around the tree for several hundred feet, seeking the water, phosphorous, nitrogen, potassium, calcium, sulphur, iron, and magnesium that the tree requires to supply its many needs. These far-reaching roots also provide a firm foundation for the gigantic trees. Little pumps within the sapwood drive those atomic building blocks up through the entire tree, up to the needles at the crown of the tree. There the branches reach out into the air and seek the sun.

The tiny roof-shaped needles of the giant sequoia are adapted to shed the snow. Within them the green chlorophyll takes the water and carbon dioxide from the air, as well as the water and nutrients that the roots provide, and then combines these with the captured photons of the sunlight to create the building blocks of hydrocarbons for every part of the tree. And in the process these needle-leaves, like the chlorophyll in marine plants, discharge oxygen that enables animal life to exist on the face of the earth. In redwoods living by the coast, the water vapor released by the needles precipitates the often-present fog, creates a light rain, and even adds as much as thirty inches of needed rain in the summer months. And the chlorophyll in those amazing green needles is an atomic factory capturing the sun's light and transforming it into life. This amazing substance is the ultimate source of all fossil fuel. We take far too much for granted. When we begin to understand them, those magnificent trees can fill us with a sense of wonder.

Although these trees look inert, swaying in the winds, they are alive, working, seeking, searching. If fire damages one of them or burns out its core, the tree heals itself, and gradually the sapwood and bark grow back over the wound. The trees don't give up but continue for generation after generation; animals, on the other hand, have given up length of life for mobility. Standing beneath these trees alone, deep in the forest, I feel a sense of friendly fellowship of spirit, of persistence and continuity. I understand why Jesus compared the kingdom of God to a tree: "What is the kingdom of God like? What shall I compare it with? It is like a mustard seed that a person took and sowed in a garden; and it grew to be a great tree and the birds of heaven came to roost among its branches" (Luke 13: 18–19, author's translation).

Seeking for the Kingdom

For me, the sequoia is a grand image of the importance of persistent *seeking*. The folk wisdom of nearly all people gives the same advice: seek diligently and you will find. In fairy tales we find that the seeker, no matter how misguided, is the one who obtains the princess; those who give up and cease their journey or their search are left behind. Indeed, is not the essential goal of every journey to discover, to find some treasure? This attitude is nowhere more clearly stated than by Jesus in the Gospel of Luke: "And so I say to you, ask, and you will receive; seek, and you will find; knock, and it will be opened. For all who ask receive, those who seek find, and to those who knock it will be opened" (Luke 11:9–10), author's translation).

Many of Jesus' parables picture the same truth in different ways. This statement in Luke about the necessity of seeking follows the story of the man who has a friend who comes in the middle of the night to get bread. Even if the householder will not get up because of the friendship, the continuous knocking will be annoying enough to induce him to open the door and produce the bread (Luke 11:5–13). In another context Jesus gives the same advice with a humorous and incisive story: "There was in a city a judge who did not fear God nor respect any human being, and in the same city there was a widow. She kept coming to him, saying: 'Grant me justice against my adversary.' For a long time he refused; but in the end he said to himself: 'True, I don't fear God or care about any human being. However, this widow causes me so much trouble that I will grant her justice before her persistence wears me out.'" (Luke 18:3–8, author's translation). Jesus goes on to say that if even an unjust judge will grant justice, how much more will Abba grant it. Is not prayer in essence an act of seeking the presence and the kingdom of God *now* as a foretaste of what we desire forever?

The kingdom of heaven requires dedicated seeking. Jesus makes this point very clearly by telling the story of a pearl merchant. This trader is constantly looking for the finest pearls, and one day he finds one of surprising value; he goes out and sells everything he has and purchases it. Without his seeking he would never have found his pearl, and without his single-minded effort he would never have possessed it. And Jesus also tells the story of a woman who is digging in a field. We do not know whether she was looking for treasure or just preparing the land for planting, but she stumbles on a great treasure and then buries it again in the field. She is overjoyed at her good fortune, and she goes and sells everything she has and buys that field. Had the woman sat at home grumbling about misfortune, she would never have found this treasure.

Few statements of Jesus are less understood by our adult-dominated and male-chauvinistic culture than those about children. Until recent years, little children have seldom been valued by our culture. Children have frequently been neglected and abused, and all this has occurred in "Christian" society (in spite of the fact that Jesus used some of his strongest language in praise of children). In the first court case in the United States to save a beaten child, the judge declared the child an animal, since there were laws against cruelty to animals and none against cruelty to children.

Three Gospel writers tell of the time that a group of women approached Jesus and asked him to bless and touch their small children and their babies. But Jesus' disciples were all men, brought up in the patriarchal society of ancient Judaism; they told the women to go away and not to bother the master, who was involved with important religious matters. When Jesus discovered what had happened, he was indignant and angry. His disciples had not caught his essential message, had not understood him, and he addressed them with one of his most forceful statements: "Let the children come to me; do not stop them; for the kingdom of God belongs to such as these. I tell you, whoever does not accept the kingdom of God like a child will in no way enter it" (Mark 10:13–15, author's translation). Jesus then took the children into his arms, laid his hands on them, and blessed them.

What is the quality of children that opens them to the kingdom? Is it not their wonder about the world, their openness to the spiritual dimension as well as the physical, and their constantly seeking, searching to know both the physical world around them and the spiritual one? Indeed children hunger and thirst to know the totality of the world in which they find themselves. Nothing needs to be done to develop this inquisitive, seeking spirit in children; all we need to do is to release their natural thirst. Tragically, so much of our formal education is involved in keeping order and satisfying the teacher that this torrent of interest in seeking and learning is turned into a measly trickle, a mere leaky faucet. The normal child is a natural seeker until, because of adult prohibitions and schooling, this questing spirit is suppressed or squashed by the rationality, rigidity, rules, and prohibitions of adult society.

Interestingly, the word "cretan"—which for our adult excessively rational culture means a person who is somewhat retarded, lacking in reason—comes from the French *bon crétien*, good Christian; perhaps in society's eyes, *any* good Christian seems retarded! In his fascinating study of the neurologically disabled, *The Man Who Mistook His Wife for a Hat*, Oliver Sacks notes that adults who have not been able to submit to our rational culture and so are considered retarded often have a grasp of reality that eludes those of us who have been able to conform. Indeed, one of the reasons so few of us ever come to our full stature as human beings is that we have lost this spirit of childlike seeking, something that is very difficult to regain once it has been conditioned out of us.

The seeking of the average follower of Christ is pale indeed in comparison with that of the scientist. Physicists bent on discovering the nature of matter spend hours and months and years of training and experimenting to unlock the mysterious secrets of this physical world around us. Most world-changing scientific discoveries have been made by people with this childlike, seeking spirit—by people, in other words, who have not accepted all the answers of their elders as the final truth. Most of these new breakthroughs of knowledge have been made by young adults who have not lost their childlike spirit, or by adults who have come in from another field of knowledge without preconceived notions. Einstein, for instance, was a high school dropout with dyslexia; he maintained a delightful childlike quality throughout his life.

Hungering and Thirsting

We are told in the Beatitudes that those who hunger and thirst after righteousness will be filled. A "hunger and thirst" is a passionate human desire to satisfy not only physical and emotional needs, but also the most profound needs of the human soul. So to hunger and thirst is to *seek*— and perhaps the most powerful (and familiar) form this seeking takes is *love*. Love is that quality of our humanness which is always reaching out, seeking the person who completes our life in one way or another. But the most mature love also tries to bring joy and peace and fulfillment *to other people*. Laurens van der Post states well the searching quality of love: "When the world and judgment say 'This is the end,' love alone can see the way out. It is the aboriginal tracker, the African bushman on the faded desert spoor within us, and its unfailing quarry is always the light."[1]

In English "hunger" and "thirst" are literally only physical cravings, but to the Greeks the words implied a need for more than just food and water. "To hunger" meant "to crave something with all one's being"; the hungry, then, would include all those who are not satisfied yet. "To thirst" also signified a strong need or desire; the words "I thirst," which Jesus cried out on the cross, were the same words that Jesus used when he spoke to the Samaritan woman at the well about the living water that she might drink and never thirst again. Indeed, the entire New Testament concludes with a call to the thirsty (and the same Greek word is used): "Come forward, you who are thirsty; accept the water of life, a free gift to all who desire it" (Rev. 22:17, NEB).

Often hunger and thirst are linked together to indicate the most extreme privation, the greatest seeking for infilling. After Jesus finished feeding the five thousand, he spoke to the crowd: "I am the bread of life. Whoever comes to me shall never be hungry, and whoever believes in me shall never be thirsty" (John 6:35, NEB). In the vision of the heavenly Jerusalem in Revelation, those who have gone through the ordeal of martyrdom and have come to the Lamb will never again feel hunger or thirst. The teaching of the Sermon on the Mount is summarized in these words: "Seek first the kingdom and its righteousness, and all the rest will be given to you as well" (Matt. 6:33, author's translation).

Perhaps we can now understand Jesus' uncomfortable words in Luke's Sermon on the Plain:

> But woe to you that are rich, for you have received your consolation.
> Woe to you that are full now, for you shall hunger.
> Woe to you that laugh now, for you shall mourn and weep.
> Woe to you when all men speak well of you, for so their
> > fathers did to the false prophets (Luke 6:24–26, RSV).

Jesus tells us that those who feel comfortable and satisfied—those who find life merry and without problems, basking in the admiration of all people—become stagnant because they lose their desire to seek further. The satisfied often become complacent; they are not drawn on to eternal meaning and fulfillment. When we cease seeking, we are likely to die spiritually. In C. S. Lewis's *The Great Divorce*, hell is described as the condition in which people can have anything *they* want, and so they are never truly satisfied. They are in hell because they do not seek for what can truly fill the human heart; they do not seek for the solid reality of heaven.

When John Stuart Mill was asked what would truly satisfy him, he replied that he couldn't imagine anything that would. Perhaps he didn't use his imagination enough. Imagination frees us to soar beyond our present world and its limited possibilities. Augustine's statement about seeking has become proverbial; he said that God made us human beings restless, and so we remain until we find our rest—our satisfaction in the Divine Lover.

The first beatitude speaks of those who are beggars in spirit, and it states that they will find the kingdom of heaven. Then those who mourn are called "blessed," because they know their poverty of spirit, and this knowledge allows them to become gentle, resilient. And then Jesus went on to bless the hungry and thirsty; these seekers are those who can adapt and change as the situation demands. They are tough like the reeds growing by the stream. They bend with the wind and survive; even a mighty gale does not uproot them. The satisfied are like the great oaks that may be torn from their roots and left to die. But seekers can take life's buffeting; they have real inner strength. They listen to the deepest longings of their hearts and continue to seek, pushing on, to find the humanly unimaginable.

In another place I have suggested some modern beatitudes:

> Blessed are the fearful and the inadequate.
> Blessed are the broken and confused.
> Blessed are those who refuse to accept human limitations and death.
> Blessed are the discouraged and disillusioned about human things.
> Blessed are the dissatisfied and the angry who find intolerable the
>   tragedy of those who suffer needlessly.

All these are blessed because they are driven to find something that will endure, something that will withstand the storms of life, even death. The angry, the fearful, the anxious, the driven are still seeking. How tragic is the plight of the depressed, for they have given up. Life seems to them too painful, and they sink down into the darkness of their own anguish and cannot move. They need our encouragement, our love, to pick themselves up and go on. And, indeed, our own experience of pain ultimately can be a gift that helps others pass through times of discouragement. Having known despair and survived, we can sometimes throw out a lifeline of hope to those who have given up. Is there any greater gift that we can give as parents, friends, family, ministers, or therapists than going out to those in darkness and walking with them back into the light? And can we give this gift without having ourselves been fearful and inadequate, broken and confused?

Dante, one of the greatest Christian poets, found himself in a midlife crisis that he pictured as a dark wood; his early promise had faded, and he was an exile from his beloved city of Florence. But he did not give up. His path toward wholeness led him, with Virgil as a guide, on a poetic, imaginative journey down through hell and up through the trials of purgatory. There he met his beloved Beatrice, who led him through the nine spheres of heaven until he came at last to the celestial white rose where he beheld the Triune God. He concluded one of the greatest works of art and religion with these words:

> High phantasy lost power and here broke off;
> Yet, as a wheel moves smoothly, free from jars,
> My will and my desire were turned by love,
> The Love that moves the sun and the other stars.[2]

He sought and found.

One of the finest statements of the value of the human search is found in Goethe's *Faust*. In this play, Faust makes a contract with Mephistopheles, who promises Faust anything he desires on earth in return for his soul. Faust seeks love with Gretchen and Helen of Troy; he also seeks all kinds of knowledge and wisdom. Then as he is dying, the devil appears to take Faust with him to hell, for Faust has signed the contract with his very blood. And then from heaven the Virgin Mary and the heavenly hosts appear and whisk Faust off to Heaven, singing: "Those whose seeking never ceases, / Are ours for their redeeming."[3] These words are similar to those written in the Letter to Timothy: "Fight the good fight of the faith and take hold of eternal life" (1 Tim. 6:12, RSV). The message of both Paul and Goethe is keep searching for the best, the deepest, for meaning, and for wholeness, and you will lay hold of eternal life.

CHAPTER 3

Seeking for What?

Toward what are we striving? What is the goal of our restless search? The answer to this question will depend on what we believe our universe is really like. But few people, unfortunately, puzzle over the nature of the world in which they live. Indeed, most people take their world for granted; they accept what has been passed on to them by their parents and teachers, and by TV and the ads with which they are conditioned. But when we have not puzzled over our view of reality, then we are prisoners of a view that we have been given; we are not free to consider in a critical way other points of view, or to learn from them. As I have mulled over the various worldviews, I have come to believe that there are three quite different ways to view the universe in which we live.

Since the nature of our worldview determines to a great extent what we search for in life, a firm belief that the nature of reality is entirely exhausted in the physical world will drive us to devote most of our effort to understanding and making use of this material world around us. We will seek to learn all we can about the inner workings of the atom, and about how the stars were formed. The wisest of those with this worldview will try to develop the most comfortable and pleasant homes, learning how to obtain the most delightful, nondamaging pleasures that life affords. Skinner's *Walden Two* provides a clear and consistent picture of the good life in a utopia founded on such a materialistic attitude. According to this view, there is no spiritual reality, and certainly no way of contacting such a reality. So the only people who pursue the way of spiritual enrichment will be simple people who follow outdated religious traditions, as well as those who are compulsive, neurotic, or psychotic—people, in other words, out of touch with reality as it is. The universe, from this materialistic viewpoint, is essentially value free and meaningless; when we die, it is the end of our loves, strivings, and hopes. For someone whose life has been difficult, an apt slogan might well be: life is a bitch, then we die.

Many Eastern thinkers, on the other hand, believe that the physical universe is essentially illusion, and the world of the psyche and spirit alone have eternal significance; such people spend enormous effort and energy in exploring the spiritual world and in methods of realizing it. We find, for example, great spiritual wisdom and deep understanding of spiritual reality in the Hindu and Buddhist traditions of India, which express this view with clarity and beauty. These religions have influenced all the religions of Asia. However, within this worldview there is little incentive to search out the structure and meaning of the physical world. If material reality is unreal, so are other material human beings; in the Bhagavad Gita, therefore, Lord Krishna can say to Arjuna as he faces battle that he need not hold back from fierce violence because the people he is about to slay are only illusion. Furthermore, if we are reincarnated into this world of illusion at the station we deserve, there is little point in works of charity or mercy—these acts only mess up the karma of those we would help.

Materialists who become disillusioned with their view of reality frequently jump into Eastern thought because so much of Christianity has sold out to materialism. But Jesus, Plato, the early church, Judaism, and Islam all believe that both of these views are only partially true. All of them believe that *both* the physical *and* spiritual realms are real. Human beings confront a complex reality composed of both physical and spiritual elements, and our searching needs to be directed to both. Indeed, the physical world and the physical body are seen as launching platforms from which the human psyche can blast off into another dimension that is quite different from our physical world. It is difficult, though, for human beings to balance two different kinds of searching: to deal adequately and well with the physical world around us that gives us our personhood and concrete reality, and at the same time to seek diligently to contact and deal with a spiritual world that has more ultimate and eternal significance than a purely physical one that ends at the grave. Such living requires reflection, balance, understanding, and guidance. We cannot live in this complex world just by rule, by rote, blindly following someone else; nor can we live well if we simply walk on unconsciously, blown by any wind that comes our way. We need some map of reality that has a place for both the physical and spiritual realms of experience. Then we can work consciously at finding our way to our greatest fulfillment.

Making a Choice

I had both the good and the bad fortune to be raised in a family in which my mother and father had totally different views of the nature of the world in which we live. My mother was the daughter of a Presbyterian minister, and her mother too was the daughter of a Presbyterian minister. Grandfather Morton Trippe, for whom I was named, was a very well-educated man who had his Phi Beta Kappa key from Hamilton College and had received fine seminary training at Auburn Theological Seminary. My mother accepted the Christian view of her tradition; her religion was very real to her, and she was gifted psychically. However, she did not have the background to deal with the agnosticism of her husband.

My father was a brilliant man with a prodigious memory, well-indoctrinated by the chemical engineering school at Cornell from which he graduated in 1905. In reaction to the naïve and literal biblical belief of his parents and armed with all the enthusiasm of the new scientism that was emerging in 1900, my father adopted the uncompromisingly materialistic view of his professors, who lamented how unfortunate he was to be a chemist at that time: all chemistry had left to do, they thought, was to work out the periodic tables a few more decimal points. This physical world was all there was; there was no life after death, no spiritual reality—though the *moral* teachings of Jesus were the best that could be found. The church was a good institution—to keep the ignorant masses in order. (Father did support the church financially, and he even served on the governing board of the church we attended.)

When I started taking some courses in philosophy at Washington and Lee University, I met a fine man and a good teacher, Dr. Morton, who introduced me to Eastern thinking, to the Upanishads, to the Vedas, and to Buddhism. This very sophisticated worldview delighted me. It was the polar opposite of my father's; in this view the spiritual world was the *only* ultimate reality, and the physical world was a strange illusory wrinkle in the nonphysical world. The great Bishop Berkeley had suggested the same kind of view to fend off the materialistic thinking that was sweeping over England in the eighteenth century, a view that was to sweep over all of Europe (as well as over the colonies that these Europeans planted all over the world). I remember prodding my father with this Eastern idealism and listening to his snorting disagreement. Still, he realized that logically there was no answer to Bishop Berkeley's arguments.

However, the materialistic point of view made a great impression on me and captured a large part of my allegiance. My father was brilliant. We lived in the acme of materialism, a company town, and my father ran the company. None of the religious voices in that community could stand up to the brash, clear materialism of my father and his associates. My mother's religious framework was ridiculed by my father, and as soon as my brother got his academic and medical training, he added his voice to the view that the only reality was that which was physically measurable. Then, when I was twenty-one, my mother died at age fifty-eight after a long and ghastly sickness. It seemed to me that if there were a God, followers of that divinity were left to perish without much help. And then I went off to the rampant agnosticism of Princeton University Graduate School to study philosophy.

One of the problems of materialism is that it offers very little hope for people wrestling with the meaning of life or with the agony of sorrow and alienation. Life has little meaning if the best are snuffed out after a ghastly death, and that is the end. If that is the whole human story, then human beings are not integral to the meaning of the universe. To face this as reality head-on can lead to utter despair; most materialists, therefore, simply shove these reflections under the rug, and such thoughts only emerge at times of sickness and death. William James wrote that materialism alone can drive intelligent and thoughtful human beings into hopelessness and depression and separate them from any significant creative life.

Those who have struggled through the awful darkness and hell of meaninglessness, cut off from any real human relationship, know what a farce materialism makes of human existence (Sartre has described this truth with all the power of his bitter pen). I realized that if I were to survive, I would have to find something else; unless there was some meaning to human life, there was no point going on. Suicide seemed a sensible option for this meaningless life in which the pain greatly outweighed the pleasure. But I wasn't quite able to give up; after a breather, while I taught in the Junior School of Peekskill Military Academy, I went off to seminary to see if the Christian church had anything to offer, although I thought the chances were slim.

The intellectual level of the faculty at the seminary was not outstanding, except for the magnificent lectures of Massey Shepherd in church history. Without a note he spoke of the vitality, courage, and devotion of the early Christian church. These early Christians were on fire with something and that something was founded on solid fact, as Hans Lietzmann's careful study, *A History of the Early Church*, shows beyond a shadow of a doubt: the "something" seems to be the continuing reality and presence of the resurrected Jesus of Nazareth. And then someone suggested that I read Baron Friedrich von Hügel. I was amazed at the brilliance, wisdom, and depth of this incredible man. He was at least as well informed as any of the agnostic professors that I had known at Princeton. He presented me with a new worldview in which we human beings share in both a physical and spiritual world. Then I was led to A. E. Taylor's Gifford Lectures, *The Faith of a Moralist*; we had used his commentary on Plato in Princeton Graduate School; this guaranteed to me his authority. Taylor supported von Hügel's view, but from another perspective. The essential Christian message of the life, teaching, death, and resurrection of Jesus of Nazareth began to make sense in the worldview they proposed. And I realized that intellectually the point of view that proposed two kinds of reality could be defended with *more data* than the materialistic one or the purely spiritual one.

The burning question to me was: how does one make contact with this spiritual reality *now*? I knew enough about philosophy and human beings and modern science to know that intellectual ideas not based on experience are seldom convincing to oneself or to anyone else. However, I received no instruction on how I could come into communion and communication with the saving reality that had been the determining factor in the victory of the early church over persecution, death, and paganism. But more about that deficiency later.

I graduated from seminary and entered parish ministry with the belief that there were as good reasons for accepting the gospel message as for rejecting it. However, I found I was able to raise budgets, attract people for confirmation, preach interesting sermons, minister to the sick and dying, and make a good general impression. After two other church assignments I was called to be rector (the Episcopal title for a minister with life tenure) at St. Luke's Church in Monrovia, California.

When I was interviewed by the vestry, one of the leaders of St. Luke's Church asked me the brand of my politics. I replied that I was neither high nor low church, but wanted to adapt to what the congregation wanted. One of the vestry snapped back: "No, what is your national politics, Republican or Democrat?" I already knew that the last rector was very liberal and marched in picket lines. I gave the right answer and was asked to come as rector. The question and the answer show the Christian level of both the vestry and the minister they were interviewing. In any case, I jumped into that "job" with everything I had; and soon the parish was growing and drawing people to services and church school. The parish finances also blossomed.

Almost as soon as I achieved the status of "successful" clergyperson, the skies fell in. As I got up to preach, a voice sitting on my left shoulder kept whispering into my left ear that I didn't *really* believe in all that claptrap I was preaching. Very disconcerting.

A dream showed me exactly where I was: I had entered the church to conduct the service. First I could not find my vestments. My second trial was that I could not find my sermon notes. In my third temptation to despair, I could not find my place in the prayer book. Then I turned around to face the congregation and saw that a dead tree had fallen through the nave of the church. Finally, in panic, I wondered how the ushers would take up the collection through the branches of the dead tree.

I awoke in a cold sweat; I was at war within. One side of me was clinging to belief, while the other was doubting the reality of the Christian belief, just like my father. Living in such division and tension is the stuff of neurosis. I grew more upset and anxious. (I have since come to think that any clergypersons trained in the rationalism of most seminaries who have no neurotic problems probably have no integrity either.)

I looked around the church for someone to give me help. I could find no one who knew the depth of the human soul or with whom I dared share all of my soul—I certainly didn't want the bishop to know the state of my inner life.

In the parish there was a wise Quaker, Dorothy Phillips, who had compiled a book, *The Choice Is Always Ours*, which compared depth psychology and the classics of Christian devotion. I went to see her, and she referred me to Max Zeller, a German Jew who had escaped from a Nazi concentration camp and was a Jungian analyst. He knew what anxiety was. First of all, he accepted me exactly as I was; I could share all of me and was never judged. This was my first experience of such treatment from anyone, family or friends or church. Max knew the nature of anxiety, and he showed me ways of coping with it. He also believed that God really operated in the present world, and he believed that he had survived only through God's intervention. He showed me that my dreams were wiser than my conscious self and were trying to lead me out of the morass in which I was sinking. In fact, Max, a Jew, viewed the New Testament as more historically true than my seminary professors did. He also showed me how I could reach out to and communicate with the wisdom that was trying to reach me in my dreams. My life began to mend, my sermons became more real, people began to knock on my door to talk about spiritual problems, and the voice on my shoulder ceased its jabbering.

I discovered a way to relate to the spiritual world, and I experienced a being of light and love who wanted my fellowship and wanted to guide and direct me; this being expressed the essential qualities of Jesus of Nazareth—wise, humble, down-to-earth, unjudging, loving, courageous even in agonizing death, and now resurrected. Von Hügel and A. E. Taylor had provided me with a possible view of reality, and now Dorothy and Max, these followers of Jung, provided me with a method of opening myself to this caring side of spiritual reality. I then read the church fathers along with my friend and copastor John Sanford. I realized that what I had learned about relating to God and the risen Jesus from a Jewish Jungian analyst were practices that had been used by victorious members of the early church and by those Christians through the ages whose lives had been most influential and transforming, the best examples of genuine love.

At a later time, working along with Dr. James Kirsch, who had collaborated with Jung back in the 1920s, I gradually came to see that Jung was offering a new worldview, or rather revitalizing and giving evidence for an old one. I reread my Plato and understood that he offered a similar one; I understood Plato this time around. Jung was suggesting that human beings were in touch with two quite different dimensions of reality, one consisting of observable energy and matter operating in the space-time world and another consisting of reality that was psychoid in nature. The psychoid reality had the quality of our human consciousness but was far more extensive than our consciousness (which led Jung to call it the unconscious—a bad name if I may say so). It took me nearly ten years of analysis and study to grasp Jung's point of view and realize that there was very good evidence that human beings were amphibious creatures, living in both a real physical world and a real spiritual one.

I was asked to write *Tongue Speaking*, and this forced me to describe clearly the worldview that was emerging before me. And I then realized that this view was the worldview of Jesus of Nazareth as well as of the basic Judeo-Christian tradition. The New Testament began to make sense, the gifts of the Spirit made sense, dreams made sense, a continuing relationship with God made sense. The spiritual value of tongue speaking made sense.

About this time I was invited to teach at the University of Notre Dame. Many of the graduate students were highly trained nuns and priests who were trying to make Christianity relevant to the modern generation. This worldview that had been given to me made sense to them. In addition, I found that this worldview made sense to the astute and critical undergraduate students who took my courses in the Department of Graduate Studies in Education. As I prepared my classes there, I read a great deal of modern science and the philosophy of science. I realized that not only Jung, Plato, Jesus, and classical Christianity opted for a more complex view of the world, but that modern physics, mathematics, anthropology, and sociology were far less dogmatic than the strict philosophical materialists. The great physicist, Werner Heisenberg, wrote that real science has become so skeptical that it is skeptical of its own skepticism.

I have discovered that although diagrams don't give the whole picture, they help people see the difference between the various worldviews. I started with a simple diagram that showed us human beings bridging the physical and nonphysical worlds. As we discussed this diagram in classes and with groups to whom I lectured throughout the country, the diagram grew and changed. It changed again as I reflected on it for this book. I now see reality as mapped out in the illustrations that follow.

A Picture and a Map of the Territory

Pictures and maps often give a clearer and more understandable idea of reality than words alone. It is nearly impossible to convey an experience by words alone to another person who has never had that experience. The English language (and most of the languages of Western Europe) are very poor in describing any experience other than our physical sensations or human emotions, those relating to contact with this physical world and our own bodies. In his book *The Doors of Perception*, Aldous Huxley points out that our worldview determines which experiences we take seriously, and therefore which experiences we have words for. Hindu culture has a great array of words about the spiritual world, but few carefully defined concepts about the "illusory" physical world, and so they developed little scientific knowledge of that world. Our Western culture describes the physical world with great care, but it has few words describing our contact with the spiritual world. Huxley wrote that in the West "this world" refers merely to one aspect of reality, to a realm of reduced awareness. But as I have lived and prayed, suffered and grown, I have come to the conclusion that there is reality, abiding reality, in *both* of these dimensions of our universe, and that we need to deal with both aspects of reality if we are to achieve our full human potential.

As I read the New Testament carefully, it became quite clear that Jesus of Nazareth viewed both the physical and spiritual realms as real. The more I study this incredible person, the more convinced I am that he had philosophical wisdom as well as moral insight. He came in the fullness of time; his view of the universe can be taken as seriously as his morality.

In order to portray Jesus' worldview, I will present a woodcut by an

Figure 1

unknown sixteenth century artist and then a map of the universe as I believe Jesus saw it. The picture in Figure 1 depicts Ezekiel, whose visions took him out beyond our physical world. (This woodcut was used and brought to my attention by the magazine *Common Boundary*, a journal dedicated to showing the close relation between psychology and religion.) The physical world is made of the sun and moon and stars as well as trees, plants, animals, other human beings, mountains, rocks, and cities. But it is not the totality of what is. Surrounding it is another world of wheels within wheels, a different kind of reality, another dimension of being, a fourth or fifth dimension. (If I had drawn the picture, I would have made this outer world more specific, a domain of psyche-like reality, of archetypes, the angelic and demonic, and reigning over all the kingdom of heaven, where the Triune God and the great company of heaven can be experienced *now*. Dante's picture of heaven in the last cantos of *Paradise* is the finest vision of heaven that I know; it would take an artist of Dante's stature, however, to give an adequate portrayal of that reality.)

The woodcut, however, shows no evil—no negative, destructive reality—in either the physical or the spiritual world. My own experience is that life is not an automatic progression toward realization of our entire potential; we find not only roadblocks that make us grow in overcoming them but also in both worlds malignant and destructive elements that can destroy us. We can experience something in both worlds that attacks, annihilates, drains our energy, pulls us off the path toward wholeness, leads to destruction. Babies are born with birth defects or are injured by uncaring parents, and even the best of humans are struck down with cancer or other dread diseases. And then there is the abyss of meaninglessness and the dark voice that tells us that we are valueless, that all is futile and that our only final options are the kingdom of hell or extinction. Or this reality allures us with insidious false goals that lead us toward those destinations. Then there are the natural disasters like the earthquake at Lisbon that killed tens of thousands of people and caused the leaders of the Enlightenment such problems—because they had no place for evil in their systems.

One of the basic purposes of all the great religions is to lead us through the snares, pitfalls, and blind alleys of physical and spiritual life to fulfillment, to human wholeness; it is very difficult for us to find our way in an unknown territory without a map. In his *Ventures into the Interior*, van der Post compares a journey into uncharted Africa to the inner journey into the soul and the spiritual realm. John Bunyan described the dangers of the spiritual journey in *Pilgrim's Progress*. The map in Figure 2 is meant for such soul travelers, and especially for travelers who have found some difficulties on the way.

Only the sweeping parabola on the left of the diagram is limitless. This represents the central creative being, reality, force that made both the spiritual realm and the physical world. (A parabola is a marvelous analogy for the Divine, since it is limitless and yet has a focus.) This reality can be experienced as power, presence, or light, or at its focus as a caring deity. The Divine is outside of space and time and more than matter or energy or the spiritual realm, and yet it is present within all five dimensions. And at its best, Christianity has seen the nature of this focus of divine reality expressed in a human being, Jesus of Nazareth.

Like this divine reality, the spiritual realm is outside of space and time, and yet it can have an effect upon the physical world. It has psychic reality (Jung calls this dimension the psychoid realm) or spiritual reality and *that reality is just as real as physical reality.* Unfortunately, it is difficult for us who have been socialized and brainwashed in Western materialism to understand that such a realm can exist. But living for many months

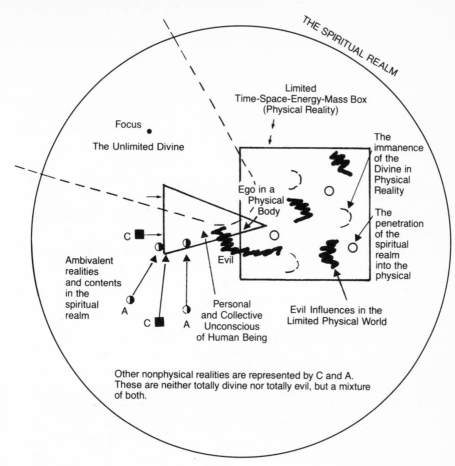

Figure 2

among Hindus and Buddhists and reading deeply in their religious and philosophical writing has made me realize how real this nonphysical world is for more than half the world's population. The spiritual world contains evil as well as good, as anyone knows who has visited a Buddhist temple or listened to Chinese, Hindu, Germanic, or African folklore. This world, furthermore, is filled with particular spiritual realities—some angelic, some demonic, some ambivalent, some lasting reflections of what has occurred within the physical world. And although the diagram shows the two worlds, physical and spiritual, as separate, they interpenetrate each other (as the little circles, parabolas, and dark smudges attempt to portray). No map portrays all of any reality.

The journey through this spiritual world is a dangerous one, as students in Zen Buddhism often discover. Zen devotees try to separate out from the illusions of this transitory world, the realm of *maya*; no one finds *satori* or enlightenment immediately. Students first pass through the morass of wild, demonic images, and some get lost in this realm, called *makyo*. Some students do not get beyond this state and never find their bearings again; sometimes they are trapped in Zen madness. People who try to go the spiritual way with weak egos and no direction or guidance can lose their bearings in the space-time world and fall into serious mental illness. They do not find fulfillment on the other side.

Many Eastern religions look on the physical world as illusion. In this view of reality, we need to get rid of our own egos and merge with the Divine, but we may well see other people as illusion as well. For many Eastern religions, caring for the physical conditions of human beings, is not the primary evidence of achieving our destiny in this world and the next; rather, what is important is our ability to lose our egos and merge with the Divine and to help others do the same. We seldom pay much attention to the nature and structure of what we view as illusion; few of the discoveries of modern science, and particularly of medical science, have originated in the East. (We must also note, in order to be fair, that the power to use nuclear bombs to destroy the earth as we know it did not come from the East. That discovery blossomed in a materialistic culture cut off from spiritual constraints.)

The most sophisticated worldview I have found sees a real physical world of great concreteness and complexity interpenetrated and surrounded by spiritual reality. Our human bodies are part of this world of matter. Life begins within the mother, and the bond of oneness with the mother continues for some months after birth. Then comes separateness, a loss and a gain; we lose our security to gain our individuality and separateness, to become unique human beings with a separate destiny of our own. It takes four or five or even six years before this physical world is perceived and accepted by children as having a reality distinct from the inner psychoid world. Young children produce answers to the Rorschach test very similar to psychotics, those who have not learned to distinguish between their experience of the inner and outer worlds. Children who never make this transition are labeled autistic.

It is possible to educate children to continue to believe in the reality of the spiritual world while at the same time introducing them to the necessity of dealing with and mastering the physical one, relating to other children, falling in love, preparing for a job, and making a living. It is possible—but it is seldom accomplished in the West, where only the physical world is granted the status of true reality. Scientism (which, thankfully, is slowly becoming less dominant in the West) simply states that we are nothing but physical beings, atomic particles crashing against each other in the specific way that our genes prescribe; when the physical organism dies and dissolves, nothing is left. This is the unexamined mind-set of most people educated in Western culture.

And this physical world is not always very kind to many people. For the few who live comfortably in Marin County or Beverly Hills, in Hinsdale or Newton, there are millions upon millions dying of starvation or on the verge of starvation, struck down by devastating malnutrition and disease. And then there is the oppression in South Africa and in so many other places as well. There are wars and rumors of wars, tornados, earthquakes, tidal waves, and the bomb. Overarching all this is the human fear of hopelessness, meaninglessness, death, and extinction.

We Americans live in one of the wealthiest and most materially affluent nations in history, and many of us do not comprehend the tragedy and pain of so much of the world; we may well think of the physical world as essentially kind and friendly. Few of us have visited our prisons, gone to the slums in some of our wealthiest cities or lived among the migrant workers, or listened to the pain that wells up within so many human hearts (even among the rich and physically comfortable). It frequently seems that the law of the jungle prevails not only in the jungle but in human society as well; the weak are often oppressed or devoured by the strong.

If we are to find the fulfilled life, we need to survive in this often cruel world. And this means that we need to develop a strong ego in order to deal with it so we can become mature adults capable of exploring the spiritual domain. One of Jung's blind spots is that he assumed that those who read his books would also read Freud, who describes the necessity of establishing a sound ego before entering into any kind of true maturity.

Realizing that love is at the heart and center of reality is not an easy process and leaves us with a tremendous responsibility. When we meet this Divine Lover, we are driven back into the world to share the immeasurable love that we have been given with those as unworthy of our love as we are of God's tender compassion and mercy.

The path toward fulfillment is a double one, physical and spiritual, and we need to balance one against the other. We need to become healthy, skillful, mature, caring, autonomous, relatable, interdependent human beings capable of dealing with this physical world and with the other people in it. We also need to know that this world alone is not enough, and that our childhood vision of love and oneness and caring was given us to draw us to the Divine Lover and to induce us to make this world an expression of the love of the kingdom of heaven. (And while we are following this difficult path, we long for the divine kingdom where evil and the Evil One will offer us far less hindrance; we will deal later on with the knotty problem of why we find these forces of evil in God's world.)

Before we go on to learn how to deal consciously and specifically with the spiritual world, let us look at the process by which we learn to deal with the physical world around us that so often does not bend to our wishes; it is this world that gives us the training and supplies a base camp for creative exploration of the spiritual one. Learning to confront this world can prepare us for the transformation that we need if we are to abide comfortably in the heavenly kingdom.

CHAPTER 4

Dealing with the Universe of Reduced Awareness

Human beings need to learn to deal with the physical world, "the universe of reduced awareness," before they can adequately deal with "the universe of expanded awareness." "This world" is the womb in which we build our individual personalities, our strong egos; we need to learn to cope with this world before we are capable of dealing creatively with the realm of spiritual reality. In order to respond to Divine Love by sharing this kind of love with others in this world, it is necessary to develop enough discipline so we can control the way we respond to and treat other human beings rather than simply acting on impulse. We do this as we learn to deal responsibly with our physical environment and with the people in it. It is no easy task to be born into this cold external world, to absorb parental love and closeness and then to step with confidence into our own separate, individual selves so that we can move on to intimacy and caring with people outside the family. (One reason that incest is almost universally discouraged is that it keeps us from developing true independence by keeping us embedded in the womb of the family; it keeps us, therefore, from the growth that can only be achieved through healthy individuality.) In addition, until we learn to have a measure of control over our fears and angers, our egotism and our discouragement, we are not mature, adequately functioning adults able to direct our own lives; we are blown here and there by every wind of emotion.

Jung remarked that the religious experiences of psychotics are just as valid as those of people with healthy egos but that the psychotics can't do anything with these experiences. Jesus said that we have to give up our lives in order to gain them; in modern parlance he was saying we cannot find our deeper souls until we give up total involvement with our earth-centered, materialistic egos. On the other hand, we cannot give up an ego that we have never developed in the first place. Discipline is necessary for any material success, and it is just as necessary for spiritual growth. Discipline is the capacity to deal adequately and maturely with the physical world and the people in it without inappropriate fears and angers. An adult with a temper tantrum is still an emotional two-year-old; such a person can seldom be an instrument for ushering in the kingdom of God. Mature people can cope with whatever crises confront them, even death.

We need a strong ego if we are to deal with the unconscious realm (the psychoid realm) and not be overwhelmed by it. And those who have not learned to deal with the physical world seldom become effective in the spiritual domain. Without strong egos we can be swamped by our dream life, by our fantasies, by our attachments, by our emotions. We need a standpoint, then, from which to deal with both physical and spiritual reality and with God. One of the characteristics of psychotics, those without solid egos, is a lack of solid personhood; when we encounter a psychotic, we sense that we are not meeting a person. Only human beings who have come to know who they are and where they stand can have real relationships—even with God, since God seems to want real people to deal with. Those who are merely masks, or who are human jellyfish with little inner structure, can seldom relate to God or become effective instruments of mature love in this world or beyond it. I am sure that God has some way of reaching the psychotic and the neurologically damaged and has a way to draw them to Love; Christians and churches should give these people loving concern, but theirs is seldom the way of conscious, self-directed fulfillment.

In his book *Hero, Artist, Sage or Saint*, Richard Coan presents what he calls in his subtitle *A Survey of Views of What Is Variously Called Mental Health, Normality, Maturity, Self-actualization, and Human Fulfillment*. The hero, for Coan, is the one who has achieved ego-strength or self-mastery; the artist is the creative person who expresses the beauty and wonder of reality in song or painting, in drama or poetry, in sculpture or dance, so that others are touched by it; the sage is one who has resolved many inner tensions and conflicts and has come to some equanimity and peace; and the saint has had an experience of transcendence and because of it lives a life full of caring and love. But if there is no hero within us, few of the other aspects of fulfillment are fully possible. The ego can become a tyrant, but properly controlled and in the service of the whole personality, it can become a guardian and servant on the way to wholeness.

Several attempts have been made to show the process by which we grow and mature. Lawrence Kohlberg took Piaget's stages of human

growth and developed a step-by-step analysis of human moral development. Unfortunately, both Piaget and Kohlberg studied the development
of males alone. In her recent groundbreaking book *In a Different Voice*,
however, Carol Gilligan has demonstrated that the value system of
women (51 percent of the population) is essentially different from that of
men. For women, relationship rather than autonomy is the essential goal
of the maturing process. Gilligan's study casts real doubt on the validity
of Piaget's and Kohlberg's work for the total human species. Dr. Beth Lie-
bert, professor of Spiritual Disciplines at San Francisco Theological Seminary, emphasizes the importance of the empirical studies of Jane
Loevinger, reported in Loevinger's book *Ego Development*. Loevinger's
work studies both men and women and sees the importance of human
relationships and transcendent experience.

Early Childhood

This is no place to go into a detailed analysis of all the stages of human
development. Judith Viorst, a sensitive and successful author who
became a psychoanalyst, provides just such a study. Her book *Necessary
Losses* presents a comprehensive and flexible exposition of the best of
Freudian wisdom about ego development. Let us look back at Figure 2
and give a quick summary of how we come to relate comfortably to the
physical world and so prepare to live in an expanded universe.

When children are born into the physical world, they are equipped
with both a physiological and psychic inheritance. This is represented by
the large base of the total triangle in the diagram. Human beings have
inherent traits, instincts (though they are not as well developed as those
of newly hatched chicks, who scurry for cover when a hawklike shadow
appears upon the ground around them; human beings are more mallea-
ble). Our most essential need in the very first weeks and months is bond-
ing with other human beings, ideally the mother and father. Some
modern maternity hospitals now allow the baby to sleep with mother
(and sometimes father) in the hospital rooms. It would be difficult to
overestimate the importance of physical closeness and touch for newborn
babies. Indeed, in foundling homes, even aseptic ones, where children
used to be left alone in cribs except for feeding, nearly a third of them
died of marasmus; this disease that caused children mysteriously to
waste away largely ceased when attendants were hired in these homes to
pick the children up, hold them, and give them human touch and warmth.

Children who have never had this kind of intimacy find it difficult to
believe that there is any caring at the center of the universe. Von Hügel's

ideas suggest that Freud had it backwards—Freud thought that our religious experience and longing is nothing but a wish to return to the womb, but for von Hügel this period of intense human closeness was created by God so that we might be prepared to relate to the loving deity at the core and heart of the universe. The theologian's logic is as reasonable as Freud's. This need of children is well met in many Third World areas, where children are often carried for nearly two years against the mother's body as she goes about her work.

My own childhood was broken into two quite different periods: the first, when I was taken with my mother wherever she went in an open Buick touring car; and the second, beginning when I was about three, when my mother became busy with my brother's activities and her social life, and I was turned over to maids. I was given both an unconscious sense of security and also a conscious doubt about its reliability. (It was immeasurably helpful that in her last illness my mother asked my forgiveness for neglecting me in the latter part of my childhood.)

The early period of closeness is followed by one in which children become aware of their own separateness and personal identity. They move away from the mother and begin to explore the world around them. They begin the development of an ego, a sense of autonomy and self-direction. (A toddler with no bruises has probably been overprotected.) During this period, there often emerges an imaginary playmate who has the same reality as the people of the outer world; gradually, though, the child clearly distinguishes the physical world from the reality perceived through the inner world. The poet William Blake was beaten because he insisted he saw spirits in the streams and trees, and although he learned to distinguish the external from the internal, he never gave up his inner vision. Hallucination occurs when we attribute to the outer world what has come to us only through the inner one. The play *Agnes of God*, as well as the movie based on it, shows the distorted nature of religious experience in a borderline psychotic without a sound ego. The ego is represented in Figure 2 as the top of the large triangle. The ego is a cork that helps us from being overwhelmed by the contents of the unconscious psyche.

During these first years we also learn a language so that we can communicate with those around us and find another level of intimacy. Without language, human beings are little more than clever animals; this truth is born out by children who have survived in the wilderness without human parents. Language provides an incredible tool for the exploration of our world. Without language we could never begin the process that results in scientific discovery. Because of our language, we can distinguish particular objects within the confused field of sensory perception. Children around the age of five become greedy and insatiable seekers after knowledge until rigid and undiscerning school systems often squash it out of them.

Our Education

The three Rs are additional tools that help us communicate and learn. Without our ability to read, we are cut off from the accumulated wisdom of the past—wisdom that can be assimilated and that saves us from having to learn everything by ourselves. And once we can write, we can begin to record our thoughts and impressions for ourselves and others. How much we forget when we do not record! The damnable Palmer method of smooth writing and the emphasis on proper spelling nearly squashed in me the desire to communicate, as a physical disability gave me crabbed and jerky handwriting. However, I discovered the typewriter when I was twelve, and then my writing was clear (and, in addition, I could excuse my spelling mistakes as typographical errors).

As we write out our hopes, our fears, our anxieties, our poetry, our fantasies, our stories, we can develop an intimate fellowship with ourselves. Recently I read over a fantasy novelette I had written thirty years ago. It was like reading a book written by another person. As we shall see later, our inner and outer lives that have not been recorded are usually lost; they cannot be used as the base of reflection in a journey toward God and fulfillment. Some people do not find writing out their experiences a meaningful way of communicating; often they are verbal types, who would find it more satisfying to record their thoughts and feelings on a tape recorder and then perhaps to have the significant dictation written out for them.

Numbers have a reality all their own. They are mysterious; we must follow their nature and rules, or we cannot use them. One of the main reasons that the Chinese never developed the science of the West is that they never took seriously the zero, which is necessary for understanding numbers and complicated numerical calculations. (The ancient Mayans discovered the zero long before the rest of the known world.) In *God and the New Physics*, Paul Davies points out that we live in a mathematically constructed universe, and that only as we learn the tools of mathematics can we begin to understand the paradoxes and intricacy hidden in the heart of the atom and electron. Unless we learn that third R, arithmetic, we are cut off from understanding the unfathomable mystery and wisdom of the physical world in which we live.

And then, in addition to the three Rs, was geography! Until this writing I could not see the reason for the emphasis on this subject so early in schooling, and yet geography really does enable us to explore beyond the borders of our own valley or village or city. Combined with history, it gives us roots, and it tells of the wonders of the past—its successes and failures. I will never forget the fascination I had with the pyramids of ancient Egypt, and I wrote a poem about them when I was ten. What a thrill I experienced thirty years later sitting on a camel beneath the Sphinx with the Pyramids gleaming in the bright Egyptian sun! The mystery of the past deepened as I climbed into the inner burial chamber in the Great Pyramid. I was in my fifties, however, before I discovered the great cultures of the East—Byzantium, India, Japan, China, Thailand, and Indonesia—and their ancient histories. The geography and history I was taught in school was extremely parochial and limited.

Adolescence and Beyond

As we mature and have wider experience, we gradually realize that our parents and teachers are fallible and that we need to form our own opinions and our own social milieu. We enter adolescence. I have sometimes argued with God that some easier transition could have been devised for enabling us to pass from childhood to adulthood. During this period we begin to separate out from parental values, to consider ways we can make a living in the world, to see where our most compelling interests drive us. And then, after knowing the fellowship of our own sex, we suddenly discover that we have missed half the world—the opposite sex, with further mystery, holds secrets that we will never wholly comprehend. We begin to seek intimacy, full sharing and relating to others. We lay the base for two of the most important characteristics of mature humanness: autonomy and the need for close relationships. Those who develop only one of these foundations of genuine maturity are cheated and stunted. These two qualities are like the two foci of an elipse; human fulfillment requires both.

Most human beings emerge from childhood sometime around puberty, age twelve or thirteen. However, some human beings remain essentially children, looking for the authority of someone else, a dominating leader or an autocratic government. Adolescents are volatile, moving back and forth from apparent maturity to childishness; they are often in revolt. And many people never pass through this stage, never come to a settled life. Real adulthood means having the ability to make intimate relationships and to step out into the world and function on our own. As adults we try to master the problems of living in our social group, relating intimately with other human beings, raising a family, making it in the world. How important a strong ego is for this stage! And even within a marriage, until children are born, there is seldom sufficient interest in tenderness, religious values, or the full mystery of human existence. It is difficult for three to be as self-centered as two, particularly when one is dependent on us parents and being shaped by what we are. When we consciously try to introduce our children to the full life, we are often forced to new levels of fulfillment ourselves.

The Midlife Crisis

And then, for many adults—particularly those who have not known consistent warmth and caring throughout childhood and who have developed powerful, heroic egos—suddenly around forty an abyss of meaninglessness opens up, or they are obsessed by floating anxiety or by compulsions and addictions they do not understand, or their intimate relationships fall apart, or agonizing depression envelops them, or they fall sick. (No one describes this crisis better than Jung in the chapter "The Stages of Life" in *Modern Man in Search of a Soul* and in his autobiography, *Memories, Dreams, Reflections*.) From the point of view of our diagram, the ego has taken control and has forgotten its base and roots in the unconscious psyche and the spiritual realm. In *The Varieties of Religious Experience*, William James makes a clear and important distinction between the "once-born" and the "twice-born." The once-born are those people who have been integrated into a family and a culture with a sound religious foundation; they seldom go through a traumatic change in midlife. Gandhi is a good example of a mature once-born individual. However, in our materialistic culture, most men and many women must be "twice-born" somewhere between thirty-five and forty-five as they come to the sudden realization that life without transpersonal meaning is not worth living. Ordinary living in the world loses its meaning, and some or all of the above problems arise. Jung suggests that the unconscious realizes around age thirty-five that life is nearly half over.

One of the problems of the very bright is that they can look ahead and see the end of the road quite young. One young man of thirteen was brought to me in depression. His was essentially a crisis of meaning after reading Jung's autobiography. Once he got his bearings by talking out his confusion, he was able to handle his life quite effectively. Jung's book had opened him to the unconscious. The problem of extraordinary mental ability can be compounded by the use of hallucinogenic drugs. Individuals opened up to the dimension of expanded awareness in their teens and early twenties may be overwhelmed by the unconscious; with the problems of learning how to make a living, to develop their own moral values, and to achieve personal and sexual intimacy, this opening to the unconscious is more than most people can handle without help. And some are destroyed.

If we have been well trained in that worldview that sees the central square (the STEM—Space-Time-Energy-Mass—box) as the only reality, we will look in vain for any meaning in life; Rabbi Kushner is wrong in suggesting that just doing our best is all we have to do. Such a worldview does not pull most people through the midlife crisis—particularly the gifted, for they see the futility of life that ends at the grave. The physical world alone is *value-free*; no moral system satisfactory to any great number of people has been devised that does not incorporate some transcendental values. Those who have been brought up in and have assimilated the rational materialism of our culture need to be provided with *both an intellectual formulation* that makes better sense of total reality than materialism and *a way of experiencing* the reality that is not exclusively physical. Some people have spontaneous conversion experiences such as those described by William James; these people sometimes find meaning without understanding why—but such acceptance is often rigid and uncritical, and it is difficult to convey to others. In *Encounter with God, Companions on the Inner Way,* and *Christianity as Psychology,* I have provided an intellectual base for belief. And in *The Other Side of Silence, Adventure Inward, Dreams: A Way to Listen to God,* and *God, Dreams and Revelation,* I have sketched out ways by which we human beings can make contact with the universe of expanded awareness. Few educated Westerners can accept only authority as a basis of belief and practice, and reason alone seldom allows us to escape the STEM box.

One of the goals of genuine education is keeping children open to the spiritual domain while at the same time helping them deal effectively and creatively with the physical world. Such an education will provide an alternative view to the determinism of B. F. Skinner and Melvin Konner, and then give growing adults methods and training in dealing with the spiritual domain. We know how much training it takes to begin to understand the mystery of the depth of the atom. Should we expect it to be simple to learn how to know and relate to the creative spiritual source of this material universe?

The Golden Age and Old Age

Individuals can pass through the midlife crisis and come into relationship with the Divine Spirit that keeps knocking at the door of our souls in religious experiences and dreams. This Spirit calls us into deeper and deeper fellowship with the Divine Lover. Then life takes on a meaning that colors everything else we do. Monumental changes may take place in how we relate to our spouses, our children, our relatives, our friends, strangers, and enemies, to the poor, the oppressed, and the forgotten. We will begin to spend our time differently, use our money differently, seek for a quality of love and experience that does not terminate with the grave.

This period of new awareness can become our most creative period of life. I call it the golden age, when our creative abilities are directed by strong egos in the service of the Divine. Our art, fantasy, or writing is not just in the service of ourselves, and it is therefore enhanced. We also discover ways of finding inner harmony. We are given a certain detachment so that tension, conflict, fear, despair, and anger no longer keep us from functioning in a way that is creative for us and for those around us. We learn ways of living in the Spirit and by doing so may sometimes have an influence on others without saying a word. Many years ago a Swiss saint, Nicholas of Flüe, came into the assembly of Swiss cantons. They had decided that they could not agree to a confederation of Catholic and Protestant cantons and that civil war was about to take place. The very presence of Nicholas changed the atmosphere of the meeting. The assembly faced their conflict once again and agreed on a form of government that has become modern Switzerland.

I have found that people need a regular amount of time each day to keep in close relationship with Spirit; this becomes a time of restoration, insemination, and direction. We are directed during these times to find our individual ways, our callings. Such callings may include ministering to the poor in a soup kitchen; taking care of the dying; organizing against nuclear war; helping the confused and depressed; struggling against the structures in society that crush and mangle people (economic or political oppression); standing up to prejudice against a group with a different color, racial heritage, or sexual preference; spending time in prayer; writing or drawing to share meanings that are significant for us; or working on AIDS research.

When does old age occur? When do we come to that time when we cease some of our activity and turn more quietly inward, getting ready for transition to another dimension of reality? I find that as I grow older, the time of old age moves farther away. I have come to see that certain of my former activities need to be curtailed, but an incredible number of new insights have come to me in the last few years. I hope that they will continue to flood me, forcing me to change opinions and to grow in many ways for many more years. There comes a time for each of us, however, when we are called to more inner reflection, to a closer attention to the kingdom of heaven, with less outer activity.

Of course, there are some people who are called to this kind of reflection early in life. The monastic life, the life of contemplation, solitude, and prayer, stands as a symbol of the reality of spiritual reality in our earthbound society. The monastery bears witness in an ego-centered and materialistic society to the universe of expanded awareness. Our society would be much poorer without those whose lives exemplify for all of us the ultimate importance of solitude, prayer, and love—of fellowship with the Divine Lover.

Many Professions

One of the most confining ideas of our specialized society is the assumption that a human being should train for only one profession, one job, one skill and stick with it throughout life. Most of us live through and out of some interests, some phases of our lives. We have children and have the confinement of their nurture and care. Then we feel a certain freedom and release when they come into their own and fly the nest. We love our grandchildren and have real pleasure spending time with them but are glad to have their parents take over the full responsibility for their care. If necessity decrees that we have to enter that role again, we can, but it would be difficult.

When I am advising young people on what work to prepare for, I constantly remind them that even though they select one profession and train for it, they can change at a later time. One of my friends, a doctor, was a missionary surgeon in the Nile Delta. Returning home in middle life, he trained in psychiatry and practiced successfully for some years, and now he has trained to treat the aging. T. S. Kuhn reminds us in *The Structure of Scientific Revolutions* that some of the most important scientific discoveries have been made by flexible people like Robert Boyle. Boyle was trained as a meteorologist and an expert in the atmospheric gases. This led him to an interest in physics, and eventually he provided the theory that is the basis of modern atomic research. In his late years, furthermore, he turned to religious writing, and he encouraged the study of science as a way to aid us in seeing the hand of God in this physical world.

A great gulf exists between the idea of a profession or job that one sticks with until retirement and a vocation or a calling that may lead one into quite different areas. Indeed narrow specialization separates people. I see my vocation as trying to understand religion *and* psychology, philosophy *and* religious experience, the questioning wonder of modern physics *and* the wonder of religious adoration. Having a vocation means listening to one's inner call and following that call wherever one is led. A real vocation is as flexible as life. A vocation in this sense will help lead us to fulfillment.

My own life has been a procession of one profession after another. First, teaching at a military academy, I learned how to deal with problem adolescents and children, a gift I have never regretted. Before that year I trained for a year in graduate philosophy at Princeton University. There I learned the necessity of stating clearly what I wished to communicate; I did this by reading Immanuel Kant's *Critique of Pure Reason* and then rendering it in meaningful English to my tutor's satisfaction. (The importance of that experience I could not overestimate.) Then came training in theology, and then over twenty-five years in parish life, where I was involved in organizing, preaching, teaching, and healing. I performed marriages and baptisms, listened to confessions, visited the sick and buried the dead.

In the midst of this activity I discovered, as I have already stated, that I was caught between two views of the universe. Psychological study and analysis opened the world of psychology for me and also introduced me to the thinking of C. G. Jung, who was as important to me as a philosopher as he was as a psychologist. He and his gifted followers in Los Angeles gave me a new worldview and a way of relating to the universe of expanded awareness. These people also taught me by action, example, and precept the centrality of love in human relationships—a lesson that I should have learned at home, in my church, and in seminary but never received in those places. My psychologist friends didn't need to tell me how to manage this physical world; I was already too adept at that. Then to my amazement, and without my declaring to anyone that I had received this training, people began knocking on my door and asking me to guide them through their emotional and spiritual problems. I was visiting with Jung and told of this experience, and he said to me: "When you are ready, the unconscious of other people will know that they can talk with you." He went on to tell me of a similar experience in his life. When I went back to my parish after the visit with Jung, the congregation's need for psychological and spiritual guidance became even clearer to me. We developed a psychological clinic at the church to carry the load the clergy could not carry alone. I found myself in a third profession—that of counselor and was licensed in that field in California.

During this period I came to know Agnes Sanford and to realize the importance of the gifts of the Spirit: healing and revelation, discernment and tongue speaking. I began to realize that these gifts are still available today for those open to them. We found the value of the small prayer group and the charismatic dimension of Christianity—and my Jungian training had given me a worldview in which these gifts and practices made sense. (Hilde Kirsch, a Jungian friend, said to me: "There is no reason there cannot be healing in the church as well as in a psychologist's office.") Little was written on gifts of the Spirit from a careful, critical, and open theological framework, so I began to write about these gifts. Many were looking for an understanding of how God touches human lives, and they found my approach helpful. Thus another quite different central focus of my life developed: the writer emerged within me and demanded time.

Because of my writing I was asked to come to the University of Notre Dame as a visiting professor in the Department of Graduate Education. Another dimension was added to my life; I began to study in earnest the whole theory and practice of education, of how we can stimulate growth and learning in others. On many levels Jung's psychological point of view provided a base for my educational theory and practice. In my classes I found a group of exceptionally bright students earnestly seeking to grow intellectually, psychologically, and spiritually so they might be able to share their new understanding with others. Another useful "perk" in university teaching was the "publish or perish" syndrome, which gave me both the time and the incentive to write and write and write. Book after book poured out from me, and from the response to these writings I learned that many other people were as confused and lost as I had been at the time when I entered analysis. I also learned that few clergy had been given any training in the practice of relating to the outreaching God revealed in Jesus Christ.

I was tenured at Notre Dame, first in the Department of Education and later in theology. I found myself part of the process of educating doctoral candidates without having a doctorate. But when I found that the University—especially its Department of Theology—was not interested in providing a program in training clergy and lay people to guide others along the spiritual way, Barbara and I started out on the lecture circuit; we spent thirty-two weeks on the road the first year. And what we had

found among the students at Notre Dame, we found among seeking people not only in every part of the United States, but in Germany, Switzerland, South Africa, Australia, New Zealand, Fiji, and Hong Kong as well:
we discovered the same hunger for a traditional faith supported by good,
clear thinking and by an experience of the Divine.

When we realized that we reached far more people by writing than by
lecturing, and when the hardships of travel and motel rooms began to
wear us down, the evangelist in us asserted itself, and we came to this
place among the redwoods where writing became our primary concern.
Although we still counsel a few people and celebrate Eucharist daily,
other professional activities take up a smaller and smaller part of our
time. Our connection with San Francisco Theological Seminary, with the
Benedictine Abbey of Pecos, and with Kirkridge and Aquaduct conference centers provide us with as much actual teaching as we desire.

Those who wish to reach their maximum potential need to be open to
various interests, even though those interests can lead to major life
changes. When Barbara and I decided to go to Notre Dame after twenty
years at St. Luke's Church, one member of my family wrote: "When are
you two going to grow up and settle down?" The answer, I hope, is *never*.
If we are to become comfortable with this world, we need to explore as
much of it as we can. Although this earth and the physical universe provide a temporarily stable home, they provide hints and signs of the
expanded awareness as well; we live in a sacramental universe. Retirement from a steady job offers many people an opportunity to use gifts
and talents that have long lain dormant.

Travel

Many people think that travel is luxury; Barbara and I, however, feel
that it is much more than that. In Germany, some villages only a few
miles apart are totally different, one Catholic and the other Protestant;
few people in each village come to know well the very different people of
the neighboring village. But human beings today live in a global village.
It is important to know those who live around us, to discover the wonders that exist over the mountain range as well as the treasures in our
own backyard. Those who can buy a new automobile (and a very large
percentage of us in this country can do this) are also able to travel; it is a
matter of setting viable priorities.

Some good friends of ours are school teachers; their summers are free
even though their incomes are not large. Several of these families have
spent months exploring our country during that free time. Even those

who are able to take off only a week or so can, in this jet age, explore all of our country or any other country of the world. Travel is geography in practice. One of the tragedies of the very poor is that often they know only their own little corner of the countryside or of a large city, and so, through no fault of their own, their vision is constricted.

My parents did not believe in travel. My father traveled into the Rocky Mountains on business, but as I was growing up in eastern Pennsylvania, the western part of the state was as much a mystery as California. (We did travel to Maine, but only because the trout fishing was good there.) My father believed that it was uppity to visit Europe, that it was putting on airs.

My own travel did not start until the early 1930s, when I went off to Phoenix, Arizona, for health reasons. I went by way of a ship to New Orleans and then by train. (It was cheaper that way.) The day in New Orleans brought me in touch with a totally different culture. And Phoenix was indeed a place of new birth for me, a totally different land. After I had a car, I scoured the United States from one corner to the other, stupefied as I looked over into the Grand Canyon for the first time, surprised as I went through sand dunes on the way from Phoenix to San Diego, fascinated by the Indian cliff dwellings and the Hopi mesas, and by the variety and color of the desert plants, so different from the wildflowers that meant so much to me where I grew up in the East. The vastness and diversity of our country continually amazed and delighted me. That diversity was nothing compared to that we later discovered in Europe, China, and Southeast Asia.

It is difficult to remain parochial as we perceive, with wonder, the beauty and the need of people all over the world. We need to pass over into other peoples' lives and walk in their moccasins if we are to know this world of ours and come to some measure of fulfillment; those who cannot travel in reality need to do so in imagination. Discovering that we belong to one world that can contain all this diversity is an important objective of the fulfilled life; until human beings know and respect other races, their personal lives are seldom fulfilled.

Money, Mammon and the World

Money is a very touchy subject, but it is a reality that is always with us. We no longer live in a barter society; our incredibly complex society runs on money. In order to survive in our society, most of us have to learn to do some task that is valued enough by society to give us (and, if we are married, to give our families) enough to live on, enough to carry us through the crises that most people face at times, enough to see that our children are educated.

But how much money is enough? Unfortunately, most people can become addicted to money. This addiction can be more dangerous than addictions to morphine or alcohol; drugs affect only a few, while wealth addiction gives a person power over others and can drive the addict to take from the poor the little they have. One of the strange characteristics of wealth addicts is that they seldom enjoy their money, as Philip Slater points out in his provocative book *Wealth Addiction*. Whenever any one aspect of life becomes the total focus of our energy—our single goal—our lives go out of kilter, and what we pursue can become demonic. In fact, single-minded concentration even on one spiritual gift can be as corrupting as any addiction within the material world—whether it be to sex, approval, drugs, power, or wealth. (Addiction to power and wealth, by the way, are intertwined.)

One of the finest outreaches of the pioneering Church of the Savior in Washington D.C. is the Ministry of Money.[1] This church organizes trips to some of the poorest sections of the planet, enabling us affluent Americans to find that we can be ministered to by the poor and that our money can alleviate the anguish of the hungry and broken people of the world. People grow as they minister with love and money to less fortunate human beings—it is so important to learn the creative use of money.

For many years, as I have mentioned, I was the rector of a large Episcopal church, and one of the tasks that fell on me was raising enough money to run the church, provide Christian education, and support the Christian outreach beyond our own church. It was sometimes embarrassing to preach on stewardship and to organize the drive for church support when my own salary was part of the package. I am no longer in that position now, however, and I can speak with a perfectly clear conscience of the necessity of giving for our own souls, as well as for the welfare of the church and of those in need. Our giving for religion and our sharing money with others are symbols of our belief in the reality of the spiritual domain. Such giving shows concretely that we wish to share our bounty of hope, love, and money with other people, just as God has shared forgiveness and mercy with us.

Money has been viewed in a very negative way by many in the Christian church. Among the Jews of Jesus' time, though, wealth was often seen as a sign of God's favor. Like Rabbi Kushner today, the Sadducees of biblical times did not believe in any really worthwhile afterlife, and some of them believed in none at all. Any rewards humans were to receive had to be received in this life. But Jesus, along with the Pharisees, believed that there *was* a life beyond this. Jesus recognized that greedy and cruel people were sometimes rich. He told the wealthy youth who came and wanted to follow him to go and sell all he had and give it to the poor, and some Christians have taken this prescription to be a requirement for all followers of Jesus.

In fact, though, Jesus did not require poverty of everyone, anymore than he demanded that all his followers be celibate. As a matter of fact, his disciple Peter was married. Luke reports that some women supported the band of apostles from their property and accompanied them to minister to them; Jesus did not suggest that they sell all their possessions. Jesus' demands on the rich young man had to do with this particular young man's circumstances. Jesus perceived great gifts and ability in the one who had come and asked what he needed to do to be perfect, but Jesus also saw that the man was addicted to wealth so he told him to sell everything he had, give it to the poor, and come and follow him. This was specific advice to a specific person, not a general rule for all.

Jesus praised the widow who placed her copper coin, all that she had, in the treasury, because her intention was that of total self-giving. But Jesus didn't tell the tax collector Zachaeus to give all his money to the poor; Zachaeus's statement that he would give half to charity and repay those he had cheated fourfold was enough. Jesus did tell the story of the rich man who lands in hell, but he ends up in hell not so much because of his wealth as his failure to notice the beggar Lazarus who lay at his gate; it never occurred to the rich man to share the crumbs from his table with the suffering beggar. The point of this story is that wealth can often blind us. On the other hand, Jesus lavishly praised the woman who poured valuable perfume over him, because of the symbolic love that this act so clearly portrayed.

Jesus never stated that the love of money was the root of all evil, a statement we read in the First Letter of Timothy. Jesus saw *many* sources of evil in the world. Any aspect of our lives that keeps us from constant fellowship with the loving God and keeps us from sharing that love with others in a concrete and practical way, can become evil.

Certainly giving away all one has—and celibacy that frees one from family responsibility—does open a pathway for radical discipleship that is impossible for those who are married and have businesses. For St. Francis of Assisi devotion to Lady Poverty was a necessity, and many other people find a call to this kind of discipleship. There are also many Christians who wish to live by faith alone, without the support of a financially secure job, trusting that the right gifts will be given by God. The Benedictine Monastery at Pecos and its daughter establishments operate on this principle of trust. Such an attitude is an important witness that God is the source of all, and that God will take care of us. But if there were not also those who are in the world with successful medical or legal practices, or with profitable businesses, there would be no one for God to touch when others are in need.

There is another sort of stewardship, however, based on the principle that we should all share a portion of what God has given us with the religious institution and with those less fortunate than we. Financial giving is a legitimate form of stewardship—but we must remember that the giving of our money does not release us from our responsibility of loving and caring first for those close to us and then for those far away. (Mother Teresa tells us to serve the poorest of the poor in our own families first.) Paul reminds us that we can give all we have, and even give our bodies to be burned, but if we are not motivated by love—if we are not showing genuine love to others—then our actions are without value.

It is nearly impossible to remain in contact with the realm of the spirit unless we give our material substance for religious and charitable purposes. It is nonsense to maintain that we want to have access to the realm of Spirit with its love and power, that we are giving ourselves with utter sincerity to God, and then to spend all but a tiny fraction of our financial resources on ourselves, on our own desires and interests, or on the quest for more money. To say that we are truly committed and still to remain in such a selfish frame of mind is worse than nonsense: it is hypocrisy. And Jesus did not have much truck with hypocrites. For those who do not give of their substance, the spiritual realm usually closes and remains closed, except for occasional flashes of lightning. Money is our congealed energy and being, what the world gives us for what it thinks we are worth.

Unless we give our financial resources for some outer religious or charitable purpose—to institutions which, however inadequately they may be performing, are dedicated to the realm of Spirit and to outreach to those who need love, medical care, housing, and food—the religious encounter usually goes dead within us. Those who give to institutions and neglect to give these things to their own families have not understood the nature of true spirituality or love. We can try all sorts of other religious practices (many of which I will soon suggest), but if we do not share our substance, we might as well not waste our time or energy on them.

Of course, in this age of TV evangelism, we need to know that our giving is not just feathering the nests of the preachers or aiding their pet projects. Another problem with TV Christianity is that it allows us to relate only to a TV screen without impelling us to deal with other living Christians, who may annoy us or get on our nerves and who require us to practice love and charity as we deal with them. How often we need to remember Jesus' words: you are my followers as you love one another as I have loved you.

Cornelius, the centurion described in Acts, continued faithful in prayer and giving. Even though he was a pagan, he persistently supported the best religious institution he knew, the Jewish synagogue. God then spoke to Cornelius through an angel and brought him new life. Such visitations of the Divine still happen to those who keep up their prayer *and* their giving.

One of the factors that was responsible for my own growing interest in the spiritual life was my own practice of tithing. I began to practice that kind of giving when I heard a speaker at a conference state that it was wicked to tithe. I pricked up my ears, since I was uncomfortable about the smallness of my giving, I had been looking for a good excuse not to tithe. The speaker went on to say that it was wicked to tithe, for this practice gave people the idea that their obligation to God was accomplished: God could be dismissed with a tip. He went on to say that real commitment requires us to give of our time and energy as well as our money and maybe more than a tip.

Right then and there I decided that I had better get into the wicked category to begin with. As I began to give actually one tenth of my income for religious and charitable purposes, the thought came to me, "This matter of religion is really important. I had better get deeper into the real business of it." I then started to spend more time reading the Bible, meditating on books of devotion, and praying. I found, like most other people, that giving is a sacramental action that reminds us in a practical way of our commitment to God and of the necessity of continuously turning to the Divine Giver. When we give for God and to God, we are more likely to make the strenuous effort that seems to be necessary for those who wish to find the reality of the kingdom now and forever.

This Fragile Earth, Our Island Home

For most of its time on earth, the species from which we humans sprang was a relatively insignificant part of earth's fauna. And then several million years ago the brain of one branch of the primates went into a gigantic mutation. A new kind of creature appeared on the face of the earth: one who could think, reflect, love, play, seek power, one with religious insights and experiences, a myth-making and artistic living being. Slowly a great matrilineal culture began to grow up, and then this several hundred-thousand-year-old culture was displaced as patriarchy developed and made power and domination the central feature of human society. The empires of Egypt, Babylon, along the Indus River, and in China flourished through the power of the sword, and "civilization" was born. The leaders placated the gods to guard against earthquake, tidal waves, and other disasters, but they cared little for the earth, unlike those in former times who lived in closer touch with it. Many species of animals were destroyed as a result of this power hunger, and they disappeared forever. Nations and empires battled for each other's wealth and power; human beings became one of the few species that systematically destroys its own kind.

Human beings gained more power over their environment and multiplied astronomically. As the years passed, secular Western civilization grew up totally cut off from value or meaning or religious ideas. Wars became fiercer and fiercer. Finally our species learned how to unlock the secrets of matter; we discovered that enormous energy, unimaginable power, lay locked in what appeared to be inert matter—and then the bomb and nuclear warfare became an ominous possibility. Before the bomb was first tested, scientists feared that it might cause a chain reaction and destroy our whole world—and yet we foolish humans took the risk and tested it anyway. Indeed, we still don't know how many nuclear blasts might trigger the utter destruction of the earth and all living creatures on it.

As human beings have learned to control their environment and to protect themselves from disease, they have proliferated all over the earth. They have cut down the great forests that once covered much of the earth's surface, forests that poured oxygen into the atmosphere. Rivers and lakes and even oceans have been polluted. Land devoid of vegetation has eroded away and become desert. We humans have even poisoned the atmosphere as we have continued to burn fossil fuels and pour other wastes into the sky. I was brought up in a town set in a beautiful gap where a river passed through a mountain range. But large chemical plants were built there, and over the years they belched poisonous gases into the air. Recently I returned to this town and found what looked like a moonscape rather than the verdant mountains I knew as a child.

This earth of ours is indeed fragile; it needs our care, or it may be destroyed. If we care about our children and grandchildren and those who come after them, we need to curb our population growth and learn to live closer to nature and to care for our island home.

Human beings are part of this physical world in which we live. Some of them live in physical comfort, free from disease, protected from other human beings by great war machines and by national boundaries that are like gigantic glaciers that cut people off from one another. However, a large percentage of men, women, and children live in poverty and under oppression; many do not have enough to eat, are wracked by disease, and live in subhuman conditions. Their life expectancies are half or less than those of the people who live in more humane surroundings. Someone has calculated that one-third of the children of the world go to bed hungry each evening. Are we caring for our total environment when some human beings prosper and others starve and die? Some human linguistic and ethnic groups are endangered species, much like many animals and birds and reptiles. If we are to care for this earth, we need to learn how to deal with other human beings with concern and care, with understanding, consolation and love. Selfishness, greed, domination, oppression, fear, hatred, and war could wipe the earth clean of the whole human race.

Taking Care of Our Bodies

Many of us have a tendency to take our bodies for granted. We want to live long and free from illness, but we don't think much further than that. We forget that our bodies are one part of the total environment over which we have a great amount of control; often we ignore our responsibility to the most personal portion of the physical world, the world of "reduced awareness."

In the next chapter we shall take a careful look at what amazing instruments these bodies of ours are; if we mistreat them we can destroy or weaken them. Paul said that the body is the temple of the Holy Spirit. But do we treat our bodies with the same kind of respect that we would the holy of holies within the temple? How do we feed them, exercise them, rest them, give them companionship, clean them, relax them, listen to them, enjoy and love them, care for them?

In some religious groups (even among Christians), the body has been seen as a deterrent to true religion. Suffering, penance, ascetic practices, rejection, denial of legitimate needs, and actual abuse of the body have been suggested as furthering us upon the religious way. Of course, the body and its pleasure can become a total preoccupation for some people, but this happens only when the body is idolized, made an end in itself. How many of us really treat our bodies well—as well as we do a plant or an animal that we love? These bodies of ours are very tough and very fragile; just like the rest of our universe of reduced awareness, they need our wise, tender, loving care. A life can hardly achieve optimum fulfillment in a body that has been neglected, ignored, mistreated, or abused.

And these bodies respond not only to our conscious care but also to our emotional and religious life. Fear, anger, depression, and stress—and excessive egocentricity—cause immeasurable damage to our physical health. The body of a person without hope, love, and meaning often is sick and sometimes dies.

And so we conclude our reflections on the necessity of dealing with the universe of "reduced awareness." This is part of the world. We can hardly deal adequately with the spiritual domain if we do not come to know our physical world and treat it with respect and love. This means that we need to become mature as persons, treating ourselves and others with understanding; we need to know the wonders and dangers of our fragile island home of which our bodies are a part. We need to use our material substance sacramentally. In this way we prepare to experience the universe of "expanded awareness."

CHAPTER 5

A Little Less than God

The Psalmist cries out to God: "What are human beings that you are mindful of them and care for them?" And then the question is answered: "A little less than *elohim*" (the word used for God in much of the Old Testament). Many translations tame down the literal meaning of the Hebrew word, but the text is perfectly clear—God made us a little lower than God (Psalm 8:5). Some translations render this passage, "a little lower than the angels" or "a little lower than the gods," but even these renditions place us human beings in quite a different category than rocks or trees, fish or fowl, amoebae or chimpanzees.

One of the real problems of the materialism of our Western civilization is that the human being is viewed as *nothing but* a complex group of cells built together in a bag of saltwater that will in time dissolve, leaving nothing but chemicals behind. This is the basic point of view of Skinner, Melvin Konner, Kushner, or anyone who sees no life beyond the grave. It is a view that seems to be manifest in the lives of most Western people (since serious daily religious observance is today a real rarity). I have discovered that most conventional Christians are afraid to look at the subject of life after death; apparently they are fairly certain that there is nothing to look for beyond the grave. When I lecture on the subject of meditation or dreams or caring, I often draw three or four times as many to the lectures as when I am speaking in the same place on afterlife. But isn't this a crucial question—whether we are more than sticks and stones, atoms, electrons, and quarks?

The Bible, Judaism, and Christianity, as well as nearly all other religions of humankind, answer that question with a resounding *Yes*. But modern materialism, which developed to dominate that little peninsula of Asia known as Europe, says *No*. Unfortunately, that little materialistic society put gunpowder to efficient use and conquered most of the known world, bringing its basic ideas with it. Carl Jung, however, suggested that if we get away from the unnatural influence of Western civilization and find people who are still in touch with nature and the fullness of life, we see how ridiculous the materialistic point of view truly is.

When we escape from this reductive viewpoint, what do we find in human beings, in these material bodies, that justifies the Psalmist's claim that we are only a little lower than God? Why does Jesus point to Psalm 82:6 as a justification for referring to himself as the Son of God—"You are gods, sons of the Most High, all of you" (RSV)? God has evidently created something quite unusual in human beings; God has given us unusual abilities.

Our Amazing Bodies

I have already suggested that we take these bodies for granted. They are, however, complex and amazing. In his book *The Body Is the Hero*, physician Ronald Glasser gives a dramatic and graphic description of the human body:

Our body is like a huge movable city, made up of many trillion individuals all with different skills, yet working together. It has its own ventilation and sewage systems, its own communications network, a billion miles of interconnecting highways and streets, a system of alleys, its own supermarkets and factories, disposal plants and heating units. All it really needs to keep going are a few basic raw materials to be brought in and a way of discharging wastes.

Yet, as with any city, there can be natural disasters. Sewers can be clogged, arteries and water mains can rupture, the communication system can be jumbled or short-circuited, ventilating can break down; or, even more important, there can be anarchy and crime. In some narrow back alley, or at the end of the spleen or in the outer part of the lung, a person or a cell can suddenly go bad and, forgetting or brushing off civilized restraints, come to think only of its own needs.[1]

Even more amazing is the fact that the health of that city that is you or I will depend to a large extent on *emotions*. Anger, fear, hatred, egocentricity, stress, and depression can cause chaos within the city. In addition, one city can learn to communicate with other cities through languages that they develop in common, and this communication is an important component of emotional development.

Each individual "city" can reach out into the world around it, learning how to get the right raw materials and learning where to dispose of waste material. In addition, these cities seem to have an unquenchable desire to know about the world in which they are located. They have studied the physical matter of the world in which they exist (and of which they themselves are made) until it has dissolved into subelectron particles (called quarks) that cannot even be imagined, into a world so full of paradoxes that physicists complain that they don't know what matter is. On the other hand, these human bodies have looked out into the immense expanse of stars and realized what a tiny part of the universe their own little solar system is, and how insignificant these many-trillion-city-bodies are in that system. Nonetheless, they know much about that universe, and they realize that they themselves are nearly as complicated as the world surrounding them: the brain alone contains billions and billions of neurotransmitting cells.

In addition, these trillion-cell bodies can communicate with each other by touch and words, by smell and taste. New colony cities (babies) have to be nurtured by food, protection, and love, or else they die. Without this nurturing, they would have no language and would be little different from the more advanced animals around them. Vast numbers of these individual cities assemble their knowledge and write it down so human beings don't have to invent the wheel all over again.

Not only do these material bodies communicate with the world through the obvious five senses, but they can also turn inward and find a whole world of images and fantasies and dreams and myths that give them meaning, purpose, direction, and even healing. These bodies of ours are transmitting and receiving centers that scour inner as well as outer space. They have other ways of knowing besides the five senses, and other worlds to explore besides the universe of reduced awareness. Like Ezekiel in the picture I presented earlier, we can emerge from the world of reduced awareness and enter another dimension of reality. And best of all, as human beings have witnessed from time immemorial, we sometimes find ourselves in touch with the ultimate dynamic center of creativity and love that most people have called *God*. This experience can be a quiet and sustaining one, giving deepening meaning and richness to life, or it can result in radical realignment and transformation of life that William James described so eloquently in his Gifford Lectures, *The Varieties of Religious Experience*. In my *Companions on the Inner Way*, I have described over thirty ways through which we can relate to this Divine Center. The Divine appears to be far more interested in communicating with us than we are in communicating with the Divine. The Divine transmitting station is operative twenty-four hours a day, every day, year in and year out.

One of the most astounding qualities of the Divine is that God has given us the power to resist or ignore the spiritual dimension of reality and to turn our backs upon God's overtures to us. The Divine has given us citadels within our hearts, and the Holy One allows them to be

stronger and more powerful than divine love. I once wrote a sermon entitled "More Powerful Than God" in which I pointed out that God gives us
the power to refuse the Divine entrance into our lives; we *can* live totally
secular lives.

We all know the ordinary in-this-world ways of knowing through the
five senses. And since most people in our Western civilization have
assumed that these are the only ways of knowing, we can be totally captured by the universe of reduced awareness. In his book *The Doors of Perception*, Aldous Huxley builds on his own experience and on the thinking
of some of the most perceptive thinkers of our time to provide a new theory of the range of human knowing. Along with many students of meditation and psychology, I believe that his suggestions are valid. The basic
idea is that we human beings are able at all times to be in touch with
everything both in the world of reduced awareness and in the universe of
expanded knowing. The function of our brains, nervous systems, and
sense organs is to eliminate much of this irrelevant data so that we can
survive on the face of this particular planet. To make our survival possible, the vast possibilities of the different worlds to be experienced are fun-
neled through the "reducing valve of the brain and nervous system."
What comes out at the other end is "a measly trickle of the kind of consciousness" that helps to keep us alive on this planet.

Huxley goes on to say that what religion calls "this world" is the universe of reduced awareness, "expressed, and as it were, petrified by language."[2] However, people have the capacity to bypass the reducing valve.
Some are born with a great ability to use this capacity, and some acquire
it through spiritual exercises; sometimes an experience of the spiritual
comes spontaneously—through a vision, an intuition, or a dream—and
sometimes it demands conscious effort.

Dreams are our natural altered state of consciousness, which reveal
the depth and range of what we human beings can experience; in sleep
we are largely cut off from the world of ordinary experience and enter
another one. Meditation and contemplation are ways of deliberately and
consciously seeking to enter into the realm of expanded awareness in
order to come in touch with the world that is revealed spontaneously in
dreams. Dreams provide perhaps our most natural access to another
dimension of reality. Whatever we can experience through dreams can be
experienced consciously when we withdraw our attention from the outer
physical world and our own inner desires and allow this other world to
emerge. However, in meditation we can direct and focus our attention on
the most creative and loving aspects of nonphysical reality. Nearly all religions suggest some method of detachment and withdrawal from the

physical world as a necessary beginning practice before meditation will bring us into substantial experience of the realm of expanded awareness.

Everyone dreams. My own dreams have continuously frightened, sustained, led, and directed me for nearly forty years. Let us look at the levels of experience to which the dream can refer. Figure 3 shows the human being consisting of an ego, with conscious will and sense perception; memory (which sometimes gets lost in the unconscious when the latter is not cooperative); the personal unconscious (which consists of experiences or desires we have had that have been repressed or forgotten); and the internal collective unconscious (a psychic reality that most human beings share in common). The diagram also distinguishes three different universes with which these psyches of ours are in contact: the three-dimensional world of matter and energy, time and space; the expanded universe, which is nonphysical, psychoid, or spiritual reality, and is as diverse and mysterious as the physical one; and the realm of the Holy, of the God who yearns for us and communicates with us, and who wishes to give us continuing growth and fulfillment within the orbit of the Divine Love—love that moves the human heart as well as the sun and the other stars. If we can indeed commune with God, a God who desires our fellowship, we certainly are mysteriously and wondrously made, a little less than God.

Figure 3 is an enlargement of the picture of the human being that is part of the map of the universe in Figure 2. The large central triangle represents the amphibious human being, who lives in both a physical and spiritual world, and who can be aware of our contact with the unlimited divine. When we become conscious of the range of our capacities, we realize that we can in fact stick our heads out of the realm of reduced awareness. (It is always sobering for us Westerners to remember that most Eastern religions view the physical world as an illusion.) In this diagram we have sketched a part of the Space-Time-Energy-Mass box, a section of the spiritual domain, and a fragment of the infinite loving, creative Divine.

Kinds of Human Knowing

Let us take up one by one seven quite different kinds of human knowing revealed by the dream and see better what remarkable beings we truly are.

Sense Experience

In the last chapter I discussed the necessity of learning to deal with the physical world if we are going to have a growing, creative, and sub-

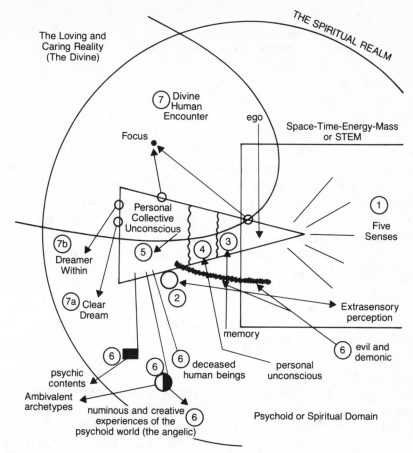

The Loving and
Caring Reality
(The Divine)

THE SPIRITUAL REALM

⑦ Divine
Human
Encounter

ego

Space-Time-Energy-Mass
or STEM

Focus

Personal
Collective
Unconscious

① Five Senses

⑦b
Dreamer
Within

⑤   ④ ③

⑦a Clear
Dream

②

Extrasensory
perception

memory

⑥ evil and
demonic

psychic
contents

⑥   ⑥ deceased
human beings

personal
unconscious

Ambivalent
archetypes

numinous and creative
experiences of the
psychoid world (the angelic) ⑥

Psychoid or Spiritual Domain

Figure 3

stantial relationship with the spiritual one. Learning to know the reality
and complexity of the physical world starts with the use of sense experience and reason. Once we have learned a language, we can learn from the
experience of others; we no longer need to learn only from our own personal experience that playing with rattlesnakes is dangerous and that running out into streets where teenagers are drag racing can be catastrophic.

Through the centuries we have tested our experience and made
hypotheses. In recent years we have built machines that can see what the
eye cannot perceive and computers that have helped human beings do
mountains of calculation. These have extended our sense experience and
reason. We have discovered much about our world. Without our
expanded sense experience and mathematical expertise, we would have
learned far less about this world.

Very few dreams simply repeat experiences of the day before; indeed, such dreams are among the most rare. However, dreams of yesterday do occur; they point out and underline the importance of special events or by little variations from reality tell us about our attitudes toward these events and the people in them. Dreams do sometimes give us clues about the nature of day-to-day reality that show us there is a deeper knowing in us about the physical world than our sense experience and reasoning mind provide. In the November 1978 issue of the *Journal of Chemical Education*, R. A. Brown and R. G. Luckcock published an article, "Dreams, Daydreams, and Discovery," showing that many scientific discoveries had their birth in dreams. And Paul Feyerabend, one of the leading philosophers of science of our time, points out the importance of training scientists' imaginations as well as their powers of perception and reason if scientists are to penetrate the mysteries of our physical world.

So the process of knowing physical reality seems to require sense experience, reason, *and imagination*. Baron von Hügel suggested that anyone who wishes to deal with God and the spiritual realm needs to take up the arduous task of learning one of the hard physical sciences, such as physics or chemistry. These studies make us take the physical world seriously, requiring us to deal with the world as it is rather than as we think or hope it is. One hundred years ago no one dreamed that ordinary matter contained the explosiveness of the bomb over Hiroshima, but it does. Von Hügel suggests that the same immutable reality exists in the spiritual world as in the physical world, as well as an even greater creative power. He believed that learning to encounter and understand physical reality can help us to perceive and take seriously what is to be discovered in the spiritual world. What we human beings can discover about our physical world is truly limitless when we explore it with care. And we need to use the same kind of careful testing of experience as we open ourselves to the spiritual realm and seek to come to the throne room of the interior castle of the kingdom.

Extrasensory Perception

The evidence keeps pouring in that Huxley was correct in his observation that we have more ways of knowing than we usually realize. We human beings do have other ways of perceiving than through the brain, the nervous system, and the sense organs. But why should we be surprised? Who has ever proven that we gain knowledge only through the five senses, and that we then extend that knowledge only by reason? Our materialistic culture has simply *assumed* this conclusion as a part of its materialistic worldview and as a reaction to the unthinking, uncritical attitudes of a more superstitious age. However, scientists are now the ones suggesting that our range of knowing is greater than our understanding of it.

In a letter dated 24 July 1921, Sigmund Freud wrote that if he were entering the field of psychology at that time, he might well choose the field of parapsychology, in spite of the difficulties of that area of study. The parapsychological research of J. B. Rhine, the pioneer in this field at Duke University, has been replicated all over the world but especially in Russia, where interest in the subject has been great. In the early 1970s, Andrew Greeley obtained a grant from the Henry Luce Foundation to discover whether Americans indeed have paranormal experiences, including the mystical (or religious) ones. The results of the project showed that in a carefully selected random sample 62 percent reported experiences of *déjà vu* (seeing an ordinary physical panorama and having the strong sense of having seen it before); 60 percent said that they had been in touch with other minds far from them (telepathy); and 28 percent reported perceiving events taking place far from them which they later verified (clairvoyance). All of these experiences gave verifiable knowledge for which there was no known physical means of transmission. In addition, 39 percent of Greeley's sample stated that they had felt they had been very close to a powerful, spiritual force that seemed to lift them outside of themselves. Twenty-five percent claimed that they had felt they were really in touch with someone who had died. (This material is from a book by Greeley entitled *The Sociology of the Paranormal: A Reconnaissance*. His results have been replicated in both Great Britain and West Germany.)[3]

Greeley anticipated that critics would claim that people with these experiences were unstable, immature, or were fabricating the data about their experiences. To avoid that charge he incorporated the Bradburn-Caplovitz scale of psychological well-being into his questionnaire. Far from indicating that these people were of borderline psychological health, the results showed a high correlation between experiences of a powerful spiritual force and psychological and emotional maturity. Indeed, Professor Norman Bradburn commented at a staff meeting of the National Opinion Research Center that he knew of no other independent variable that correlated as strongly with psychological well-being as does frequent religious experience. If people with this capacity are indeed dealing creatively with *all* aspects of reality and particularly with a source of more than human wisdom and caring, this result might well be expected. Other researchers in the field of religious experience have noted the same correlation.[4]

A little later than Greeley's study, Dean Robert F. Jahn of Princeton's School of Engineering became interested in the nonsensory ways of knowing which we human beings are capable. In 1978, Jahn discussed his ideas in a speech entitled "Psychic Process, Energy Transfer, and Things That Go Bump in the Night," which was published as a special issue of the *Princeton Alumni Weekly*. Jahn's work continues at Princeton and is well summarized in an article in *Proceedings of the Institute of Electrical and Electronic Engineers* entitled "The Persistent Paradox of Psychic Phenomena: An Engineering Perspective."[5]

When we look at the verifiable data about our capacity to know the physical world through nonsensory means, two conclusions seem inevitable. First, those who would dogmatically confine our knowledge to our sense experience are not looking at the facts and are *operating out of faith in materialism*. And second, if we can establish that we are capable of receiving nonsensory data from the physical world, then there is little reason to deny the reality of the data referring to experiences of the Divine, of the deceased, and of other nonphysical realities.[6]

Experiences of precognition and retrocognition also give verifiable data that are baffling within the worldview of rational materialism. Though it may be possible to imagine how events of the past might be stored in some psychoid bank, in the linear world of physical cause and effect, precognition—knowing the future—is simply absurd. And yet there are many well-substantiated examples of people having intuitions about the future or seeing in dreams events that later took place. Sometimes people have intimations that these events are a foretelling of the future, but there is no way of testing the validity and truth of such experiences until after the events have transpired. Indeed, people who have this ability find it a terrible burden not knowing when their dreams and visions are predicting the future or what to do with the information if they are convinced that their dream or intuition is predictive.

A priest referred a woman with this gift-burden to me. He did not know how to deal with her. He knew that she was speaking the truth, but he had no worldview from which to respond to her. She talked with me several times, and I listened and assured her that some people have this ability; there was nothing abnormal about her. It is helpful to be secure enough in our view of the universe of expanded awareness that we can listen to such people, reassure them, and relieve the isolation they often feel. Certainly clergy and psychological counselors need to have a wide enough worldview to listen and guide these people. However, most counselors either dismiss such stories or see them as demonic influences rather than as natural capacities of the human psyche.

When we view the world as a reality of many dimensions, a world of fluid time and space, we become far more open to the mysterious reality of which we are a part. How different our country might have been had Lincoln listened to the dream that came to him several nights before his assassination in which he saw his body lying in state in the White House.

Memory

Few people would deny the eerie quality of the experiences I have just described. Our capacity to remember is nearly as strange, but like so much of the rest of our capacity to know, we simply take it for granted — until our memory fails us. Jung has remarked that unless our unconscious psyche is working with us, we cannot draw fully on our memory bank. Personally I believe that our memory is only partly recorded in the brain. Once we take seriously the ideas of brain researcher Candace Pert and of neurologist Oliver Sacks (author of *The Man Who Mistook His Wife for a Hat*), we find that it is difficult to equate brain and mind. Psyche (mind) and brain are certainly interconnected, and they influence each other, but they are not identical. Some of memory may be stored in the brain, but probably all of it is stored in the psyche. What incredibly vivid memories dreams can evoke! Events of thirty, forty, sixty years ago can be presented in dreams with the vividness of yesterday. We can return to third grade and remember the names of all those around us and even the clothes they were wearing.

Recently I began to record for my children something of the life I lived as a child — a way of life that has vanished and that none of our other living relatives experienced. (I am the last remaining member of my immediate family.) I began to turn the searchlight of my conscious intention back through sixty-five years of memory. The memories of childhood sickness, of plum pudding and hard sauce, of the Buick touring car came flooding back, just waiting to be recalled. As I continued my reflections, I felt real admiration for the little boy that was me as I watched him struggle against almost insurmountable odds. We all have an inexhaustible bank of data within, and yet we too rarely draw upon this reservoir; we seldom look at what was really there, seldom note how faulty many of our ideas about the past can be. But I doubt if we can truly come to personal fulfillment until we spend some significant time with this unfathomable storehouse of memory and try to understand the patterns that emerge. Until we see as clearly as possible who we have been, we have little chance to see who we truly are and to become what we can be.

Our memories provide an incredible tool for growth and development. We can look back on the most critical moments in our lives, on the times that we have achieved and received recognition, on the love that we have received, on those moments when we felt the presence of the Divine and were lifted out of annihilating darkness. And we can also look at the pains we have experienced and see how they have passed; we can remember friends that we had forgotten, and moments of intimacy in communion with those we have loved. We seldom become aware of God's continuing presence in the present until we have seen that the gentle, sometimes hidden, hand of grace has guided and led us in the past, even when we were not aware of it.

Personal Unconscious

What we forget is nearly as mysterious as what we remember. Freud and Jung have both maintained that unpleasant or disagreeable memories can be quietly squeezed out of consciousness and buried. Our dreams, however, often pierce through the veil lowered over what some psychologists have called the *personal unconscious*. Within this vault lie those aspects of our lives that are simply too painful to remember— failures, actions that we despise and fear, parts of us that we do not want to face. In many Western cultures, these hidden things often have to do with sexuality; our Western societies have much more tolerance for violence than for sexual deviation from the mores.

Jung's word association test illustrates in a dramatic way how human beings hide from themselves. The psychologist reads a list of words, and the client provides associations to those words. Usually the person responds in a few seconds, but then a word causes him or her to pause for twenty or forty seconds or even longer; the association has touched the individual's unacceptable personal unconscious, and he or she can think of nothing to say without revealing a secret. Prying into this secret reservoir of fear and pain can be dangerous unless we are with someone who can accept us as we are; these things are not hidden without reason. When, however, the inner dreamer finds that the time is ripe and we are ready, the dream can safely reveal some fearful event or action with which we can now deal safely. It is perilous, though, to push people beyond the safety limits of their memory.

One college student came to me many years ago because each semester at exam time he came down with pneumonia. I asked him if anything traumatic had happened at college, but he could think of nothing. We met each week for six weeks, and then he came in with excitement to tell me of a sexual relationship he had engaged in throughout his first year in college, a relationship of which he was most ashamed. He had totally forgotten the entire affair. Once this was revealed, we were able to talk it through and see that experiences like his were common and that no permanent damage had been done. He went back to school and never had exam-time pneumonia again. What he had totally forgotten had a grip upon his health until he could face it and deal with it. Our health, our slips of the tongue, our missed appointments, our quiet reflection, our mistakes, and our dreams can all reveal this dungeon in which we try to imprison our unacceptability.

The Personal Collective Unconscious

Beyond the dungeon of repressed memories is a still deeper well of personal psychic life. We reach it in many different ways. All of us have access to it in our dreams, some of us through fantasy and imagination, others through meditation, and some as they paint or draw, dance or sing, out of the depth of their being. We also touch this basic area of our lives when some myth or story grips our inmost being and stirs us to our very depth. Jung calls this area of our psychic life the *collective unconscious*, because we are unconscious of it most of the time. We share this common psychic foundation with most other human beings, and particularly with people of our own lineage and race. Just as all human beings share a common genetic heritage, so we share a common psychic heritage. And just as there are differences in physical inheritance between racial stocks and between individuals even within a family, so each of us has our own common and unique psychic inheritance. I have a tiny extra spur of bone on my big toe common to one side of the family; in the same way I also have specific, inherited mental-psychic characteristics.

Following the lead of Descartes, our Western civilization has accepted as real only what is clearly conscious and has neglected, ignored, and forgotten the mysterious depth of the human soul, its complexity and structure. Plato, however, understood the amazing capacities of the psyche. And Jesus spoke of the forces that could seize the core of our being, and he told stories using images that are common to all human beings—the very images of which dreams are formed. (This is one reason his message continues to have a universal appeal.) Those who have been caught up in the view that our minds consist only of what is conscious and logical have lost touch with our right-brain functioning and with a whole basic substratum of our personality. Myths, dreams, and spontaneous images (that often emerge in us when we enter utter silence and detachment) speak a common language. I have sketched out some of these common symbols in several places.[7] The unknown man in women's dreams, the unknown woman in men's dreams, the whirlwind, the attacking figure, the ocean, the automobile, the horse, other animals, fire, the spider, war,

death and the grave, the tree, the classroom—to name a few--all often
have a common meaning, even though personal associations sometimes
provide a more important personal meaning.

The Psychoid, or Spiritual Realm

I have already noted the strange capacity of the psyche to obtain information about the physical world through extrasensory perception,
through means other than the ordinary five senses. The psyche can also
reach out to and receive information from a universe of seemingly nonphysical reality. Jung calls this realm of experience *psychoid reality*; he
means that this dimension of reality is similar in nature to the psyche or
mind. Usually this has been called the realm of spiritual experience. In
most thinking derived from Hinduism and Buddhism, this is the only
realm of existence with any abiding reality. (Sometimes when he uses the
term "collective unconscious," Jung is referring to this vast area of experience; when he describes the collective unconscious, however, it is often
unclear whether he is referring to the depth of the personal psyche or to
what people of most cultures throughout recorded history have called
the spiritual domain.) But how can we know an aspect of reality without
brain, nervous system, or sense organs being involved? Human beings
have a kind of primal knowing that is in touch with both physical and
psychoid reality as well as having the sense organs and a nervous system
that have developed as vehicles to help us focus on the external world.
Indeed, human beings seem not to be the only creature that possess such
primal means of knowing. Some interesting work, for example, has been
done showing the reactions of plants to various kinds of stress. The most
impressive example that I have seen of this primal knowing is a film or
video entitled *The Embattled Cell*, available through the American Cancer
Society, in which one can see the apparently purposeful activities of lym-
phocytes as they attack and finally enter cancer cells, causing a subse-
quent explosive death of a colony of cancer cells.

So our mind/souls/personalities have quite different modes of knowing. Through sense experience and through extrasensory perception
(ESP) we know a common outer, physical world. We can also turn our
knowing in on ourselves and know that we know, and dip into the personal reservoir of memory as well as into our personal unconscious. And
we can even come to know the mysterious and strange depth of our collective unconscious mind. And in addition to these possibilities of knowing, we can experience a world of reality that is not the same as the
physical world, a universe in which time and space and logic do not

operate as they do in the physical one, a psychoid world that is similar to our psyche but beyond it.

It is important to distinguish the contents of the deep personal unconscious from the contents that belong to a spiritual reality that lies beyond the borders of our psyches and is independent of us. This psychoid domain often appears to be more complex and powerful than the physical one and to have a much greater range and power and complexity than our individual psyches. But learning to distinguish between what is part of our own psychic identity and what is coming to us from beyond is not easy; the lines of separation between the two are often fuzzy and blurred. As we begin to deal with the spiritual realm, we are once again like newborn children, who as they grow up need to learn that they are separate from their mothers and from the physical world, and are, in part, separate, autonomous human beings.

As we enter the realm of nonphysical reality, we come into the territory of religion and mythology, into the realm of widely varying religious experiences—the realm of the gods and goddesses, the good and demonic, evil and God. Jung calls this the realm of the numinous. Contact with this aspect of reality gives a sense of awe of the powerful other—sometimes fascinating, uplifting, and sometimes fearful. Jung uses the word as Rudolph Otto does in *The Idea of the Holy*. Sometimes we have contact with deceased people we have known or have not known, with mythological images and patterns that seem to have no connection with our personal psyches, or with powerful contents that seem good, evil, or ambivalent. In his seven novels, Charles Williams has described the boundless depth and variety of the spiritual dimension of reality, its magnificent love and goodness, and its hideous evil. C. S. Lewis gives the same perspective, as do the fathers of the church. Jesus, too, spoke both of the demonic, the angelic and of Abba, the daddy-mommy divine center of reality. One of the chief reasons for religions is to lead us to a helpful God and to spare us the destructiveness of evil on the way.

To deny the reality of spiritual evil is to deny one aspect of the exciting and frightening religious journey. Walter Wink has provided the definitive study of the principalities and powers in the New Testament in two books, *Naming the Powers* and *Unmasking the Powers*. Jeffrey Burton Russell has traced the history of our human struggle with the problem of spiritual evil in his exhaustive four-volume study, *The Devil, Satan, Lucifer,* and *Mephistopheles*. He has summarized his conclusions in the *Prince of Darkness*. For some people the inward journey that leads into the spiritual realm is not marked by great struggles with evil, but for others this is an essential part of the journey. In Figure 3 we have distinguished five differ-

ent kinds of numinous experience: psychic contents, ambivalent archetypes, deceased human beings, the angelic, evil and the demonic. All are
indicated on our diagram by the numeral 6.

The Divine

One of Jung's most important contributions to our understanding of
the psychoid world was his introduction of the idea of the Self. He produced evidence that in addition to human consciousness and reason,
something beyond the ego touches and informs our human lives with a
wisdom greater than our own. This reality can speak clearly to us in
English or whatever language is our own. When the message is clear, we
need to use care to discern which aspect of spiritual reality is relating to
us. It can also speak in the mysterious symbols of dreams. Sometimes
these "big dreams" are presented like plays on the stage of our souls. The
dreamer within, who presents the drama, knows all about us; where we
come from, how we got off the track, how to get back on the track, where
we should be going, and how we can get there.

Sometimes in dreams, visions, and religious experiences we are
brought directly into the presence of the light and love of God. We know
that we have met the Divine Lover face to face. In Figure 3 we distinguish
these three different experiences as the direct encounter with the Divine
(7), a clear communication from the Holy or its messenger (7a), and a
dream or vision that conveys its meaning in symbols and appears to be a
message from the Holy Spirit (7b).

Few children abandoned in the wild survive. Similarly, if we are to
deal with the realm of expanded awareness, we need the guidance of an
historical religion, and we need a spiritual friend or guide who has
already explored some of the territory and will accompany us on the journey, helping us to avoid the pitfalls and snares that may be found along
the way. For me, the way pointed out by Jesus of Nazareth and expressed
through the last two thousand years by the saints of the church, provides
the safest, most comprehensive, and most fulfilling religious journey.

In the twenty volumes of his collected works, Jung has supported the
factuality of the psychoid or spiritual universe, and the values and dangers of encounter with this domain.[8] The historical religions are important because they have tested our religious experience for thousands of
years and people are still led by them into experiences of spirituality and
the Divine. New religions are among the most dangerous and subversive
aspects of our society. Jesus only made a half-dozen changes in the Judaism in which he was reared. How much easier it is to project our wishes
and hopes and fears into the spiritual domain than into the physical one.

New religions often offer a way to avoid both the reality of the physical world and its insecurity as well as offering a wish-fulfillment vision of the spiritual domain. Sometimes they demand a mindless adherence to a leader or a text that gives psychological security and removes human responsibility for action in a confused and frightening world.

Whatever the nature of the spiritual domain, the spiritual or religious journey will not be taken seriously by people who deny its existence. When people deny the reality of the physical world or are unable to distinguish the contents of their inner world from those of the outer one, they are usually labeled psychotic; they do not perceive the physical world in the way other people do, or they refuse to acknowledge the reality of the physical world and live in their own fantasy world. But people who refuse to perceive and deal with the reality of the psychoid-spiritual domain often fall into equally serious psychological problems; we might refer to them as spiritually psychotic.

This latter disease is far more common than the former among those who have been influenced and brainwashed by Western civilization; indeed, this disease is considered normality on Wall Street and in the power centers of the world. I was brought up in such a materialistic environment, and I fell into a neurosis that was only relieved when I began to deal experientially with the other aspect of reality. In 1945 Carl Jung wrote to P. W. Martin, a Quaker who was one of the first in the religious community to perceive Jung's religious significance: "You are quite right, the main interest of my work is not concerned with the treatment of neuroses but rather with the approach to the numinous. But the fact is that the approach to the numinous is the real therapy and inasmuch as you attain to the numinous experiences you are released from the curse of pathology."[9]

Is it possible for us human beings to come to our full potential if we use only a portion of our knowing capacity? Is it possible for us to have fulfilled lives if we deal only with the universe of physical experience, of reduced awareness, with just a small portion of total reality? Wholeness is probably not possible for us if we avoid that aspect of reality. Many of the most influential people of all times have described this realm as the most desirable, as one that contains the most satisfying and abiding experiences available to human beings. If this is true, then how do we deal with the realm of numinous and expanded awareness? How can we find our way into Abba's kingdom, into the life of eternal growth, mercy, and love? The rest of this book describes various ways that my wife, Barbara, and I have found helpful in coming into closer contact with Abba and the kingdom.

CHAPTER 6

Finding a Way to God

My wife, Barbara, is one of the greatest gifts that life has given me. Not only has she given me support, caring, understanding, and commitment in a relationship that has grown into a genuine mutual sharing of our lives, but she has also provided me with an intimate experience of a way of finding God quite different from my own. Her way of quiet contemplation has sustained her through several major crises; she has seldom doubted the reality of God and ultimate meaning. (Later on in these pages she will describe in her own words her way of experiencing a divine presence using few concrete images.) My way, however, has been at times a violent struggle, filled with doubt and agnosticism and with a struggle to find divine caring in the midst of darkness, turmoil, and evil. The use of images, particularly the image of the risen Jesus, has often enabled me to be lifted out of a dark abyss in which Evil was a palpable reality.

Every one of us needs to find our own unique way of reaching the universe of increased awareness. I have come to be quite certain that no one way is any better than another. Whatever leads each of us to our destination of relationship with the Divine Lover, with the central core of meaning in the universe, is the best one for us. In one Roman Catholic Eucharist the priest prays for "all those who seek God with a sincere heart . . . and all the dead whose faith is known to God alone." Those who maintain that they have the *one* universal way to God often fall into bigotry.

I do not know why there are different ways, but I do know that we need to respect and honor and support those whose way of prayer is different from our own. I have speculated that those who, like Barbara, were nurtured in a family in which there was genuine equality and sharing between husband and wife and between children and parents are more likely to find the universe friendly and to have less difficulty in believing in and relating to a God who cares. Those of us who have not known that warm and caring nurture seem to be more open to the dark aspects of reality. Our souls seem to be more open to the intrusions of doubt, fear, depression, and evil; the lack of love and acceptance has worn thin the boundaries of our souls. Many of these people find that only with the help of concrete, saving images can they be lifted out of the pits into which they sometimes fall. (I am sure that there are exceptions to this generalization, as there are to almost all sweeping statements.)

My Personal Journey

The best way to speak of my own way of relating to God is to describe the way I found it. My first experience of the nonphysical world was an experience of threat and malevolence. I began to realize this quite recently at a conference at which it was suggested that we try to remember and draw our first experience of encounter with the numinous. My childhood was a struggle with sickness, rejection, and discouragement. My religious education was practically nonexistent, and I was torn between my mother's unsophisticated faith and my father's very rational and well-developed materialism and practical atheism. My first sense of nonphysical reality was of a hostile realm of trolls and ghosts, of demons and malicious spirits dwelling in the third floor of our house and in the dark. I wanted to believe in something kinder, however, and I found a sense of belonging and a presence of the Holy as an acolyte serving at Holy Communion.

As a young man I went to a college far from home, and I found the fellowship of the church family important to me as a stranger in a strange land. Then came the news of my mother's sickness and impending death. I clung to church and to hope through that ordeal, but when she died, I felt alone and hopeless. It seemed to me that the kindest and most loving person in my life had been slowly crushed and destroyed. All sense of meaning collapsed. And when I read Immanuel Kant's *Critique of Pure Reason* in my graduate studies at Princeton University, all vestiges of belief were swept away from me. I was plunged into total despair. The friendship of a neighboring family gave me immeasurable support, and the necessity of making a living forced me to find a job teaching fifth, sixth, and seventh grade boys in a military academy—in reality, a polite reform school.

During that year I realized that I had to find some meaning if I were to survive. I had talked with several ministers about meaning, but I found little light for my darkness. And then I happened upon a little church in Lake Mahopac, New York, where the rector, Dr. Walter Boardman Wright, was not only well-read and very intelligent, but he and his wife were personally warm, caring and friendly. They welcomed me into their home, showed genuine intellectual interest in my agnosticism, and offered much emotional support. They never judged me for my doubt and searching. As I reflect back over fifty years of Christian ministry, I realize how important it is for the church to provide all these gifts to seeking people.

With Dr. Wright's example, I decided that I would go to the source, to seminary, and see if Christianity could offer meaning to fill the aching void within me. My father was willing to support this venture as he believed that clergy could provide a helpful kind of social service.

This decision to search for meaning is an essential first step in finding a way to God, whether one is struggling to climb out of an abyss or is seeking more of the light one already has. One reason that the beggars in the spirit, the mourning, the hungry, and the thirsty and the persecuted are blessed by Jesus is that they have to find some meaning in order to survive; for the same reason, the contented and satisfied and well-filled are warned by Jesus of the perils of complacent satisfaction, particularly in their spiritual lives.

The seminary that accepted me was an ecclesiastical bastion of intellectual respectability. On the one hand, the teachers there did not condemn honest doubt, and they introduced us seminarians to the latest thinking in biblical criticism and theological exploration. But nearly two-fifths of my time in seminary was spent in studying the Bible in Hebrew and Greek; and although it has given me confidence in my own interpretation of scripture and has been important for much of the writing that I have done, I fear that the emphasis on learning these languages was wasted on most of the students.

What I learned about the incredible growth of the Christian church in spite of three hundred years of horrible persecution made a deep impression on me. During this period, any Christian man could be executed or thrown to the lions (or much worse), his wife and children could be sold into slavery, and his property could be given to the person who informed the government of his religious practice. Few people suffer such anguish for illusion. Something had indeed happened at Easter; as Pinchas Lapide has eloquently pointed out in his recent book *The Resurrection of Jesus: A Jewish Perspective* the power that raised Jesus from the dead and the presence of the risen Jesus were living realities to those early Christians.

But none of the professors at the seminary knew enough about the science of that day or about the history of philosophy to offer any sensible explanation of how the resurrection might have occurred or how a spiritual reality might touch our lives and sustain us. Fortunately, while at seminary I discovered the writings of Baron von Hügel and A. E. Taylor; both of these writers were more brilliant than the agnostic professors at Princeton, and they believed that Christianity contained the essential seeds of ultimate truth.

Another great lack in my seminary life was the almost total absence of Christian love and community. I found less genuine interest in the students by the faculty there than I had in four years at two different colleges. The faculty were academic judges. World War II was in full swing, and the members of the faculty were afraid that some of us might be there to avoid the draft; students were even used to spy on other students and inform the dean. Instead of a sense of caring and mutual concern, I felt a sense of competition and one-upmanship. There was little faculty emphasis on Christian love, little facilitation of the spirit of love among the students. Indeed this seminary had one of the most barren and loveless atmospheres that I have experienced. Recent seminarians from many different schools have told me that the general quality of relationships has not greatly changed in most seminaries today.

Any direction on how to pray or relate with God was notable in its absence. The seminary faculty worked on the dangerous assumption that each of us had found our own way to God before we arrived in seminary. Spiritual formation was not their business. I suspect that underlying that assumption was a hidden fear that no real communication between God and human beings was possible. Personal, private, intimate divine-human fellowship was hardly considered a possibility. We had our daily chapel services using Morning and Evening Prayer according to the rite of the *Episcopal Prayer Book,* and once a week Eucharist was celebrated. Those who did not attend the services were regarded as not really sharing in the life of the community and of questionable sincerity. These services were supposed to fill our every spiritual need.

I was most faithful at the services. Indeed, I was a bit compulsive and came to the services five minutes or so early. I found that nearly a dozen students—no faculty—were already there. Being a curious soul, I came earlier and earlier and discovered that a handful of students met a half hour before the stated service to be quiet, to pray, and to read some of the classics of devotional literature. I added another person to this informal group. I found something in the quiet fellowship of those early morning times of prayer, reflection, and reading classics of the devotional life that

I did not find in the formal services themselves. But I realized intuitively that the faculty viewed this group with some suspicion. Years later I discovered through a strange series of synchronistic events that we were considered dangerous "enthusiasts," people whose judgment was not to be trusted. Also, over a weekend during Lent I attended a retreat led by a member of an Anglican religious order, and I found a sense of holy presence and the numinous in the reserved sacrament, in which the consecrated elements of Eucharist are kept between services.

I found a reality in the chapel services, the quiet, and the retreat, but I was given no way to integrate this experience into my theological framework. Then I graduated from seminary and found myself trying to bring the Christian gospel to a small church in East Syracuse, New York. And without the daily services and the quiet fellowship of others, I soon lost these sustaining practices. Instead I became an excellent social worker. I called on every family in the parish and knew them well. I could speak with real empathy about the crucifixion, but with less vitality about the resurrection. I found that what I had endured in the six months that my mother was dying enabled me to minister to the dying and the bereaved; funerals for me were a time of close communion with people and with God. Because of my own struggle with the abyss, furthermore, I had no fear of other people's doubts and darkness, and I found that people would talk with me about their fears and questions.

Something, however, was lacking in my life, and I did not know what it was, but I kept busy enough so I did not have time to pay attention to this feeling. During this period I was introduced to Charles Whiston's book *Teach Us to Pray*, and I realized that I had abandoned any regular time of quiet or daily prayer. I began to keep a list of people for whom I wanted to pray regularly, and I began reading Morning and Evening Prayer daily by myself. During this period Barbara Jones came to me for confirmation instruction, and within a year we were married. She, too, was interested in the spiritual life, but spiritually we were babes in the woods. The set services of Morning and Evening Prayer did not feed Barbara. I continued using them for several years but finally realized that they alone did not bring me into a personal relationship with God or the risen Jesus.

In 1946 I was called to be the assistant to the dean of Trinity Cathedral in Phoenix, Arizona. We arrived several months before the dean, and I continued my systematic calling and social service ministry. I also did most of the hospital calling in that large parish. When Dean Carmen arrived, I was given great freedom and responsibility. I noted that the churches that had healing services were attracting large crowds. A short service for the laying-on-of-hands for healing followed a service for the dying in the Prayer Book. With the dean's permission, I added this service to the communion service that I conducted each Wednesday morning. A significant number of people began to attend the services for healing, and a group of them suggested that we meet afterwards for a weekly prayer group.

We began meeting, and together we read Charles Whiston's *Teach Us to Pray*. We invited Whiston, a professor at the Church Divinity School of the Pacific, to conduct a mission on prayer. Then one of the group introduced me to Agnes Sanford's book *The Healing Light*. When I read this book, I agreed with Barbara that this author was either lying, crazy, or speaking an incredibly important truth. I tried using her method and found that spiritual healing could happen today just as it did in the early church. We went to hear Agnes speak at Estes Park, Colorado. She was real, humble, earthy, powerful, a wounded healer. Since the dean trusted my judgment, he allowed me to invite her to give a healing mission at the Cathedral. Barbara and I came to know her well, and we saw some amazing healings take place before our eyes. She believed that the risen Jesus was still available to those who wished a relationship with him, and that the Holy Spirit still healed just as in New Testament times.

During this period, both of us were also introduced to the writings of the remarkable depth psychologist, Fritz Kunkel. His book *In Search of Maturity* opened me to the realization that real psychology and real religion could go hand in hand. We also found that keeping a journal for reflection and for the recording of dreams was a spur to the spiritual life. We started to keep track of our dreams and also discovered that listening quietly with a journal before us brought us in touch with a wisdom greater than our own.

How grateful I am to Dean Carmen, later Episcopal Bishop of Oregon, for his suggestion that I had been an assistant long enough and it was time for me to find a parish of my own. I enjoyed being where I was, but later I realized how right he was. In my new position as rector of St. Luke's Parish in Monrovia, California, I had full authority. I was called for many wrong reasons. My personal motivation was no better: I was going to be the finest rector the parish ever had. I worked fourteen hours a day. I called on all seven hundred and fifty families within eight months, provided an accurate and up-to-date roster of members, and spearheaded a successful every-member canvass that put the parish on sound financial footing. In addition (to the horror of some of the more conservative members) I asked Starr Daily, a converted convict and an associate of Agnes Sanford in the Camps Farthest Out, to conduct a prayer and healing mission in the church. He lived in Monrovia, and we became close friends. We started a weekly healing service during our midweek communion service, with a prayer group following it—a group that continued for the twenty years I was rector there.

In the midst of all these "positive indicators," my life came to a screeching stop. I continued to keep my journal, and my record of dreams became increasingly ominous. Anxiety began to rise within me. Barbara's father became ill in what became a terminal illness. She took the children and drove to the East Coast to be with him, and I was left all alone to face myself. It is dangerous to look deep within and see all that is there when one has no one with whom to talk. Luckily my omnivorous calling had introduced me to a fringe member of the parish, Dorothy Phillips, who had been ill for many years. Through her I contacted Max Zeller, about whom I have already written. He knew the depth and capacities of the human soul and was one of the least judgmental people I have ever known, as well as one of the most caring. When his son was asked what he wanted to become when he grew up, he replied without a pause: "I want to be the patient." Is not this kind of caring the ideal of Christian ministry?

My dream the night before my first visit to Max Zeller brought forth an aspect of my life that I had never discussed with anyone, and the following dreams showed me a way out of the hopeless dead-end street in which I was stranded. With Max's help I saw that in my dreams I encountered a wisdom far greater than my own, trying to reach and direct me. I found a presence that knew me far better than I knew myself, who knew where I had strayed off my path, how to get back on it, and where I should be going later. I carefully studied the Bible and the vital early church leaders, and I discovered that most of the early Christians leaders believed that God communicated with human beings through their dreams. My experience with dreams, therefore, was a continuation of early Christian practice, not a strange aberration. Barbara and the children were gone for only nine weeks, and during this time my life came together in a way in which I would not have believed.

The most important aspect of this experience of direction and caring was that God became real to me. I began to realize that my faith had been built on inference rather than experience and encounter. I came to see that the root of much of my anxiety was a deep split within my psyche. Part of me believed and was trying to help other people believe, and part of me was caught in the materialistic agnosticism in which I was brainwashed in my childhood and youth. But my experience with the wisdom of dreams gave me evidence that my materialistic view of reality was inadequate, and this new understanding usually silenced that persistent negative voice. Neurosis and anxiety usually arise within us when we are divided at a deep level.

I came to see Max on one occasion feeling like death warmed over. He sensed my mood and asked me what was wrong. I told him that I had awakened at three that morning and had not been able to go to sleep again, and I had a fourteen-hour day ahead of me. He asked me: "Do you know why you couldn't sleep?" I groaned that I didn't, and he replied: "God wanted to talk with you." My response was a sarcastic: "Now really!" He went on to say: "This is the way Yahweh got in touch with Samuel. Do you think that God has changed?" That night I awakened and got up with my journal in hand. In the silence of the night I asked somewhat rudely: "Lord, what's on your mind?" And an inner voice spoke back: "I just want your company." I responded: "At three o'clock in the morning?" Again a voice within spoke, not in audible words, but with clear meaning: "It is the only time that I can get your attention." This conversation continued for a half an hour or so. I recorded it in my journal and then went back to bed and went to sleep.

I learned two important lessons from this experience. I discovered that I need not just wait for dreams to give me relationship with God, that I could initiate the relationship with this caring, inner wisdom when I was relaxed and quiet. When I awoke in the middle of the night, I was already quiet, a perfect time for my communion with God. I have naturally awakened at this time for many years. It was a good time for me to meditate, but I realize that it is an impossible practice for many people, and my own practice sometimes changes now. We all need to find our own individual way and to realize that our time of quiet with the Divine Lover needs to change as we change.

During these times of relaxed quiet I have reflected over the previous day and I've dialogued with the Inner Presence, letting it lead me with its divine wisdom. I have also found that when I read and ruminate on scripture quietly within the fellowship of this presence, I have been led to a deeper understanding of its meaning. The life, teaching, and parables of Jesus revealed level after level of significance for me—and ultimately for my congregation. Sometimes these times of quiet were periods when I could simply bask in the presence of a loving, caring luminous reality and be rested and strengthened. Out of these times of initiated relationship with the Risen One and the Holy Spirit have come much of my understanding of the gospel, and most of my ideas for sermons, lectures, and books.

At times of outer and inner turmoil the old doubts and fears would press in on me, and I learned to use Christian meditation—what Jung called active imagination—to deal with the dark moods into which they threw me. (I suspect those who think they have conquered every difficulty and have nothing more to deal with have not faced the agony of our world.) Moods are as difficult as mercury to pin down; seldom can one argue one's self out of them by logic and reasoning. However, Jung discovered that behind every mood lay an image, as James Hillman, in his book *Emotions*, describes in detail. Instead of running away from the oppressive moods, I learned to enter them and let them reveal themselves in images.

Sometimes these images were horribly hostile and destructive, but I did not remain in the hopeless chaos—as Sartre and Camus, for instance, do in most of their stories. I would then invite into this demonic chaos the risen Jesus, the one who faced the worst that human beings and Evil could do to any of us and conquered it. The dark figures then would retreat, my own torn and broken being would be restored, the mood would dissipate, and I could go on again. I found that this practice was seldom effective unless I wrote out a description of my encounter with the hostile, destructive darkness and of my restoration from it. These practices, which I learned from Jung, are not new. They have been used by Christians for centuries. Ignatius of Loyola systematized them in his ground-breaking manual of spiritual practice, *Spiritual Exercises*.

My spiritual practice was largely pragmatic. I used it because it worked. But after many years of attending to my dreams and of prayer and meditation, it suddenly dawned on me that Jung provided a world-view in which there was a spiritual realm of experience as well as a material one. He also experienced in this realm a creative organizing principle, wiser than human beings, which wanted to relate to us and guide us to our wholeness, to fulfillment. Jung called this reality *das Selbst*, (literally the itself); the church called it the Holy Spirit. Jung had come to propose this view of reality as he dealt with his own inner struggle and as he helped his patients through their emotional crises and on toward wholeness. And this view, I realized, is very similar to that of Jesus of Nazareth and of the leaders of the early Christian church. Eventually the various parts of the puzzle fell together for me, and I developed a diagram that has grown and changed over the years, until the most recent revision of it became that worldview I described in earlier chapters (see Figures 2 and 3).

Within this view of the universe, the idea that the Spirit gives us "gifts" makes sense. This is God's world; the Divine Spirit penetrates the spiritual and physical world and seeks relationship with human beings. When I was asked to write a book on tongue speaking, I could examine the experience within this worldview without either denying the gift or seeing it as the most important manifestation of God's Spirit. I also found that my Jungian friends were far more open to this spiritual phenomenon that most clergy, and that Jung himself had studied the tongue speaking in his early years. Since I had first felt the direction of God in my life through dreams, I started a ten-year study that demonstrated that throughout the Bible and the history of the church (except in recent years in Western Christian practice) dreams had been considered one of the most common ways that God reaches out to human beings. This resulted in my book *God, Dreams, and Revelation*. I also studied the other gifts of the Spirit, since they had been ignored by most serious theologians, and wrote on healing, prayer, the gifts of wisdom and knowledge, and the gift of discernment. Indeed, if this view of our universe is correct and yet we fail to seek relationship with the caring center of reality, we are neglecting our most important resource for actualizing our human potential.

For many years Barbara and I each went our different ways of prayer alone. My way of using images was not helpful to her. She developed her own way, and also found the Eucharist increasingly meaningful in her prayer life. At her suggestion we began to celebrate Eucharist daily together. This has brought us together both spiritually and emotionally. I experience Eucharist, the most ancient and central Christian way of worship, as complete prayer, embracing all elements of communion with God. In it we come quietly into God's presence, we confess our failures, receive absolution, meditatively listen to scripture, let ourselves go in adoration, live through the ritual that Jesus gave us before he was betrayed and crucified, have fellowship with the risen Jesus, commune with God, offer thanksgiving, and receive God's blessing. This daily ritual has added another dimension, a great depth, to our life of fellowship with God. We have found that we can celebrate Eucharist wherever we go—in motel rooms and in airports, as well as in our home or in a church. God is not confined to church buildings.

Barbara's Spiritual Journey

Barbara has had a very different spiritual journey from mine. She writes:

I was always aware that I had been a very-much-wanted first child, who arrived ten years after my parents were married. My family were church-attending Methodists who believed in a very personal God, and I was taught early to talk with God about my desires, problems, and hopes, and to give thanks. Most of my very early prayer time was at bedtime, and for me bedtime prayers were a good, permanent habit; each night, even now, I find it helpful and necessary to review the day, ask forgiveness for what has been amiss, give thanks, and pray for those I love and those in need. And I end by asking God to watch over me.

When I was nine years old our family doctor discovered that my mother had cancer. In those days, that was a sentence of death. In our family, children were not excluded from the joys or the sufferings. For example, I always knew what the family financial situation was, and I was allowed to help decide how what we had would be spent (these were the depression years, and we didn't have very much). So the fact that my mother was considered terminal was shared with my brother and me. My mother had faith that life continued after death and that her influence on us would also continue. I never questioned this, but the sad years that followed the revelation that she had cancer were years when I pleaded with God nightly not to take our mother from us.

My parents were soulmates and were deeply in love with each other, and therefore I now realize how much my father was suffering. During the next eight years my mother managed to live in spite of nine operations and deep X-ray therapy, which left her skin burned to a crisp. During all this time I pleaded and pleaded with God. Meanwhile, at the age of nine, it had become my duty to do the cooking and to take care of my mother during the night if she needed care.

At age seventeen I went away to college. I had been brought up in a liturgical Methodist Episcopal church, and I discovered in my new city that my denomination was not liturgical, it did not have formal services or frequent Eucharist. At that time I also discovered how much I needed this more structured outer worship with others at least once a week. The Communion service seemed to bring me an experience of the Divine that I received in no other way. So I began to attend the Episcopal church, which was more like the church in which I was raised.

The day before Thanksgiving during that first year in college, my mother died. I was devastated. I felt let down by God. It seemed to me that just when I left home and turned my back, God let her die. After two weeks of being home, I returned to college, and each night I would cry out to God for leaving me without a mother.

For the next several years I kept attending the Episcopal church, and I finally met Morton the month after he graduated from seminary, when I went to him for confirmation instructions. It was not love at first sight, because I was engaged to another man, who was away in the war. But I became active in Morton's church and circumstances intervened, and the man I was engaged to was no longer available.

After some time Morton and I were married. Being a priest's wife was a more or less prescribed role forty-five years ago, and I admit that, though I worked hard at it, many parts of the prescribed role I did not enjoy. At that period in our lives I continued the daily conversational "talking things over" with God, and Morton and I read the Bible each day together. However, we did not pray together. These were busy war years and I taught at school, did case work for the Red Cross, and faithfully attended all meetings and services connected with church.

As I look back on my life, I realize that my great experiences, both positive and negative, were really religious experiences, but at the time I did not interpret them in that way. For me the sexual experience was one in which God was present. In many of the more negative experiences, I railed at God for not hearing me, but I realize now that until I could be honest with God and be angry, I could not be real. Later I often felt guilty for these angry feelings and words, and I had to learn to feel forgiven for them.

My first pregnancy ended in miscarriage and was a crushing experience, but perhaps the most difficult time for me was shortly after our second child was born. Morton suffered his darkness experience, about which he has already written; most lay people would refer to this experience as a nervous breakdown. I was terrified. Here we were in a parish. I knew something was radically wrong with my husband. I kept up the outer appearances that everything was all right, but in this time of need I found myself praying ever more intently. I learned to pray just for each day.

At this point in my life, my father was taken seriously ill in the East, and I needed to go and help care for him. I hated to leave Morton, but he and I decided I had to go. I took the children, and nine weeks later I returned and found that Morton had received help, as he has told you, and that I was living with an entirely different person. Before I had been needed, but now I had the feeling that Morton was so happy to be able to stand on his own two feet that he was like an adolescent who wanted to go his own way. I felt I was no longer central in his life, to his work, or to his needs. In desperation I went to see his analyst. Over the long period of time that I was in analysis, I discovered that I was more than a wife and mother. I was me and Morton was Morton, and I just had to allow these two individuals, ourselves, to work out a new marriage. All of this I now know was spiritual growth for me, painful as it was, but at the time I hated having to recognize this and to allow it to happen. At that time, society was not supportive of independent women, and I really had had very little drive towards independence. But I did learn to let Morton go—railing at God all the time!

Out of these several years of great trauma for me, I learned that Morton had discovered a way of having a personal, one-to-one experience of the Divine. I spent many hours trying to make his method of going to the Lord work for me as it did for him. The Lord seemed to speak directly with him, but with me he just didn't seem to want to communicate! During this time I read most of the devotional classics, and a few gave me some help. The ones that did just encouraged me to keep up my conversational way of talking it all over with God and telling him honestly what I felt, not what I thought God would want to hear.

Years later, a Roman Catholic priest who had known me for several years leveled with me and told me that I was a completely different type of person than Morton, and that I had had such a different childhood and background that I was wasting my time trying to meditate in the way Morton did. The priest said that I should find my own way and that not everyone found images and imagination real for them or a way to God.

I then discovered a way that I call contemplation (only because Morton labels what he does meditation, and I need a word to distinguish his from mine). I observe something closely, preferably in nature (but music and art can be useful also). After asking God to be in this with me, I concentrate for a few minutes on this experience and only this, and then in some mysterious way I experience a real "sense of presence." I seem to feel I come into rhythm with the total universe or become one with it.

In *Companions on the Inner Way* I wrote my description of this process:

The basic idea is that the spiritual and physical worlds are one in the sense that they totally interpenetrate each other. Whenever we touch the physical we are also touching the spiritual. Contemplation (from this point of view) is an attempt to deal with our spiritual lives in the same way that we human beings handle most situations in life. This is a threefold process:

1. We experience something.
2. We mull it over or think about it.
3. We try to discern what implications this experience and our consideration of it has for our lives.

As a method of religious discovery, we need first of all to become aware that we have lived all our lives in a society that has given us a sensory overload of noise and smells and colors. We have become desensitized to sensory experience, and we need to learn to truly *experience* once again. We need to concentrate *totally* on a limited area of sensation for a short period of time without blocking any aspect of it and without thinking about it—just experiencing the *what* as it is now. We can usually enter that sensory experience and stay with it for only a short period of time. Any analytical thought at that time immediately turns off the process.

The process begins with relaxation, quieting of the body and the mind as much as possible. After a few minutes of experiencing and concentrating on the sensory data that is presented, we can then withdraw further into the silence, into the absence of any sensation, and rest in it, just experiencing whatever comes. What comes may be a dazzling darkness, a sense of presence, a deep sense of peace, a cessation of struggle, or we may be presented with a word, a thought, a number, a color, a musical sound, etc.

As we pull out of the depth of the quiet we begin to mull over that which has been given, thinking about it, seeing where this experience leads us. This can go on for several minutes or an hour. The last stage occurs as we pull out of the depth of quiet and try to understand what the experience means to us, how it applies to my everyday life, where I am now, what it tells me about my relationship with God, with other people, and with the world around me and finally what I am going to do about it.[1]

Eight years ago I had a severe accident and was literally crushed. I spent months on my back in the hospital and at the home of a friend. I discovered that I did not rail at God so much. I really felt an inner peace (there was little outer peace during that time). I had learned to take each day, one day at a time, to give thanks for the little things that were pleasant (like having my position changed or being given a cold drink) and to say "ouch" to the Lord when I hurt—and I had a sense that God was with me all through that long experience of being helpless and in pain. I seldom felt down or discouraged; I knew that however it turned out, it would be all right. I learned that my contemplative way of coming into this presence was even a good way to control pain. When I was in God's presence I just knew that whatever was to be would be all right. It might not be the way I wanted it, or Morton wanted it, and I wasn't even sure it was the way God wanted it, but whatever it was, my Lord would be there with me. All I needed to do was to stop and become aware of the Presence, and then I knew things would fall in place. In many ways Morton and I are closer in our feelings, in understanding each other's values, in our intimacy and sexuality, and in our prayer life than we have ever been before. In meeting together daily in the Eucharist we find that we can be present to each other and with the Divine.[2]

We have just passed through the most traumatic experience of our life together, the death of our younger son. We found that the same practices have sustained and carried us through with hope. God will receive and redeem what we have lost.

Reaching into the Spiritual Realm

More and more people from all walks of life are coming to see that their lives cannot develop to their full potential unless they learn to deal with the realm of expanded awareness, the psychoid, the spiritual. Returning from a conference in New York, I sat in the plane next to a vice-president of one of the nation's largest brokerage houses. He was on his way to a conference center in Colorado to study meditation. He told me that only with this help could he survive the pressures of his life. (He was surprised to find that I, as a clergy person, had an interest in meditation and that I had even written a book on Christian meditation.) Various national opinion polls bear witness to this increasing interest. As many as 10 percent of the American populace have tried Transcendental Meditation. And yet very few mainline Christian churches have weekly prayer groups or regular classes teaching people to pray, to open themselves to the spiritual realm, to find a close and intimate relationship with God. In addition, few churches provide adult education classes that teach us how to deal maturely with the world of reduced awareness. We have already indicated the dangers of dealing with spiritual experience before we have learned to deal creatively with our physical world and the people in it. If our religious practice is going to help us toward human fulfillment, we need the wisdom of historical religions to guide us in both of these areas.

The journey toward wholeness involves bringing all of ourselves—both our conscious life in the ordinary world and the depth of our psyches and our experiences of the spiritual world—to all of the divine reality we can know. As we grow in knowledge of ourselves and the Holy, our practices will change. Prayer and meditation are a conscious attempt to facilitate the encounter of our total psyches with the divine center of reality for our transformation and guidance so that we may realize our maximum potential. I have described how two different ways of seeking wholeness developed and grew. One uses images of the Savior to help us survive; the other, like Barbara's, enters into an imageless presence. They are different and yet they have much in common. They give us a way to begin to deal with spiritual reality inside of us and beyond us and to open ourselves to God and the fullness of life. These two methods offer two roads that diverge, and yet these divergent ways complement each other. Indeed, they need one another if all people are going to be open to the mysterious reality of the unsearchable richness of God.

The Redwood as a Symbol of the Growth Process

We have already pointed to the great redwoods as symbols of fulfillment and seeking. They also give us a pattern of elements and processes
necessary to the fulfilled life. What does it take for a redwood to grow
from a ridiculously tiny seed to the largest living creature on earth? First
of all, only an intact and undamaged seed can grow into a majestic tree.
Second, to begin the process of growth the seed must break out of its
hard casing: until it does this, the seed is only potential. Seeds can
remain dormant for thousands of years. And moisture is, in fact, another
necessary element for the tree's growth; without moisture, the seed cannot break out of its cocoon, nor can it survive once it has shed its skin.
Water brings the seed the agony of birth, and then it becomes the seed's
very blood. Furthermore, the fledgling plant can survive only a short
time without an environment of soil, air, and light, from which it takes
the atomic building blocks it needs for growth.

The tree must also have warmth, the warmth of the sea, of the fog
drifting in over the mountains and valleys, the warmth of summer. And
redwoods are, in a sense, communal: they most often grow in groves,
where they protect one another and create an environment that enhances
the chances of reproduction and great growth. They produce a canopy so
dense that only minimal light filters to the forest floor, so most other
plants cannot survive there and compete for nutrients in the rich soil. But
most of all, they need time, year after year; time gives the trees the opportunity to *become*.

When a human's saw or a great storm has laid one of these giants on
the ground and it is cut across the trunk, one finds a thousand years or
more of history written into the fabric of the wood. The rings reveal each
fire, every dry winter, and the years that trees along the river were
flooded and covered with new soil. Silently, secretly, the tree has written
its own story within its wood.

How is it that these trees live so long when others rot and die? The
answer, it seems, is that the wood and bark of the redwood are impreg-
nated with tannin, which discourages hungry insects in the soil. And this
tannin protects the tree in yet another way: this complex chemical produced within the redwood-tree factory also retards fire. Most great forests
expire when fire strikes them, and nothing is left but charred ghost trees.
But only the most violent fire can pierce the redwood's tannin-filled bark.
Indeed, fire is a friend to the coast trees and a necessity for those in the
Sierra: fire sweeps the tall redwood forest damaging and scarring some

trees, but removing all competition for the forest environment. Other trees are simply swept away, and the redwoods have everything they need to fill in their scars quickly.

For many years the vigilant Forest Service quickly extinguished most fires among the massive mountain giants. However, an observant ranger noted that where there were no fires, there were no new young trees. Careful research showed that the seeds of the giant trees didn't germinate until a fire cleaned away the branches and leaves and fallen trees that littered the forest floor. Researchers also noticed that the cones opened most fully during the fire and could then drop their seeds on ash-covered soil. Like gold and silver, and some human beings, redwoods are refined and made stronger through fire. Persecution often fosters vital Christian faith and fellowship.

Tirelessly the tiny pumps within the living sapwood work day and night; they are like the human heart, which keeps alive the many trillion cells within the human body. These pumps force the life-giving sap from the most distant rootlet to the needles three hundred feet above the ground. The coast redwoods continue to live even after they are cut down. From the roots of each cut tree, many saplings spring up around the great stump and over time a cathedral-like vault emerges deep in the forest's heart. Immortality, in a real sense, belongs to them. They can rise again and again from the same roots.

The wisdom that guides this germinating and growing tree is contained in a fragile, minute seed, almost lost in a wrinkle in my hand. The complexity of this living tree is just beginning to be understood by scientists as they discover the nearly innumerable life secrets of this ancient tree.

Growth of the Tree and the Soul

Some seeds and some human beings are damaged. They cannot survive well, if at all, on their own. They must be cared for. People who have never learned to deal adequately with the physical world, the world of reduced awareness, are not good candidates for the inner journey. They can get the spiritual and physical worlds mixed up and so become confused and immobilized. Some people can even get so caught up by the spiritual world that they become inflated and believe they have a personal pipeline to God. Our time of inward turning, our contact with the world of expanded awareness, is healthy only if it helps us grow *and* enables us to share more love with others. Christian meditation has failed unless those around us feel more cared for because we have spent time with the caring core of spiritual reality, the Abba that Jesus revealed.

Seeds must die and lose their identity as seeds if their potential is to be released, if they are going to grow into redwood trees, and seeds need water to start this process of transformation. Jesus spoke to Nicodemus in the night and told him that he needed to be born again. Nicodemus took him literally, but Jesus was speaking in a parable: until human beings consciously realize that the ordinary world around them is not enough, they are like seeds that have not sprouted.

Moisture makes the seed swell until the pressure is so great that it rips apart its husk, a violent process. And sprouted seeds—like newborn humans—are tender and require a nurturing environment if they are to continue to live and grow in this difficult world.

I wonder if spiritual birth is any easier for many of us. Some seem to make the passage easily, but few of us become very strong in the spirit who have not known some tension, trial, and testing. I don't like it that way, but this has been my own experience and that of most of those to whom I have listened. And even after the process takes place, life can remain difficult: spiritual birth often makes us quite different from those around us, and it can leave us in a lonely place.

And when does such birth occur? I have known it to occur even in a person's teens; I doubt, however, if genuine spiritual birth can take place until a person has achieved some autonomy and self-direction, until childhood dependency has been largely outgrown. It often occurs in midlife, when suddenly we see that life is half over and what we have already found is dust and ashes. It can occur on a deathbed or in the process of dying, a process that in some ways is very much like birth. And I believe, along with C. S. Lewis and Charles Williams, that we may have a chance to be reborn in the world to come. I believe that the loving Abba whom I have known will always be open to all those who finally decide that the kingdom of heaven is what they want more than anything else.

The physical seed, as I have said, must have water to give birth and grow. There is a comparable water of life that opens us spiritually, rips us open, and sets us on a new path enabling us to become new creatures in the Spirit. No matter what else we are given, unless we continue to be bathed in this living water we dry up and die. Water is the substance from which we sprang, so it is an apt metaphor for this spiritual life-giver. Often we dream of water as the vast reservoir of psychic life of which we are a part; it can represent our own spiritual nature.

Water was a symbol of life for the Jews, who lived in a semiarid country and saw the desert come to life when it rained. Isaiah tells how God will transform the desert of Israel into the garden of the Lord (Isaiah 55). And Ezekiel envisions the heavenly temple as the source of water that

brings abundance and joy to God's people (Ezekiel 47). Jesus and his followers carry on this tradition. After Jesus asked the Samaritan woman to
draw some water for him from Jacob's well, he said to her: "All those who
drink of this water will thirst again, but whoever drinks of the water that
I shall give them will never thirst; the water that I give them will become
in them a spring of water welling up to eternal life" (John 4:13, author's
translation). Later Jesus spoke at a festival and told people that those who
thirst may come to him and drink. And John comments that when Jesus
speaks of water he is speaking of the Spirit (John 7:38–39).

Water became the instrument and symbol of baptism through which
followers of Jesus shared in the Spirit. One of the last statements of Revelation is this: "And let them who are thirsty come, let them who desire
take the water of life without price" (Rev. 22:17, author's translation). Are
we not bathed continuously, both within the depth of us and in our outer
world with the Spirit? Our task is not so much to seek for God, but to let
the water of life, the Spirit, seep into our lives so that we become new
creatures and then to keep ourselves open to the stream of living water so
that we may grow into what we are capable of becoming. The Spirit
opens us to life and nurtures us into mature members of the kingdom.
Like light, water is a powerful symbol of the Spirit of God.

Jesus also spoke frequently of seeds. He told a parable of how various
seeds fell on different kinds of ground. Some fell among the thorns and
were choked by brambles; others fell on rocky ground, where there was
not enough moisture for the roots; some fell on the road and were
crushed into the earth by hooves and feet. The soul, in other words,
needs the right environment if it is to prosper. There is good news here,
however: once we are born into new understanding, we can *choose* the
soil we need. Unlike the plant, we need not stay among thorns or on
pathways or in shallow rocky soil. One of the main purposes of religious
fellowships is to provide good ground where sprouted souls can be nurtured and grown; monasteries, for example, were developed when the
outer environment seemed particularly hostile to spiritual growth. The
church should offer an environment in which men and women can grow
when the outer world is little more than brambles and rock, the chaos
and confusion of a dog-eat-dog world. The most significant reason for
individual churches is to provide a place where the soul-seed may sprout
and then be protected, nourished, and nurtured so that we may grow
and bear much fruit. We humans are more fortunate than seeds scattered
by a sower or the wind: we can select an environment in which to grow.

Jesus was trampled down on the crowded roads and crucified, but he
rose again to let us know that *there is always hope*. Even when we are

choked to death by brambles, trampled down by unconscious, dominating, and oppressive people, or dried up in soil covering bedrock only by an inch—even then we can be raised up by the power that coursed through Jesus in the tomb and raised him. So many Christian saints remind us that it is never too late: Peter who denied Jesus; Paul who persecuted him; Augustine and Francis of Assisi, who were choked with weeds but who sought other soil. We, too, can be raised up in this life or in the next one and planted in good soil. The soul-seed has infinitely more potential than any merely physical seed.

Living in the Light and Spirit

Insight into maturity or fulfillment may come in a flash, but the embodiment of that insight takes time. Just as a redwood spends centuries reaching up toward the sky and stretching out its branches to receive the light and energy of the sun, so we human beings need time to open ourselves to the Holy, the divine Light, and let it transform us. The Light that created us to be receptive to itself wishes to give us more than we can imagine or desire. We need times of quiet and relaxation, when we do nothing more than wait ready to receive the Light.

It is no wonder that many ancient people worshipped the sun as the source of life. John wrote of Jesus: "In him was life, and the life was the light of human beings. The light shines in the darkness, and the darkness has not overcome it. . . . The true light that enlightens every person was coming into the world" (John 1:4–5, 9, author's translation). Just as the tree ceases to grow and gradually dies when cut off from light, so we humans never mature to our full potential unless we find the true light and expose ourselves to it. But how do we learn to live in the light and drink the water of life? How do we open ourselves to the Spirit?

Nearly every historical religion tells us that we need to be detached from total preoccupation with the world of reduced awareness if we are to be open to the Spirit. This requires that we quiet down, relax, and enter into the silence. When we enter a theater with a good friend, we may be in lively conversation, but when the lights go out and the curtain rises, we miss the play unless our conversation ceases and we focus on the stage. And meditation-contemplation, similarly, is turning toward the central stage on which the cosmic drama is constantly portrayed.

During daylight the chlorophyll in the redwood needle turns off its processing activity, thus opening itself to receive. We need to do the same thing if we are to receive the true Light. First of all, most of us need a place where we can be still. Only the most developed meditators can pray

in a busy street with a jackhammer breaking concrete; we need to go into
a quiet place and stop everything else. We relax as we put everything else
out of our minds and begin to breathe deeply and evenly, just as we
breathe when we awaken from a deep and restful sleep. We then try to
relax our muscles, remembering that muscular tension represents an
unconscious, congealed movement. I find it helpful to have my journal
open in my lap. When I begin to get quiet, I find myself remembering the
things that I have forgotten to do and the things that I have done wrong
that need to be corrected. If I try to hang onto these thoughts, I cannot
remain open to the realm of expanded awareness and to the Light. If I jot
them down, I can then return into the silence.

Once we are quiet, we can open ourselves further in several quite
different ways. Some people learn simply to withdraw from all their sensations. This practice is advocated by many Christian meditators and is
described well in *The Cloud of Unknowing*. Adepts in Zen suggest this
method, and the sensory deprivation tank offers a physical method of
coming to this receptivity by allowing an individual to float in water in a
dark and soundproof space. I find that stopping my inner talking to
myself helps bring me into a state of silence. Some people find it helpful
to concentrate on a cross or the flame of a candle. The constant repetition
of a phrase can also bring people into the realm of expanded awareness.
The repetition of the Jesus prayer, "Jesus Christ, son of God, have mercy
upon me a sinner," has been used for centuries in the Orthodox tradition.
Many Hindu religions, similarly, offer mantras to help us in centering.

At this point I wish to offer a word of caution about which I shall say
more later. The spiritual world is real, and it contains both light and
darkness—and even darkness masquerading as Light. I taught once a
class entitled "Practicum in Religious Experience" in which we used the
Jesus prayer to be still; it opened one person to an aspect of herself so terrifying that she became hysterical. If we decide to enter the silence, we
need both a religious tradition and a companion who has been on this
way before us.

Both Barbara and I need several different kinds of detachment and
quiet before the Light. Both of us need at least a half an hour daily in
which we open our souls to God. During this time we lay our lives open
before the Spirit for correction and direction and enlightenment. (I find
that a journal in hand helps me concentrate my attention on my encounter. She finds that a pencil in hand destroys any real quietness.) When I
wish to understand the meaning of scripture, I like to enter into the quiet
and expectantly listen to the text. At such times the Bible often sings its
own message, a message far more profound than I could have discovered

on my own. I find the same experience in reading great books of devotion, Thomas à Kempis's *The Imitation of Christ*, Ignatius's *Spiritual Exercises*, the writings of Augustine and Luther and early church leaders. We also need to set aside time for celebration of Eucharist together.

At least once every three or four weeks I need to set aside three or four hours in which I do deeper listening and reflection. I often find that I need to make significant changes in my life as a result of this longer and deeper communion with the risen Christ. This becomes a regular spiritual housecleaning.

We know that the Light is constantly shining, and on our better days we try to experience in very practical ways the presence of God (so well described by Brother Lawrence in *The Practice of the Presence of God*). As I sit down at the typewriter, for instance, I pause and ask that the Spirit direct what I write. As I get up to speak, I ask: "Lord, take not your Holy spirit from me. If you do, I have nothing to say." As I listen to a counselee, I ask that I may be guided and directed to hear what I need to hear and speak what I need to speak and feel what I need to feel. Barbara has already described how this sense of constant presence has sustained her through many difficult times. At one school of meditation where I lectured, five minutes of every hour all talking ceased and each person stopped and tried to enter the presence of God in this very concrete way.

Sometimes the darkness of the world overwhelms me, however, and this practical experience of the presence is not enough. At such times, I need two to four hours in which I withdraw and enter imaginatively into the void or face the evil that has dragged me to near immobility. In the midst of the darkness and inner violence and pain, I call upon the Risen One and am rescued and regenerated. This experience of darkness and rescue happens again and again. This, however, is not Barbara's way; for some people this kind of imaginative visualization is neither fruitful nor necessary. My soul-tree has been damaged by the forces of life, and I may need these special times to repair my wounds more than some other people. Yet many people who have had encounters with hopelessness and despair thank me for sharing this method; they tell me that this way of reaching the risen Christ has saved them too. (Later I will give more specific examples of this process.)

At least once a year, I need a time of retreat, thirty-six hours to several days or a week. (One good friend, a marvelous extrovert, recently made a three-month silent retreat.) My retreat time provides the space for examining what my priorities have been and then setting up an ideal set of priorities. The difference between the two often requires major life changes for me. I realize that certain activities are no longer good for me and that I need to spend my time in quite different ways. Sometimes such enforced periods of quiet can open us to radically new visions of life. Ignatius of Loyola's life was transformed as he listened to God while recovering from a wound sustained in battle. He left military service and became a soldier for Christ.

Both Barbara and I find that we need a time when we awaken to record any dreams that may have come to us during the night. And then we need a time to listen to their meaning. Our sleep detaches us from our ordinary life and opens us to the dimension of expanded awareness. If we do not listen to our dreams, we may be ignoring the soft, persistent knocking of the Spirit.

Detachment and Attachment

What do we experience when we open ourselves to the Light? Some people find a dazzling darkness that sings that all will be well. And sometimes we find a Divine Lover within the Light. Catherine of Genoa in her deepest experience of God would simply repeat over and over again: "Oh Love, Oh Love, Oh Love." Hassidic Jews, Sufis, and some Hindus speak of the same kind of experience. Some Christians have written of their experiences of this divine Light, and they have often found that this Love at the heart of being cannot be described in ordinary prose. In other books I give many ancient and modern poetic examples of our contact with God. Here I give only one—George Herbert's encounter with Love:

> Love bade me welcome; yet my soul drew back,
>   Guilty of dust and sin.
> But quick-eyed Love, observing me grow slack
>   From my first entrance in,
> Drew nearer to me, sweetly questioning,
>   If I lacked anything.
>
> "A guest," I answered, "worthy to be here."
>   Love said, "You shall be he."
> "I, the unkind, ungrateful? Ah, my dear,
>   I cannot look on Thee."
> Love took my hand, and smiling did reply,
>   "Who made the eyes but I?"
>
> "Truth, Lord, but I have marred them; let my shame
>   Go where it doth deserve."
> "And know you not," says Love, "who bore the blame?"
>   "My dear, then I will serve."

"You must sit down," says Love, "and taste my meat."
So I did sit and eat.[3]

If Love is the source, the spring, from which this universe emerges, then we are out of sync with ultimate reality when we do not try to love others with the same kind of love that can be found at the heart of being. Catherine of Siena was asked by one of her nuns what she might do to show her appreciation for God's love. The great saint wrote back that it would do her friend no good to add further penances or to build the most beautiful church in all the world; what she could do, however, would be to find someone as unworthy of her love as she was of God's love, and to pour out upon this other person the kind of love that she had received from God. Such loving would convey her gratitude to God. Indeed, when we do not try to go out in love to other human beings who are as broken and unconscious as ourselves, we are likely to cut ourselves off from the Divine Lover.

Prayer, Love, and Action

The growth and survival of the redwood also gives us hints concerning the importance of several other aspects of the human journey toward fulfillment. Like redwoods, human beings need warmth and love, the practice of keeping a record of their lives, continued working at growth, courage, playfulness, a way of overcoming adversity and evil and a vision of immortality. We will look first at these processes in the redwood and then in the chapters that follow we will examine in depth these elements of the full life.

Redwoods need warmth and grow best in communities. Human beings are similar; we need warmth and caring, love and nurture. We do not even become fully human, let alone fulfilled men and women, unless we are cared for by other human beings. We have already shown that love gives us our humanity. Love also heals and helps us grow; love is one of the necessary elements of an environment where the kingdom of heaven can exist among human beings.

As a redwood records its past in the rings within its trunk, so we humans record in memory all that we have done and been and thought and hoped for. However, unlike the rings laid down in the tree's trunk, our remembrance can fall deeper and deeper into the unconscious and disappear. Unless we keep some record of those we have known, of those who have been kind to us, of our religious experiences, of the great moments of our lives, of our dreams and fantasies, this important personal data can be lost forever. In the last few years I have been reflecting back over my life. I have learned much about myself, but I have also realized how much of my past is irretrievably lost. I wonder if literate people who fail to keep a journal record of their experiences can realize their full potential. If we do not routinely keep a record of ourselves, we tend to neglect our need for self-reflection.

Standing tall, with its branches swaying in the breeze, drinking in the sun, the redwood seems inert—quiet and at rest, like a woman sleeping comfortably. The tree is working and resting at the same time; its play and its work can scarcely be distinguished. Human beings are more conscious if no less mysterious. We have choices; we can labor or rest. However, if we do not balance our work and play, we can become addicted to one or to the other. Fulfillment is a combination of playfulness and work. Barbara is a wonderful help for me in balancing work and play. I can get so caught up in work that I forget that work alone makes for one-sided, warped, and dull people. I need to set aside times for recreation—simple enjoyment of a quiet meal together, a walk in the moonlight, a play or movie. When play, laughter, rest, and relaxation are not mixed with directed purpose, focused energy, and goal achievement, we fail to be human, let alone fulfilled. Either work alone or play alone leads to a moonlike desert.

One reason that redwoods can live so long and rise to their enormous stature is that the tree is provided with a system of defenses that is always alert. Humans also need to struggle to survive; we need courage to withstand the attacks that can destroy us. Sometimes these evils come from the outside world in the form of natural catastrophe, human oppression, sickness, poverty, a loveless childhood, or prejudice against our race or color. We shall examine later the sources of inner strength that can be tapped by people in the most desperate of circumstances: hostages held in a plane for fifteen days, another hostage chained for eighteen months, a majority of blacks surviving in a country where they have no rights.

Few living things come closer to immortality than the redwoods. Although the individual bristlecone pine does live even longer than a giant redwood, the coast redwoods, even after being felled, live on as long as their root structure, the rhizome, is left intact. In order to clear a valley once covered by redwoods, the great roots must actually be pulled out or a blazing fire must be set around each stump. What is three score and ten or twenty years compared with a continuing life like this? If we human beings, therefore, are truly snuffed out after our brief lives and become nothing more than dust and ashes, then human life does appear meaningless and futile. The redwood, that springs up from its roots again and again, reminds us of immortality and resurrection and gives us hope that our infinitely more mysterious psyches may continue beyond the grave.

Many people who have meditated deeply on life and death speak of the close connection between our belief in a significant life after death and our capacity to love. In *Death to Life*, Karl Jaspers stressed this relationship:

The consciousness of immortality needs no knowledge, no guarantee, no threat. It lies in love, in this marvelous reality in which we are given to ourselves. We are mortal when we are without love and immortal when we love. . . . I achieve immortality to the extent that I love . . . I dissipate into nothingness as long as I live without love and therefore in chaos. As a lover I can see the immortality of those who are united to me in love. [4]

Emily Dickinson points to the same connection in four brief lines:

> Love—is anterior to Life—
> Posterior—to Death—
> Initial of Creation, and
> The Exponent of Earth—[5]

So we now turn to love, that quality of life that undergirds a full life, both here and hereafter.

CHAPTER 7

Fulfillment as Love

Within most religious traditions prayer and love cannot be separated. Both are essential aspects of the fulfilled life. If we listen deeply in the silence, sooner or later we will hear and know that if we wish to remain in close communion with the Holy One, we need to try to love others with the same kind of unconditional love that God pours out on all who will receive it. Full human existence requires both devotion and caring.

I have already told the story of how my eyes were opened to the importance of love in my relation to God and to all other human beings. Once we are aware of a truth like this, we often see it everywhere. I have discovered that most of the perceptive people in our Western civilization have called attention to the divine nature of love and to the emptiness and futility of lives that have not experienced and expressed self-giving love.

As I discovered the importance of love, I began to understand Plato, who called our human capacity to love a "divine madness" that opens us to an experience of God. The great historian Will Durant, at age ninety-two, stated that the final lesson of history could be summed up in three words: love one another. He went on to say that love is the most practical thing in the world, and that he agreed with Jesus' teaching of the centrality of love. I also studied the life of Francis of Assisi, whose prayer had awakened me from sleep, and I found that by the powers of love, Francis had revived and renewed the dormant and cynical church of his time. I also realized that in the letters of St. Paul the words "love" and "Holy Spirit" could be interchanged without altering his meaning. And a counselee drew my attention to a passage at the conclusion of Jung's autobiography, *Memories, Dreams, Reflections*, in which Jung states that the essence of love is hidden in the mystery of God and that the two experiences cannot be separated.

Richard Coan, a student of human wholeness and maturity, writes that saintliness is one essential ingredient of the actualized life. He describes saints as those who reach out to others with compassion, caring, and empathy, using the same kind of devotion with which they open themselves to God. He quotes the novelist James Baldwin: "The moment we cease to hold each other, the moment we break faith with one another, the sea engulfs us and the light goes out."[1] With his characteristic incisiveness, Aldous Huxley points out that we cannot avoid the subject of love:

Of all the worn, smudged, dog's-eared words in our vocabulary, "love" is surely the grubbiest, smelliest, slimiest. Bawled from a million pulpits, lasciviously crooned through hundreds of millions of loud speakers, it has become an outrage to good taste and decent feeling, an obscenity which one hesitates to pronounce. And yet it has to be pronounced, for, after all, *Love* is the last word.[2]

In his recent book, *Love, Medicine, and Miracles*, Bernie Siegel, a cancer surgeon, tells of his work with his patients. He writes that healing involves psychology and spirituality, as well as surgery. He states again and again that a loving environment and the patient's capacity to love are often the determining factors in *all* cures that defy statistics. Most psychological and religious healers similarly emphasize the vital importance of love as the catalyst in healing.

After Jesus had taken the place of the lowest slave and washed his disciples' feet at his last supper with them, he told them that this was a sign of his love and an example of how they should treat one another. Then he said: "A new commandment I give to you, that you love one another; even as I have loved you, that you also love one another" (John 13:34, RSV). Jesus concluded by pointing out that people would know that they were his disciples by their love for one another; loving others as he had loved them made them his followers. Jesus came to give us life— abundant life. It is clear, then, that one basic foundation of any consummated living is the self-giving love we show one another.

What Is Love?

What is the nature of this love that is so vital for our civilization, for human harmony, for our individuation, for our religious integrity, and even for our physical health? After mulling over Scott Peck's description of love (given in his book *The Road Less Traveled*) and discussing it at many conferences with many people, the following description came to me: love is the disciplined will *and* desire to extend ourselves for the purpose of nurturing our own and another's spiritual, emotional, and physical growth and healing in order to guide people through their crises and on toward their full human potential.

A recent trip to South Africa brought me in touch with traumatizing tension and injustice *and* also in contact with a vital church that is as much alive as any I have encountered anywhere in the world. In South Africa, many Christians are reaching out to those who are disenfranchised and oppressed, and they may suffer persecution for doing so. Many of the churches' leaders are wrestling with the meaning of Christianity and with ways of bringing love and fellowship to that torn and divided land. One Christian chaplain in a prison called my attention to *Christian Theology: A Case Study Approach*, by Robert Evans and Thomas Parker. In it they come to grips with the meaning of love within a broken society: "Love, agape, is the equal and unalterable regard for the value of other human beings independent of their particular characteristics. It extends especially to the helpless and hopeless, to those who have no value in their own eyes and seemingly none for society. Such neighbor-love is costly and sacrificial. It is easily destroyed. In the giver it demands unlimited caring, in the recipient absolute trust."[3]

Many Christian theologians put a great gulf between two different kinds of love: *eros* (desiring love) and *agape* (self-giving love containing no element of personal desire). In my experience, actual loving of the kind we are describing contains an element of both. Love with no personal involvement can degenerate in what the theologian Nicolas Berdyaev calls "glassy Christian love," of which he wants no part. I agree with him; I want no one to love me out of duty alone. Eros, on the other hand, can easily slip into unconscious possessive desire or mere sexuality unless it contains concern for the other person.

One of the greatest cop-outs in genuine relationships is the idea that I need to love everyone, but I don't have to like them. This frees us from considering the kind of love that Jesus lived, the kind of love that transforms our lives and leads us toward fulfillment. Eros and agape are united like the two poles of a magnet; together, they create an integrated love that flows from *both* the will *and* the heart.

Jesus told a story about love that has been called the gospel within the gospel. Many refer to it as the parable of the prodigal son, but would it not be better to refer to it as the story of the prodigal father? The father in Jesus' parable is far more extravagant, profuse, and lavish in his love than the son is in his folly. The father gives his son freedom, and then he receives him back home without judging him. He pours out on him gifts that the son needs—new sandals and the best robe—and then he adds the gift of a ring, a detail that many people miss when they listen to the story. The son does not need this ring. It is pure grace. The father then orders that a great feast be prepared, so the fatted calf is slain and all the neighbors are invited. When the hard-working elder brother comes in from the fields and hears the music and dancing, he sends a slave boy to the house to see what is going on. And when he is told that the lavish feast is for his returned brother, he refuses to go in.

The father then leaves the party and his guests, and he pleads with his elder son to come; thus he ignores his son's insolence (the older brother had broken Semitic custom far more by his refusal to come to his father's banquet than the younger brother had in his waywardness). Jesus' point was that God treats any of us human beings who will receive his love in this way, whether we are self-righteous like the elder brother or extravagant and immoral like the younger one. And if we are like God and living up to our potential, we will treat one another as that father treated his sons.[4]

In his Letter to the Romans, Paul describes the radical nature of the love that Jesus lived and taught: "It is a difficult thing for someone to die for a righteous person. It may even be that someone might dare to die for a good person. But God has shown us how much he loves us—it was while we were still sinners that Christ died for us! . . . Now that we are God's friends, how much more will we be saved by Christ's life!"(Romans 5:7; 8, 10, TEV).

The church that Paul had founded at Corinth had rejected his authority and was in turmoil. He wrote to the Corinthian Christians, pleading with them to realize that love was the basis of all the spiritual gifts about which they were quarreling. In poetic prose Paul describes the nature of genuine Christian love: "Love is patient and kind; not rude, or jealous; neither arrogant nor boastful; neither self-centered, irritable, nor resentful; it does not rejoice at other's wrongs but in their goodness. Love bears all things, believes all things, hopes all things, endures all things. Love never fails" (1 Cor. 13: 7–8, author's trans.).

As we have already pointed out, Dante struggled on until he finally found ultimate meaning in God. He found love a part of the fundamental structure of the universe. We cannot hear frequently enough those words with which he concluded one of the finest works of human art:

> Yet, as a wheel moves smoothly, free from jars,
> My will and my desire were turned by love,
> The love that moves the sun and the other stars.[5]

Dante withstood persecution, rejection, and condemnation, and yet he continued to love and forgive. Divine Love, operating through Virgil and

Beatrice, guided Dante and led him to his experience of heaven and of the Love that ultimately governs all reality.

From the time that I began to realize that love was one of the essential foundations of the truly actualized person, I have been searching out how I could be a more genuinely loving person. Throughout the last twenty years I have been given insight after insight into the mystery of transforming, divine love, and into the ways that I can embody that kind of love in my life. I have come to see that this kind of love, like the fulfilled life itself, is a mosaic of many pieces. The image came to me recently that love is a many-faceted jewel set into the larger mosaic of the maturing life, and this jewel binds the rest of the picture into a fiery unity.

Why Is It So Hard to Love One Another?

If love is such a significant human quality and so vital for human well-being, why do so few people make it the central focus of their life? There are many reasons why more of us don't base our lives on the foundation of love. First of all, few of us were raised in families where all of the members of the family were treated with the kind of unconditional love that I have described. Often punishment and even spanking were considered better methods of changing others than firm, loving understanding. One of the sure results of psychological research is that battered children can easily become battering parents, unless they awaken to self-awareness and to the supreme importance of love, both human and divine. (We usually give to others what we have received.) The church has called this inherited lovelessness "original sin." In addition, most societies (our own included) base their legal systems on a form of punishment that takes the rotten apples out of society and puts them into schools of crime (that is what prisons really are). The only programs that produce transformation of legal offenders are those that treat people as human beings who need caring concern rather than displaying calculated punishment.

Most social and ethnic groups within our society are concerned only with their own self-interest and will use any means to gain their ends. How few international power struggles show any concern, let alone love for the other country! Global cruelty is merely a reflection of the frighteningly real dark side of all of us.

Sometimes when I listen to the very depth of me, I hear a destructive voice speaking to me to attack and destroy those that oppose me. In his deeply moving autobiography, *Report to Greco*, Nikos Kazantzakis tells of discovering this demonic, barbaric aspect of himself. He was walking along a mountain road with a good friend on a moonlit night, and he saw the lights of a village below. "At that point an astonishing thing happened to me. I still shudder when I recall it. Halting, I shook my clenched fist at the village and shouted in a furor, 'I shall slaughter you all.'" He wrote that the voice was not even his own and that deep within us "there is layer upon layer of darkness—raucous voices, hairy hungering beasts."[6] In *A Leg to Stand On*, Oliver Sacks tells of his protracted recovery from a serious accident and his spiteful rage when he watched a group of young people playing rugby because he could not participate.

When this demonic level of us is not confronted, it frequently takes over the leaders of a government or group: the result is oppression, slavery, pogroms, gas ovens, and annihilating, aggressive war. Such atrocities are often called "bestial," but it is unfair to refer to these drives as the animal part of us, since no animal species other than humans systematically kills its own kind with blind, destroying rage. The fact that religious wars are among the most vicious and brutal is a sobering realization— Hitler serving Wotan, the conflict in Northern Ireland, Islamic conquests, terror in Palestine, and the Afrikaners viewing their great trek to central South Africa as an exodus to *their* promised land.

Biological impulses lie beneath these fierce activities. Built into our very bodies is the instinct for survival—no matter who suffers. (No wonder that people viewed the willing martyrdom of the early Christians with such amazement; martyrdom seems biologically unnatural.) Under attack, our sympathetic nervous system prepares us for either fight or flight, for attack or withdrawal. At adolescence, testosterone begins to flow in young men, and they become more aggressive and violent; indeed, studies of young offenders in jail show a highly increased level of this male hormone.

If we believe that we live in a purely material universe, human nature amounts to nothing more than this biology. There is no place for good or evil; the universe is value free. Within this mechanistic framework, what gives a person the most power to indulge in the most pleasure becomes the only criterion for human behavior. No truly satisfactory system of morality has been devised within a meaningless, materialistic universe.

The leaders of the so-called Enlightenment dismissed God—and then they became frightened when they realized that they had opened the door to the very logical and terrifying ideas of the Marquis de Sade. If the god we worship is Wotan, a god of war, vengeance, and violence, love can be viewed as weak and degenerate; Nietzsche propounds this point of view when he describes the superman. And if we see the final revelation of the Bible as a vengeful, punishing, destroying, and angry God rather than Jesus, who died on a cross to reveal the unconditional love of God, then we Christians will not see love as the central reality in the universe anymore than Nietzsche did. We will then not be forced both religiously and morally to make love the main source and spring of our actions.

Unfortunately, many nominal Christians have *not* really heard the message of Jesus; they view God as an arbitrary potentate who can be angry and destructive one moment and friendly and merciful the next. Such a God is not essentially motivated by love but by power; this God can be approached only in fear. In *Paradise Lost* John Milton portrays this kind of God in deceptively magnificent poetry. Jesus, however, revealed a God of love, who created us in order that we might receive God's unconditional love and then share that love with other human beings and with God. And unless we truly believe that God is love, we are not likely to put forth the effort that is necessary to shape our lives by self-giving love and caring.

Most people don't like to have their religious views challenged. Socrates was condemned and given hemlock to drink because he taught and lived a way of love. Because Jesus put love above religious law and national interest, he, too, was put to death. And many Christians have suffered death because they followed Jesus' way—from Stephen and Peter to Martin Luther King, Jr. Preaching and living love can be dangerous to one's health and life.

If, indeed, God is love, and if God created human beings so that they might love one another and love and enjoy God forever, where did all the evil, sickness, oppression, war, police brutality, child beating, and nasty gossip come from? That is a big question that we take up in another chapter. For now, the best answer I can give is that something that God created free, good, and capable of love turned against God and has tried to drag the rest of the universe along with it.

How Can We Love One Another?

Although those who have been nurtured in unconditional love may have a deep understanding of and desire to love, there are, as we have seen, strong forces pressing on most human beings from within and from outside, turning them in another direction. Learning to love is a life-long, sacrificial, and heroic way of life, and it takes single-minded devotion. Few people will make this effort unless they see that love is at the center of the universe and is the essential nature of God, and that for all eternity (if not here on earth as well) God will give to those who love joy, wholeness, and the deepest existential satisfaction.

The first step in loving is making a decision that love is the most important human action. In spite of all the evidence to the contrary, in spite of all the evil that we feel within us and around us, God is love. Love is at the heart of being. If I do not follow love, I miss the meaning of life. This conviction is the foundation of faith. It calls us to commit ourselves and our best energy to God's way, Jesus' way, the way of unconditional love. If we do not make such a commitment, we are not truly faithful people. In a very real sense we worship that to which we give the most of our time, effort, and energy. What we do is the best indicator of what our faith truly is.

Jesus lived and taught the way of love more fully than any other person in human history. Thus, had he been crucified and died, but not raised from the dead, his life would have been the most tragic of all time. It would have written in the fabric of history that love does not work on earth, that heaven may well be an illusion, and that those who follow Christ and love are of all people the most to be pitied. Without the resurrection of Jesus and the meteorite emergence of the Christian church, it would be difficult for me to hang on to faith in Jesus and Abba, the God of love.

And this brings us back to prayer, meditation, communion with God. I have already related how I have found a loving, caring presence as I have listened to my dreams, listened in the middle of the night, and meditated on scripture and particularly on the life and teachings of Jesus. In my deepest experience of public worship and Eucharist, and in my times of quiet fellowship with God, I have met a Divine Lover—one who, as Augustine said, would have died for me if I had been the only human being. I find that this Loving One is always there desiring to draw me closer to Love. Again and again I hear gentle suggestions, when I listen in the midst of troubles, that my best way through them is by practicing unconditional love. Sometimes, though, the darkness overwhelms me, and I need to walk into the darkness, listen to its destructiveness, and find that even in that darkness the Resurrected One is present and can lift me out of hell.

Unless my faith in Christ and my love are reinforced again and again by my continued fellowship with the Christ, my love begins to lose its fervor.

One of the great values of learning to deal adequately with the universe of reduced awareness is that we learn discipline. Without discipline and a strong ego, one cannot become effective in either the physical or spiritual world. Until I begin to take responsibility for my life and try to control it, I will love and have fellowship with God only when I feel like it, and I will ignore God when I feel like it. Both prayer and real love require discipline. Love that comes and goes like the wind is often worse than no love at all. Indeed, children who are subjected to that kind of environment are often more neurotic than those who exist in a continuously hostile one. God's kind of love is *action* springing from the hidden depths of us, leading us to respond to others with kindness and caring even when we don't feel like it. Love is not just our feeling of love, but the movement of our entire being toward others so that they can feel loved. In other words, love is transitive, not intransitive. The final test of whether I am loving or not is whether the other individual feels loved by me. This is one reason why real love requires such patience.

But many of us also find it difficult to allow ourselves to be loved. We need to learn to be loved as well as to love, and it requires great trust to allow ourselves to be loved. Few are able to love who have not allowed others to love them. It is very difficult to love ourselves until we have accepted love from others. A psychologist once told me that his first task was to love the patients so that they could find themselves lovable and love themselves.

Genuine love for another human being is nearly impossible for us unless we love ourselves. Often what we think is love for another is the projection of the perfect parent or friend on another person. We see in others the angel hidden within us, and when we find that they have feet of clay, we are likely to project the image of the betrayer, the unfaithful one, the enemy itself on them. And then we feel anything but love toward them. But these negative images are really projected parts of ourselves that we haven't been able to face. Thus, until I know myself with all my failings, anger, lust, fraud, and destructiveness and can still love myself, the chances are slim indeed that I am going to be able to love any other person or race or nation with patience and consistency.

Jung has written that loving one's self is the hardest of all tasks, and that it can sometimes make us livid with fear. I find myself harder to love than any other person. I personally can love myself only if I return again and again to the One who loved me so much that he died for me. Then I can rest in the Source of Love and find that the risen Jesus, who died to defeat the evil that attacks us humans, is there waiting to pick up my wounded, fragile, erring soul and body and heal me. By hating myself, I actually reject God: I am hating the one that Love has taken such pains to show is loved. Indeed when we think that our evil and ugliness are more than God can tolerate, we are making ourselves more powerful than God.

I find that sometimes I can feel God's love most vividly when I allow my dark mood—with its oppressive sense of evil, darkness, and valuelessness—to be translated into images. I ask the risen Christ to deliver me from the horror of the images that arise and to give me the kind of love of which St. John of the Cross wrote so eloquently. I am most genuinely able to love when I feel myself loved, released, and transformed by God's love.

Reaching Out to Others

It is impossible to love others until we learn to listen to them. I learned this not at seminary or by reading, but from my colleague Ollie Backus, who directed the educational program at St. Luke's Church for many years. As soon as we see how many of our reactions to others are the result of our projections, we realize that we need to learn what other people truly are. And we can best learn about others by listening to them. When we are open and receptive, most people are happy to let us in and tell us about themselves; human beings have a profound need for one another. Without listening, there can be no genuine caring, whether we are dealing with friends, family, or children. Unless we listen to another, we are treating him or her as an *it* rather than as a *thou*, a human person. When we do not listen, we take others for granted, assuming that we know all we need to know about them. But when we truly listen to them, we become present to people. And we cannot creatively do anything for people until we are present to them.

We will find that few people will truly open up to us if we contradict, argue, or judge them. Active listening involves suspending judgment. And this sort of listening is healing—both for them and for us. One well-known psychotherapist told me: "Half of all psychotherapy is warm, receptive listening." Some rare people have a natural knack for listening, but most of us need to learn to listen. Listening is an art and a science that can be taught and learned.

Considering the importance of love in any fulfilled life, it is strange that more opportunities are not offered to help us develop our ability to listen, this essential prerequisite for all genuine love. Any institution that stresses the primacy of love without providing opportunities for mastering the fine art of listening is defeating itself, yet very few Christian churches provide their members classes in listening. Except in certain specifically structured, confidential groups, or in a one-to-one relationship with a good listener, few emotionally healthy people will casually expose their fears, angers, and oddities. Children, in particular, need time alone with each parent if they are to feel truly listened to, valued, cared for, and loved. Real love demands time and deep sharing. Sometimes I feel annoyed when effusive people come up to tell me how much they love me before they have taken the trouble to know who I truly am.

Loving and listening to people can be difficult until we see that human beings are very different from one another. Like the needles or leaves of a tree, each of us is slightly different, and some of us are very different from one another. Our complex society would cease functioning without many kinds of very different people. God knew what was necessary when the great variety of human beings were created. People differ in the way that they perceive the world and in the way they function. They also differ greatly in what they value and in what they deem important. Until we are awakened to the reality of these differences and their importance, we are likely to view people unlike ourselves as impossible to tolerate if not evil.

Barbara and I had been married nearly twenty years before we came to understand how different we were. We had been in analysis for many years, and both of us knew ourselves well, but we did not know each other very well. We knew about Jung's theory of types, but until we had a method of measuring our differences, we did not deal with them. Using the Myers-Briggs Type Indicator, we found that we were nearly opposite types. Barbara was an introverted-sensation-feeling-perceptive type. I was an introverted-intuitive-thinking-judgmental type. She felt my intuition went beyond facts and my thinking was not useful in child rearing. I thought that she did not understand my best gifts. (Often people wonder if the type opposite to theirs really belongs to the human race.) Few revelations have so helped us to relate to and care for each other as an understanding of our differences and a realization that the other has not only a need but a right to be who he or she is. Barbara and I have come to understand that the other person is not consciously obstinate—just different.⁷ Until we come to appreciate and honor other people's differences, it is very difficult to love them.

People can differ in their basic values about what is right or wrong, insignificant or important. Again, if we are going to love others, we need to be able to realize and accept the idea that decent people can have values quite different from ours. Values clarification attempts to show people how to assess what they view to be important. Barbara and I have been working on this for twenty years, and we are still making headway. The most dramatic example of how different people are—people who we might think would share a common point of view—occurred when I was lecturing at the Benedictine Monastery in Pecos, New Mexico. I told the story of Alligator River, in which people with *very* different values interact with one another in a dramatic way. We discovered that within this group of seeking religious people every character within the story—from a seducer to the seduced, from the conventional to the violent—was ranked by some people as the most admirable and by others as the least.[8]

When we cannot listen to people whose values are different from ours without judging, we really cease listening and our love no longer reaches out to the other person. Jung reminds us that even when our judgment is not expressed, the other person usually is aware of our reaction and the desire to share dries up.

Dealing with Hostility

Whenever we believe that we have overcome all our hostility and have no more anger in us, we are deluding ourselves. Hostility and anger are the natural physical and emotional response to threat. If I think that it is wrong to have any hostile feelings, I usually repress my anger and drive it into the unconscious. On the outside I become one of those people with the never-failing sugary smile with whom no one can have a real or honest relationship. (I sometimes call this the adoption of a *ministerial persona*, an attitude that proclaims: "I have everything in control; I have no doubts or threats or fears." One doesn't, of course, have to be a minister to wear this mask.) This sugary attitude discourages most mortals, who are struggling through an avalanche of those very burdens of hostility and anger. It keeps most ordinary human beings from sharing where they are and also from receiving the help and encouragement that they need in order to survive. People who are out of touch with their hostility and fear are unreal and impossible to relate to on a deep level.

Fear and hostility are largely the opposite sides of the same coin; behind most hostility lies fear and hurt. I find it so much easier to deal with the anger that people express toward me when I remember that they are really hurt or that I threaten them. When I am most conscious, whole, and mature, I can absorb others' anger without being destructive. I realize that most anger masks helplessness and fear and is a reaction to a threatening situation. Hurting and angry people need my concern and love, not my angry response.

When I am not conscious of what my inner reaction is, I have no way of controlling it. When as a minister I swallowed my anger and did not face my resentment at the meager salary the church gave me and of the constant demands of church members, I found that my anger was coming out in my home. When I face my inner fear and anger, then I have a chance of utilizing that energy and not hurting others; I can respond appropriately to each situation in which I find myself. I cannot deal with others as a fulfilled person until I know who and what I am, until, by the grace of God, I can bear what I find within myself. Then I can respond in the most concerned and caring way that is possible to the angry person. What I refuse to face within often explodes with violence and hurts both myself and the other person. Whenever I see people judging others, I wonder what they are hiding from within themselves. The recent TV evangelist scandals speak eloquently of the dangers of refusing to face our own sexual and hostile shadows.

Love and the Family

Some marriage counselors suggest that people learn to fight fairly with each other. But I wonder if fighting is really the way to true closeness and intimacy. I agree with Luciano L'Abate's statement that intimacy is not assertive confrontation so much as a sharing of hurt feelings.[9] When we human beings can trust each other enough to share our hurts and weaknesses, then true caring, intimacy, is possible in the family, with friends, in the community, and the world as well as in the church. Few social groups or even families provide this openness and trust, but this vision gives us an idea of what the kingdom of heaven may be like.

If I had a chance to live my life over again, I would make one major change: I would spend more time with my family, particularly with my children when they are young. As I have reflected before God about love, I have come to realize that the most important place for me to pour out my love is within my own home. Indeed, my love for others has a touch of sham until I learn to give love to those closest to me—and this is not always easy. I can love anyone for an hour in my office, but in the conflicts and tensions in a family situation most of us are hard pressed to continue loving others twenty-four hours a day. Although celibate ministers do not have to bear the tension between their ministry and their immediate family responsibilities, those who live in community know how hard it is to love those with whom they live day in and day out. However, difficult as they are, these family groups are the very crucible in which our love is refined; they mature us.

We have already shown how much the quality of our childhood shapes our adult lives. Children who are loved and given reasonable limits usually become caring and reasonable adults. Neglected and abused children find it more difficult to be instruments of consistent love. Neglected children, those who do not feel cared for and loved, find it difficult to open themselves to the experience of an intimate, loving God. The quality of their parents' relationship will usually shape the kind of intimate relationships these children are likely to develop as adults. When students in a class at Notre Dame read Frances Wickes's remarkable book *The Inner World of Childhood*, they often expressed fear about having children. It had not occurred to them before how much parental actions and attitudes create the foundation on which children build their lives.

Many couples have children with little or no sense of the responsibilities involved. They have children for their own sexual gratification, or because of their need to be parents, or simply because marriage and sex usually produce children. They have little idea of the love and patience that real parenting requires. Unless the tensions and conflicts that so often occur in families awaken the parents' own child-selves to a desire to seek human understanding and divine love and guidance, parents are likely to live empty and unfulfilled lives; they prepare their children for barren lives as well.

Love and human sexuality cannot be entirely separated. If marriages and sexual unions are to be sacramental of love, leading people toward fulfillment, they require solid foundations. Both partners in the union need to perceive each other as equals, and sexuality needs to be experienced as God's beautiful, ecstatic, and unifying gift, not as an ugly, debasing, or evil aspect of life. Sadly, however, surveys indicate that few married people grasp the importance of these prerequisites for fulfilling, permanent sexual unions. Those who do not understand the complexity and potential of a marital relationship, who simply seek "happiness," rarely discover the existential satisfaction that a full intimate relationship can provide.

In his remarkable book *Marriage Dead or Alive*, Adolf Guggenbüh-Craig suggests that marriage can be a pathway to salvation, God, and fulfillment. And a renowned psychiatrist and expert in family relations, Dr. Charles Whitaker, has said: "The greatest ordeal in life is marriage—it is the central focus for enlightenment and the natural therapeutic process in the culture."[10] Such total relationship is one of the most important pathways to the fulfilled life.

Barbara and I share our reflections on forty-five years of our own married life in *Sacrament of Sexuality*. We also share our observations about love and sexuality after a greal deal of study and after listening to many hundreds of people. We concluded that genuine relationships of love can develop in marriages with hard work, among celibates who try to experience an inner union of their masculine and feminine sides with equally hard work, among homosexuals who are working at being expressions of divine love, and among bisexual people who find both sexual responses active within them and who are honest with their partners. This last group is little dealt with or understood. Men and women, who have buried their sexual talent, however, may find that warm, caring love with other human beings is difficult, and a genuine relationship with a passionately loving God is very threatening.

The Outreach of Love

Jesus said that if we love only those who love us—members of our families, say—we are no better than the heathens and tax collectors. (It did not seem to occur to him that love would be lacking even within a family.) Fulfillment for all of humankind will come only when the kind of love we have been describing is found not only within families but among races and nations as well. But how can we begin such a colossal task?

We can start with our families and friends. (Friends are those whom we treat as though they were members of our family circle and feel a commitment to relationship with us even when we are wrong.) And then we reach out to acquaintances: the people we work with or for whom we work, the clerk in the store, the people in our service club or in the PTA, those in the altar guild, our social friends, members of our church (including the ministers, their spouses and children), neighbors down the street.

Jack Smith (his actual name) was a close friend who ran a medium-sized industrial company. The company was not doing well, and one day in discouragement he thought he would pray. He went into his office, became quiet, and asked God how he could run the company more creatively. Almost immediately the answer whizzed through his head: "Create the conditions whereby individuals can come to the maximum of their potential within the opportunities at hand." Later in the same intuitive way he was given eleven rules for implementing this principle.[11] This basic way of treating others is ideal for nearly all of our more casual contacts. It is also considered by management experts to be the best method of creative management.

Reaching out to strangers is as difficult for introverted people as spending time in quiet and in solitary meditation is for extroverts. And yet we do need to reach out to strangers. Have you ever been a stranger in a strange land? Those of us who have our own social group and are comfortable there can hardly imagine the pain and destructiveness of loneliness. Loneliness can actually destroy people, as the psychologist James Lynch points out in his books *The Broken Heart* and *The Language of the Heart*. We *are* our brothers' and sisters' keepers, and we can help destroy people that we ignore or reject. We need to be conscious enough to see the strangers around us, and then make the effort to reach out to them.

Some human beings are strangers to our society, in a particularly radical, painful way, cut off from nearly all meaningful contacts with others. Jesus said that those of us who reach out to the homeless and hungry, to the shut-ins and dying, to those who are thirsty, and those in prison are actually ministering to him. The plight of the homeless, the shut-ins, and the prisoners in our country is a festering sore within American society.

We are one of the wealthiest nations on the face of the earth, and yet two million homeless people wander our alleys and sleep on the streets or in boxcars. There are many reasons why this situation arose but no reason for it to continue.

Another scandalous situation exists in those places that are euphemistically called "rest homes," where most Americans discard the elderly when they are too much trouble for us to care for. In most societies the elderly are honored, but in ours they are usually put away and often forgotten. They desperately need friendship, care, and a loving touch—gifts that any of us can give. Barbara and I welcomed her grandfather into our home after both of his children had died. He was as much a gift to us as we were to him in the years he lived with us. We left everything to care for our dying son, a painful and blessed privilege.

Most of us know virtually nothing about prisons; few of us have ever visited one. Most prisons are utterly degrading, and, in addition, they are the finest schools of crime humans could devise. Take fairly innocent or confused men and women (and most criminals are psychologically disturbed people), and put them in the average prison, and in a few years they will be truly skilled criminals, thoroughly antisocial members of society.

Also profoundly in need of love are the dying—so often ignored by family, friends, and even hospital staffs. These people must face alone the transition to another dimension of reality. Our own fear of death often keeps us away from these lonely people, but if we know the God of the living and the dead, and have faith the size of a redwood seed that something better than this life awaits us, we can bring incredible fellowship, comfort, and healing to dying people.

Most of us are afraid not only of the dying but also of those who are broken, discouraged, depressed. If the pain and lostness of others, however, causes us to be overwhelmed by our own darkness, we can at least find someone else to minister to them. Such depression manifests itself in many ways: most people who turn to alcohol and drugs, for instance, are those who have found life more than they can deal with. They need our understanding and concern, not our rejection and judgment. John Keller, who has worked for over thirty years with alcoholics and their families, shows in his book *Let Go and Let God* how we all can learn from the Twelve Steps of Alcoholics Anonymous to reach out to suffering people of every kind.

Our love and caring can even be healing for the physically sick. When human touch is empowered by faith and love, miracles sometimes occur as surgeon Bernie Siegel attests in *Love, Medicine and Miracles*. We do not have to be physicians to spur healing in people; there are religious and psychological as well as physical dimensions to the healing of body and mind. (I have described how we can participate in the healing thrust of ministry in the concluding chapter of *Psychology, Medicine and Christian Healing*.)

In order to rescue the enslaved, the oppressed, the poor, the rejected, the prisoners, we need to do more than minister to their immediate situation. Part of love involves social action, which changes the structures of society that have created these abominable conditions. Each of us needs to be aware of the pain and degradation under which so many people live, and then we need to take up some project in which we can reach out to these people—at the same time doing what we can to change our indifferent society. When Evelyn Underhill, for instance, came to Baron von Hügel for spiritual direction, his first suggestion for the development of her *spiritual* life was that she go into the slums of London and visit there one day a week. I should add that we cannot take on all of these different miseries, or we will drown in them. Rather, we can each take on some specific project that we support with our time, energy, and money. Isabel Briggs-Myers, who developed the personality type inventory, has warned feeling intuitives, in particular, not to take on more than they can do.

If the world gets better, it isn't usually because a few people make a major impact or write books, but rather because each of us listens to the ever-present voice of God deep within us, and then responds as well as he or she can. That all is not so ill with you and me as it might have been is largely due to those who "lived faithfully a hidden life, and rest in unvisited tombs"—to use the concluding words of George Eliot in her novel *Middlemarch*. Someone asked Mother Teresa, "How do you stand it? Here you are in Calcutta. You probably don't touch more than one percent of the suffering and dying in the city." Mother Teresa replied: "I was not called to be successful; I was only called to be faithful."

In addition to all this, we are told by Jesus even to love our enemies.

Charles Williams, writing during the blitz in London, said that there are those things that need not be forgiven (where we have just misunderstood another person), those that need to be forgiven (ordinary actions of hurt and thoughtlessness that we all commit), and those things that cannot be forgiven (the horrors of war and the systemic oppression and torture that occur all around the world)—and that the Christian needs to forgive all of them. Anyone striving for fulfillment needs to learn how to forgive. As long as we harbor within us hatred for others, we restrict the flow of love in and through us—and we end up psychologically tying ourselves to the people we like the least. And we need to remember that the enemy is not only the person that we can't stand, but also the person who can't stand us. At times we find that as we go further on the way of wholeness, some people are annoyed and disturbed by us. Starr Daily, for example, learned his spirituality in prison, where many of those found it distasteful. He often told me that we are forced to grow spiritually as we try to take our enemies into the sphere of God's love within us. To forgive is to have mercy. Those who have mercy receive mercy as well.

How Can We Love?

How can we go out toward those who have betrayed or misused us, oppressed and tortured us? The answer comes in the words *forgiveness, reconciliation, mercy.* When we know ourselves well and realize how unconscious and destructive we have been or could be, then even in our agony we can say with the crucified Christ, "Father, forgive them, for they know not what they do." When we know our own capacity for evil, we are much less likely to harbor hostility or to strike out at others.

Turning the enemy into a friend involves several quite different thoughts and actions. First of all, we have to admit that there are those who do not like us, and those whom we neither like nor love. Then we simply have to stop doing anything unkind to those with whom we are trying to be reconciled. Every unkind action wears the ruts of hostility deeper. The next step is difficult indeed: I need to stop saying anything critical to others about that person. Sometimes my tongue seems to have a life all its own, but when I gossip about my enemies, I nurture my animosity toward them. I also find that when I pray for my "enemies," it is much more difficult to strike out in word or deed at them, for such hostile acts would put me in conflict with the loving God to whom I am commending them. It is, then, extremely important to pray for them with whom we are at odds. The fourth step is to look for some fine quality in the person I am having trouble with, and then to speak of this when others are verbally dissecting this individual. It is difficult to continue being hostile to a person who I defend. And last of all, I try to do something that gives the person real joy, and I do it anonymously. It is difficult not to feel warmly toward those to whom we have given joy; one reason we love our children so much is that we have given to them freely and fully, often expecting nothing in return.

When we look at what it means to love, we can be frightened at the immensity of the task. One of the best responses to this very reasonable fear is found in the words of Father Zossima in Dostoyevsky's *The Brothers Karamazov*:

Never be frightened at your own faint-heartedness in attaining love. Don't be too frightened overmuch even at your evil actions. I'm sorry I can say nothing more consoling to you, for love in action is a harsh and dreadful thing compared with love in dreams. Love in dreams is greedy for immediate action, rapidly performed and in the sight of all. Men will even give their lives, if only the ordeal does not last too long but is soon over, with all looking on and applauding as though on stage. But active love is labor and fortitude, and for some people too, perhaps, a complete science. But I predict just when you see with horror that in spite of all your efforts, you are getting further from your goal instead of nearer to it—at that very moment I predict that you will reach it and behold clearly the miraculous power of the Lord who has been all the time loving you and mysteriously guiding you.[12]

CHAPTER 8

Moving toward Wholeness

Few people have written more profoundly about the process of human individuation and fulfillment than Carl Jung. He describes four stages through which we usually pass in our journey toward wholeness. (Arthur Miller describes much the same process in his profound and moving play *After the Fall*.)

First of all, we need to face who and what we have been, are, and can become. Seldom can we do this realistically unless we share this process of self-discovery with another person; alone, we can easily deceive ourselves. So we must find someone we trust, and trust is usually accompanied by genuine caring.

The second stage is closely connected with the first. It involves the willingness to be vulnerable, to allow ourselves to be loved and cared for, to love and to care. As we have already seen, without love we do not become the amazing beings we are capable of becoming, fulfilled women and men. (Most recoveries from chronic illness, it should be noted, require an environment of love at least as much as miracle drugs.)

Jung next reminds us that, like any pilgrimage, the journey toward fulfillment requires determination and hard work. The third stage, then, is that of working to be what we are capable of becoming. And one important part of this work for most people is keeping a written record of it. Most explorers would never have found their destination unless they kept a log of their journey; often they discovered unexpected treasures on their way. Likewise, Jung's magnificent journals record his route. A journal is an invaluable aid in finding our outer and inner ways. (The outer and the inner work cannot be separated.)

By our unaided humanness we seldom find integration. But the Divine knows our need and gives us momentary experiences of wholeness and totality. The fourth step is given to us—grace. People do not earn grace, and yet it is seldom granted to those who do not seek after something or to people who are closed to the possibility that such a saving and transforming reality might be waiting in the wings. These grace experiences are given again and again. They give us a new depth of revelation about ourselves, new insights into the meaning of love. And then we have more work. We return to the never-ending journey, the spiral staircase that brings us back again to the same place but at a higher point. As T. S. Eliot put it:

> And the end of all our exploring
> Will be to arrive where we started
> And know the place for the first time.[5]

Keeping a Journal

Keeping a journal is one of the most helpful practices in our working toward human fulfillment. Most of us stop and reflect far too seldom on our journey, unless we have made a commitment to keep on growing. And we are more likely to forget our great joys, our transforming religious experiences, and our visions of wholeness than we are to forget periods of darkness, pain, and sorrow. When we fail to record and reflect on our peak times of light, we seldom fully experience or integrate them. The deep despair that we don't deal with, however, seldom ceases to haunt us.

In reflecting back through my memory, I came on six or seven people who had made a critically positive impact on my pilgrimage. I had forgotten how much they had touched me. I wrote to them and received appreciative letters in return from those still living. Several old friendships were renewed. I had not seen one family friend in forty-nine years. We arranged to meet and as we began to talk, it was as if only a week had passed rather than nearly fifty years. This was a real experience of grace.

How does one go about keeping a journal, a record of significant happenings that provides a launching pad for further growth and development? The first decision that someone has to make who wishes to keep a consistent record of his or her journey is to take seriously the idea that each of us is a unique individual who has an infinite value and a destiny that no one else can fulfill. We can keep such a diary out of vanity, but it is worthwhile only if we keep it because we are called to live to the full our personal destiny.

Many people are impeded from the attempt to plot out the curve of their path because of an unacknowledged belief that they are insignificant or valueless and that what they do makes little difference. But Jesus made a revolutionary and radical proclamation: each human being has immeasurable value, and no single human being can be sacrificed for the purposes of another. Jesus also stated clearly, in the tradition of the Hebrew prophets, that what we do in the world has eternal significance. Religious beliefs that regard this world as only illusion seldom suggest the value of worldly actions, or of attention to such actions. The keeping of a record of actions, thoughts, and experiences can be far more than an exercise of vanity. It can be a sacrament and symbol of my increasing relationship with the Holy One and of my desire to realize my potential.

Once I have come to the conclusion that I am worth considering and planning for, worth thinking about and reflecting upon, then I need to own a notebook or composition book and a pencil that can be clipped to the journal. (Those who keep their notings, their reflections, on scraps of paper are usually announcing that their lives have no more significance than scraps of paper.) Having a journal by my bed and then carrying it into my office reminds me that I have value and have a destiny that no other person can live out. I prefer a bound book to a loose leaf binder. This is a permanent record; I don't want to lose any of it.

I use only one journal at a time and write both from the front of the journal forward and also from the back of the notebook toward the front. I put my logical, practical, left-brain material in the front of my notebook: address, telephone numbers, lists of people I want to pray for, and other important information to which I wish to refer. I also write in that section outlines for talks and for the writing that I am doing, schedules, and conscious planning of all kinds. My log book emphasizes both the outer practical world as well as the inner, unconscious, prayerful, and reflective aspects of my experience. (Augustine's *Confessions* is a model for today's journal keepers; it is one of the first literary attempts to show the eternal significance of both the outer and inner journey.)

Starting from the last page and moving forward, I date each entry and where I am at the time. (I travel far too much, and this locates me solidly in space and time.) Dating each entry also reminds me when I last stopped to reflect and write. I find that I need to stop and reflect at least once a day and at a specific time when I have ceased my outer doing and am able to reflect; my busyness can crowd out my reflection. Jung's remark to a friend of mine about our busyness is classic: busyness, he said, is not of the devil; busyness *is* the devil. Busyness is probably the most effective way of keeping us out of touch with the inner loving Wisdom and of tying us to lesser gods, unconsciousness, and egotism.

If I awaken with a dream, I usually write it down, because dreams that

are not recorded in the first ten minutes of awakening are usually forgotten. If I have little time, I write down significant words from the dream.
If I pick up my journal at other times, I need to quiet down and relax and
detach myself from my most pressing concerns. Breathing deeply twenty
times can quiet me and prepare me for reflection and listening. Then I
usually record what I am feeling, what the world seems like, what the
day before has brought me, and what meaning it has had for me on my
journey. I cannot deal with what I do not honestly face within myself—
my joys, my experiences of grace, my fears and angers, my moments of
bad temper, my sexual feelings. I also need to describe my feelings of
being misunderstood, my psychic and physical pain, and the beauty of
the world around me: the cliffs falling into the sea, the towering redwoods, the waves breaking on the lava rock.

After recording these reflections, I usually take time to address the
Holy Inner Voice and discuss where I have been, where I am going, what
I need to do to integrate a grace experience, and how to deal with the
darkness within me and outside of me. Sometimes nothing comes
through, and I wait in silence. Usually, though, something answers back,
not in an audible voice, but in a meaning. Usually some clarity comes to
me if I wait long enough. (When the darkness seems overwhelming I use
another method that I will describe later.) Sometimes during this period
of quiet I read scripture and listen deeply to it, or I read some other book
that speaks to the pilgrimage toward wholeness. I also look back at my
recent dreams and try to understand the message that the dreams have
tried to give me.

In addition, this time of inner quiet, after I have relaxed and become
silent, is a good time to hold up those for whom I pray: those I love, those
who have needs, those who don't seem to love me, and those I find it
difficult to love. Jesus told us to pray for our enemies, and there is no better time for that practice. Sometimes I write about the places in which I
have experienced the Holy: in the world, in people, in worship with others, and directly within the sanctuary of my inner being. Occasionally I
try to describe my experiences in poetry or prose.

Honestly written reflections are extremely personal and confidential.
Our jottings will be concerned with our reactions to those around us.
They will describe how we have been hurt, and what we should do about
it. Such a written record can be very destructive if it is left lying around.
Curiosity and anger can often prod people to pick up what is the private
property of another person. Thus, if parts of our log could injure another
who might break confidentiality and read it, these parts should be writ-

ten in code. If one is living with others, everyone in that community must agree that such journal records are confidential. Otherwise, we need to find a safe, private place for these written records.

When I begin a new journal, I look back over the years past and I ask myself a number of questions. Anyone who wants to begin a journal might find these questions provocative. They reveal something of the range of concerns that we can profitably record:

1. What are my good qualities? How often have I noted them and appreciated them? What are the gifts with which I have been endowed?
2. What significant religious experiences have I had that have revealed God's love?
3. How have I grown and matured during the last five years? the last year? Or have I ceased to grow? have I fallen backwards?
4. How have I handled the hurdles that have been in my path?
5. In what situations have I felt closest to God?
6. How have I succeeded in loving difficult people?
7. In what situations have I experienced another's lack of concern for or interest in me, and yet I have reached out in concern and care?
8. How do I need healing in body, in attitudes of mind? How do I deal with my egotism and self-centeredness? What spiritual healing do I need?
9. What are my addictions—money, sex, drugs, TV, closeness, dependency, workaholism, compulsiveness, over-neatness, laziness?
10. Where have I found real enjoyment and relaxation? Have I kept time for these activities?
11. Have I considered myself of enough value to treat myself kindly?
12. How have I taken time to relate to the Divine Lover who wishes to strengthen and guide me?
13. Have I stopped to reflect on and record in writing the beauty of the world, wildflowers and forests? on my good fortune? on experiences of caring from my family and friends and the strangers around me?
14. When have I turned to God in darkness and despair and felt this Inner Presence bring me to life and joy and set me on my journey once again?
15. How do I experience the world around me? As friendly? ambiguous? hostile? indifferent and uncaring?

16. Have I brought my pain and sorrow, my loneliness, my fears and tensions, my misfortune and anger and sickness to the healing presence of eternal Love?
17. Have I given myself enough time with the Holy One?

Writing down our personal reflections and personal inventories, our dreams and experiences of grace, makes them more real and substantial. When we are discouraged, we can turn back to our moments of hope and enlightenment and love and realize that we have indeed had such experiences. We can turn the pages back to times where we have been lifted up from catastrophes and inner prisons, and then we can hope again. The concrete written record has the mysterious effect of making our journey more real. It also helps us to change what needs to be changed, to integrate our peak experiences, and to struggle out of dark moods, and it can stimulate us to develop our positive traits. What is only thought about usually disappears, like seeds in shallow soil. What is written down often produces eighty- or a hundredfold.[2]

Clarity

To my surprise, I have learned that some of what I have written in my journal just for myself has been most helpful to others. Writings in which I exposed my own struggle and lostness—*and a way out of them*—have often spoken most deeply to some of my readers. Others have thanked me for sharing personal communications with friends who were fighting through the swamp and mire, like the hero in the film *The Neverending Story*. On the other hand sermons that I have written for others have often helped to clarify my own thinking. When I have not come to clarity in dealing with my own issues, intellectual or emotional, I cannot help others with theirs. My journal writing can give me distance from myself—detachment, objectivity, and clarity. Only a trusted friend listening to me and reflecting with me can give me the same kind of understanding of myself. I do not always have such a friend with me in the middle of the night or in a far city. My journal, however, can always be with me.

It is almost impossible for me to have an idea or feeling or mood and at the same time to be critical of it. However, when I look at my recorded thoughts, feelings, and actions, then I can read them just as if I were reading another person's log or listening to them in person. The journal gives me the opportunity to look at myself critically, to see myself more and more as I really am. Only then can I make changes; I cannot change what I do not know about myself.

Like many other people, I have found that *written* autobiographical reflections can give me a new understanding of what I am and a new appreciation of the journey that I have taken so far. I have been engaged for several years in such writing. I began with my earliest memories, and then I progressed on through the years. I described the lonely and frightened little boy that I had been, and of whom I had been ashamed. As I looked at him objectively, I came to appreciate his grit and courage under physical and emotional handicaps. I came to admire that child, to be proud of his drive, and to be thankful for those who had helped him realize his gifts. This new attitude changed the person I am now and gave me an increased confidence. Those who have never attempted to record the story of their journey may have neglected an important growth experience: the redeeming of an injured past.

Nearly any writing that I do, whether just for myself or for others, brings its rewards. When I am writing for publication, I find that I need to make at least two or three revisions. I seldom see confused thinking, places where connections are not made, or writing that embodies prejudice until it leaps out at me from the typewritten page. I can then rework the sentences that are unclear and without foundation, and I can overcome some of my blind spots. My next step is to read over my clarified writing to see how my train of thought fits in with the new insights that I have gained from listening to others, from the dramas I have witnessed on the screen or read about in books, and from the tragedies and comedies that take place within me and among those who touch my life. I can also reflect on how my conclusions compare with those of others who have written on the same subject. Out of this critical and careful consideration of what I have tried to express, new solutions and possibilities arise. I learn much about myself, even when I am writing to share my experiences and thoughts with others. An excellent editor once told me that only those who can be critically objective about their own manuscripts have the ability to produce worthwhile books.

Gaining clarity and objectivity about our emotions and moods is even more difficult than getting rid of confused thinking—and equally or more important. Sometimes our angers, our fears, and our attachments seem to possess us rather than being under our control. In English and most Western languages we say, "I am afraid" or "I am angry." Such statements imply that *all of me* is fearful or enraged. Some languages, however, describe emotions by quite a different use of words: "Fear has invaded me" or "Hatred has seized me." When we are seized by an emotion, we often can feel nothing else. In fact, however, we are more than that emotion. Recording and describing our emotions can enable us to look at them and see that they are only a part of us. When I experience fear or anxiety, for instance, my first step in releasing me from its grasp is to describe it in my journal; this simple process helps me realize that I am more than my fear. In other words, keeping a journal can actually help us not to be overwhelmed by emotions. Many alcoholic recovery programs, in fact, recommend the use of a journal to help free people from this addiction.[3]

We have seen that anger is a natural part of our humanity. Sometimes this anger gets hooked onto some person in our environment so that we can hardly abide being around this person or we strike back at him or her. We find it impossible to shake off this hostility. We wonder how we can obey Paul's injunction: "Be angry, but do not sin" (Eph. 4:26, RSV). Again, as I express these feelings in my journal I begin to see how silly and out of proportion they are. I also realize how stupid it is to be tied by my anger to the people that I like the least. I examine what in me is like the person that stirs up my wrath. And I realize that even though my adversaries have problems and give me a hook upon which to hang my inner hostility, they are not intentionally as bad as they seem. When I begin to compare my own unconsciousness with theirs, my ire begins to melt away. But without a journal in which to wrestle with these feelings, I seldom take the time or have the objectivity "to be angry, but sin not."

At times the conflicts, tensions, and responsibilities around me and within me seem more than I can bear. I can either go on struggling in confusion through the morass, or I can take time, get out my journal, quiet down, and write one by one those issues and problems that I am confronting. I have discovered that I can handle each element of the overwhelming situation once the different elements have been identified. I sit down with my journal and write: "I feel oppressed and hopeless. I feel like I am lost in a jungle, but also I realize that life isn't all bad. Why am I so upset and confused?" I then list my concerns one by one:

1. I am not physically up to par. I have had this problem before—but I know what I can do about it.
2. I have three deadlines to meet—but once I write down the three dates, I can see a way to get the work done and I make my plans.
3. I have too many details to handle—but I can delegate several of these to others.
4. I have inner tensions and conflicts—but I have had these before and as I write about them, I can put them into perspective. I can also talk to a trusted friend and be reassured.

5. I am worried about money. One of my children needs my help—but as I review my whole financial picture I realize the fears about the situation are unfounded.

6. My son is dying. His pain and frustration are almost too much to bear. Another person close to me is very sick. It seems too much. But then I remember that life does not end at the grave and that the resurrection tells us that what we suffer on this side will be swallowed up in the love and glory of the kingdom of heaven. What we shall receive will more than compensate for present suffering. Resurrection followed crucifixion, and my son has great confidence in life after death.

Forty or fifty minutes have passed. The mountains have indeed turned into hills (though not necessarily to molehills). I can deal with the situation. I have a new energy to put a workable plan into action. (When this process does not produce results, or when I recognize that I am fighting a different kind of battle, then I use a method that I will describe later.)

Setting Priorities

Jung once wrote that the essence of sin is unconsciousness, unwillingness to become conscious. God gave human beings the ability to be self-aware, to think, to reflect, to choose, to be conscious. Refusal to use this capacity, this giftedness, reduces us to acting on the whim or feeling of the moment. In fact, unconscious people may be more dangerous than those who are downright evil. Good and evil flow from them without discrimination. We don't know what to expect next. If we are to be truly human, we need to be as conscious as possible. That means that we need conscious goals, a direction for our life journey. This requires that we establish priorities, because lives without conscious priorities are likely to be governed by unconscious attitudes and to run into blind alleys.

What do I wish my years on this earth to accomplish? What do I want to become? It is mandatory that I ponder such questions *at length*. When I first set up a list of priorities for myself, I need more than a few hours or an afternoon. I need at least twenty-four or thirty-six hours directed toward this purpose alone. Some people find they need even longer, one week or several. The lengthy Ignatian retreat, for example, is essentially directed toward guiding pilgrims in establishing priorities for their journey.

As we continue on our way, we need to review and revise what we consider important to us. Without openness to change and growth we can become rigid and fixed; we fall again into the confusion of unconsciousness. Reviews of this kind, therefore, are essential. More courage and time, in fact, may be required to review my values and gauge how well I have lived up to them than was necessary to set them in the first place. As I engage in this process, I need to remember that what I have done is a better measure of what I really believe and value than what I thought or said that I believed. So I should write a description of how I actually have been spending my time, and how I now see that it should be spent. I need also to remember that priorities change with the different stages of life. I may have experiences that show me that some of my previous values were misplaced, or are wrong at the present.

As I wrote these words, Barbara and I were far from home for several months caring for our middle-aged unmarried child, who was terminally ill. Most of the regular patterns of our day-to-day living had been broken. I found my time filled with tasks I have seldom done before. I found journal keeping a stark necessity, and my first three priorities were patently clear. I list these and my other values in descending order as an exmaple of setting such goals. (Each person's goals will be unique in many ways. What I write is not a prescription for others, but my view of my values for this day and for some days to come.)

1. Keep open to the Divine Spirit.

Facing a situation like this I realize very quickly that I do not have the wisdom, strength, courage, and love that I need. I need to keep in touch with the saving God whom I have experienced in my deepest distress, the One who has given hope to many people in times of crisis. The Crucified and Risen One offers me a God of love who knows that depth of human pain and agony, a God who cares, a God who offers day-to-day help, wisdom, and strength, and at the same time promises a life beyond the grave that infinitely makes up for what we have suffered. An abstract metaphysical principle or an unmoved creator of the universe is of little value as I face the pain and suffering and death at an early age of one I love. At such a time, morally ambivalent pagan gods enrage me; they give no help.

A recent trip to South Africa introduced me to a vital Christian church among both blacks and whites. Both races were struggling against prejudice and oppression without losing hope and they give me hope in my situation. Real hope is contagious. The blacks, who make up 82 percent of the population and yet have no voice in deciding their own destiny, had faith that they would finally receive justice. I understood why Christianity spread in the Roman Empire, where three of every five human beings were slaves at the whim of any master, bought and sold like pigs. I also learned why Jesus spoke harshly of those who knew only laughter, filled stomachs, freedom, and riches. Those who have known only these things do not plumb the depths and mysteries of human existence – or its divine potential. Evil and pain and suffering are real and awful, but as we pass through and beyond them, we discover a new dimension where they are overcome and transcended.

But this does not make evil good, even though God has conquered it and can always conquer it. Evil is still evil. It is not the essence of the universe, but it is nonetheless potent, and I must not be overcome by it or taken in by it. (But more about the reality of evil later.)

I have already described two quite different spiritual practices, the prayer that finds salvation in images and that which finds fulfillment in the imageless presence of God. There are many variations on these different methods of staying in touch with the Divine. We maintain this relationship because it gives us joy, fills a deep need, stimulates growth, and protects us from inner evil. Each method of doing so, however, takes time. How do I stay open to the Divine Spirit?

First of all, I need the time to quiet down and come into the presence of the Holy, and then I must remain in silence or in dialogue with the inner voice of the Spirit – at least twenty to forty minutes a day.

During the day I need to come back again and again into that presence. (Unfortunately I find this easier in times of tension, sorrow, and pain than in times of satisfaction and laughter. I wish this were not so, but this is my truth. When my need is great, I find that I am calling continuously for help and seeking the Holy with real fervor.)

Out of this spontaneous, frequent turning toward the Mother-Father, loving God there flows quite naturally the attempt to practice continually the presence of God. Brother Lawrence, Thomas Kelly, and Frank Laubach have all described this practice well. In this practice, we try to find the Divine through everything we experience and to serve the Abba of whom Jesus speaks in all our actions – even the simplest ones like sweeping the floor or washing the dishes or picking up a pebble.

And then there is Eucharist, a more structured kind of Christian worship in which we not only think and pray, we act out the death and resurrection of Jesus and come into communion with the Risen One. Sacramentally we take the risen Lord into us. We are active but also passive. Eucharist has many different facets. We are actors in a divine drama; Eucharist is a divine play in which we enter another dimension of reality to share in the heavenly banquet and share it with our beloved departed who are part of the whole state of Christ's fellowship. We offer to God a tiny portion of what has been given to us, and these gifts are transformed and given back to us as the very life and reality of God permeating every part of our psychological and physical being. We recognize that what we are about to receive is far more than we could hope for. We acknowledge and confess our unconscious, our failures at love, our bitterness and our doubts, our self-centeredness and stinginess. We listen to and meditate on the words and actions of the one who defeated evil and death and on the story of the people who prepared the way for these events and of the amazing church that sprang to life among the people whose lives had been transformed by the reality of the risen and glorified Jesus. We also pray the prayer that Jesus gave us. Then we reach out to those around us to offer them peace, a real action of caring and at the same time a symbol of the love we hope to exemplify as individuals and as a group. We give thanks for all that has been done for us and for the love that welcomes all who feel unworthy to receive the overflowing fullness of divine compassion. And we praise God with our hearts, in songs that lift us up and inspire us to go out into the broken, sick, and hurting world, living our lives as Jesus lived his, living out our destinies, bringing the love that we have received to others.

You may object that the practice I suggest takes too much time, an hour a day or so. But what is our time for? I know that in the steep and narrow places of my journey, few practices give me surer renewal than Eucharist. If we are too busy to turn regularly to the center of Being, the soul's lodestar, then perhaps we are simply too busy.

As soon as I have come to *know* Love, then I realize that I am out of sync with the central core of the universe when I do not try to practice the same kind of love toward others. My limited time limits my giving, so I must decide what my priorities are in giving love. The other values I will list indicate these priorities.

2. Love myself.

I have already suggested that I cannot love others until I have spent time on loving myself. I have to keep the channels of my life open to Love if love is to flow from me. And then I need to realize that I am a human being and not an angel. I find it so difficult to accept my human limitations. I need sleep, time for relaxation, and nourishing, healthy food. My body needs exercise if it is to remain capable of continuing to give love in the midst of tension. At times Christianity made a grave mistake when it despised the body, praising those who abused the flesh because it was considered evil. Most saints entered willingly into intolerable situations because of love for the unfortunate, without any tinge of self-hate. I wonder, though, how much Symeon Stylites, who sat on a pillar for decades, was motivated by love and how much he was driven by masochism. We can overdo self-indulgence, and we can also indulge in too much self-denial, austerity, and asceticism. I need to love myself as a person whom Jesus valued enough to die for—a love that produces a healthy body-mind-soul capable of serving fully.

3. Love my family.

God gave me my family, but I was also actively involved in bringing my children into the world. So my family has first call on my time, money, and energy. If I do not love my family, the rest of my love may be only a facade. (Sometimes divorces do become necessary for the physical and mental well-being of members of the family group, and these situations pose complex problems.) Jesus *assumed* that we would love our family, even though he also said clearly by word and example that we need not be blindly or unconsciously tied to our family group. I have already described how much our children need us when they are small if they are to be healthy, normal adults. And if our love has been real, we will continue as parents to love them no matter what they do. When they need us for some genuine reason—financial stress, emotional crisis, or critical illness—our first duty is to them. There was no question that my son's illness required my presence. I could not let him face death alone. Everything else was cancelled.

The celibate undoubtedly is freer in some ways to serve than married people or parents. But celibacy needs to flow from commitment to service and outgoing friendship, not from a view that sexuality is ugly and unholy. When it does, it is a special vocation for some Christian ministers and a symbol of spiritual commitment in a secular world. Celibates, of course, are not freed from the pains involved in loving others. Celibates have community members to love, and they can be as difficult to love as the most impossible wife or husband, children, parents, step-parents, brothers, or sisters. Some unmarried people develop friendships to a high degree and make it one of their first priorities.

4. Nurture friendships.

A tragic practice in much of monasticism was the discouragement or forbidding of particular friendships. Without close friends with whom we can share our tensions and conflicts, our fears and anger, we can find ourselves trapped in an inner prison. This is not to say that married couples or those who live together intimately should share their every thought and feeling with each other. Unless we have internally processed our reactions and emotions and determined that our sharing is an attempt to strengthen and heal the relationship, we can fall into pure vindictiveness and egotism: a fine line is all that separates necessary honesty and unconscious hostility or psychic sadism. But real, generous, intimate sharing is necessary for all of us. (One of the reasons that the counseling profession flourishes is the absence of true, wise, close friendships that give us the wisdom and trust of our peers. We pay for what we seldom find among our peers.)

We need, therefore, to be taught how to achieve the depth and complexity of real relationships. Such learning is far more important than Euclid's geometry or parsing sentences. We have few more important tasks than learning how human beings relate to one another. Sadly, our scientific knowledge has far outpaced our ability to live with one another. I have learned that I need several close and frank friendships if I am to love myself and my family and if I am to wisely share the love of God with those whom God places in my path.

5. Love and serve the world.

Each of us has our particular way to express love in the world. One good friend accomplished this by having a company that treated employees as human beings and created a general atmosphere that was more caring that most church communities. Another sells insurance so that widows and children will not be in misery when premature death occurs. But there are some occupations in which it is more difficult to express love than others. (Of course, even such seemingly moral occupations as the religious ministry can be an ego trip rather than genuine service.) In meditation in the presence of the Divine Love two of my most important questions are: What do you want me to do? How can I best fulfill my destiny?

The answer to these questions will change along with our stage in life. Children need to be children and allowed to be children. Adolescents need to have the opportunity to experiment within a safe environment, and going away from home to college may provide this opportunity better than any other alternative. Each of us needs to assess our talents and our preferences and to plot out the options that are open to us for the use of our time and resources in this ravaged and paradoxical world—a world of great wealth and humanitarian effort and of incredible poverty, oppression, and sickness. If we never pause to consider the misery of the world (and those who operate from within a purely materialistic framework have little need to give it a thought), then our actions will likely be shaped by parents or by compulsiveness, unconsciousness, or greed.

I have already indicated that my life has been a series of professions; my primary work goals and service goals have changed over the years. For many years my first priority was my profession as a clergyperson. I regret to say that I was often more interested in my ministering than I was in God, in family, or in my own well-being. It took a severe crisis to startle me into that realization. Lecturing, counseling, and teaching each had their turn as my prime motivation in serving, and each of them at times became too consuming. When I dreamed that I was driving a truck backwards down a hill and that the brakes gave out, I immediately knew that thirty weeks of lecturing on the road with Barbara was self-destructive.

I have come to find that now my first goal—after relationships with the Holy, with family and close friends, and with myself—is writing. Outer pressures can keep me from my writing, but if I don't keep at it, then I am not sharing what God has given me in the way I seem to be called to do. In addition, when I write I find that I am renewed and refreshed, even though the writing is sometimes trying, and rewriting can be tedious. (Agnes Sanford describes a similar experience in her autobiography, *Sealed Orders*.)

6. Keep in touch with people's struggles.

I do some lecturing. It keeps me in touch with the problems people are struggling with. I also do some teaching for the same reason. And I also find that counseling/spiritual direction (I cannot separate them) and listening to the dreams and problems of other seekers keeps me in touch with the incredible depth and mystery of the human soul. These relationships keep me aware of the continuous presence of God in people's lives, a presence that, as Jung once wrote, is present whether it is sought or unsought.

In his remarkable book *Awakenings*, the neurologist Oliver Sacks describes the necessity of meaningful work for recovery from illness. He goes on to say that few people are able to maintain health of mind or body who have no meaning in their lives. His conclusion is a wise one, and it is based on his vast clinical experience. Medicine cannot maintain health and vital living unless people have genuine caring (received and given) and a meaningful way to express their gifts.

7. Study and learn.

If I do not keep learning, keep in touch with the developments in many different areas, what I say loses its relevance. Among the most important areas of learning for me are psychology, literature, physics (sometimes the most mystical of subjects), biblical study, philosophy, theology, parapsychology, and sociology. I try to keep one serious book going all the time. Friends and strangers often provide me with surprising new insights by sharing books with me.

8. Respond to casual friends.

We have close friends and we have casual ones. The latter reach out or we meet them, and if we are living in the spirit of love we will respond to them. One of the best examples of Jung's genuine concern for people was his practice of answering every serious letter written to him. His answer to my first letter was an experience of real grace and a turning point in my life. Correspondence unanswered is like a greeting ignored or avoided. So although letter writing can be a chore, it is an important chore.

9. Deal with daily tasks of living.

Finally we have to deal with the exigencies of daily life or with supervising those who help us do so. There are errands to be run, and bills to be paid. We must steward the resources we have been given so that we will not be dependent on others and so we can help those who need our help. When we forget that we live in a world of cars with blowouts, mail to be mailed, groceries to be carried home, and income taxes to be filed, we become ethereal and lose a portion of our humanity. Barbara and I try to share these tasks. They keep us rooted to reality. Many of the very poor have little time for anything else beyond this; they bleakly scratch for a living and hardly survive reality.

These are my priorities as I now see them. I was working on this priority list in the midst of a tense and demanding situation that drove me back to this very writing. As I struggled with these conflicting concerns, I found that I could make time for writing and that I was not being true to myself until I made that time.

Listening to the Dark Speech of the Spirit

In the book of Numbers we are told that God spoke to Moses face to face, but to other human beings the Holy One speaks in dreams, the dark speech of the Spirit. I have already described how listening to my dreams awakened me to the reality of something active within my psyche that was wiser than I. My dreams were leading me from death to fulfillment. I also discovered in a kind of detective-story search that dreams that been deeply valued in the biblical tradition and in the early history of the church.

If understanding dreams in indeed important, why are they so difficult to understand? What can we do to begin to uncover their meaning? Dreams speak in the ancient language of symbols, a language generally used by humans before the development of logical thought and still used in poetry, drama, and story. Symbols speak of realities that are too complex to be reduced to the level of logical thinking. This is not the place for a lengthy description of dream interpretation, but the subject is too important to ignore. The following simple suggestions will give some clues to the meaning, direction, and power of the dream. The suggestions can at least start one on a voyage of discovery.

1. If we wish to understand dreams, we must first be serious seekers for deeper meanings in life, searchers for a contact with the Holy that we do not already have. We must at least entertain the possibility that there is a dreamer within us who is separate from our ordinary ego and has wisdom and insight that this Holy One, who speaks softly in an ancient language we can learn, wants to share with us.

2. The second step requires possession and use of a journal. Dreams seem to pay more attention to those who pay attention to them. They are easily lost from memory as we leave the world of sleep and the unconscious and focus on the morning newscast, breakfast, getting gas, and arriving at work. One study of brainwaves reveals that 90 to 95 percent of our dreams are lost within the first ten minutes after awakening. Unless we consider them important enough to record immediately, we very seldom remember them. Since the dream can disappear in the few minutes taken to find a pad and pencil, I keep my journal and its pencil by my bedside. If I do not have the time to write the whole dream, a few notes or key words will enable me to recall it later and write it down in full. The dream needs to be written down simply with significant detail. As with any real *experience*, one's description of a dream can go on forever, and we can actually obscure the meaning of the dream by retelling it in too much detail.

3. Then we can take the written dream (either when we write it down or later) into the silence, where we can refer back to the areas of experience to which dreams can refer. The dream can refer to all seven areas of knowledge diagrammed in Figure 3. Then we can mull over the dream asking ourselves questions like:

· Is there any clear message or meaning emerging here that strikes home to us?

- Is the dream speaking of pains and guilts of the past or of the present?
- Could it be telling us that we have lost our way on our journey?
- Could the dream be giving us some hints how to get back on our journey and out of the dead-end street in which we find ourselves?
- Could the dream simply be giving us guidance on our inner journey? (St. John Bosco, the great humanitarian priest-teacher, found the voice of God speaking through his dreams, and his pope directed him to write down all his dream communications. *The Dreams and Visions of St. John Bosco* is a detailed account of how this great spiritual leader was led by his dreams—one of the most complete records of religious dreams available in any religion and culture.)
- Do we find at a later time that a dream has given us a hint about the future? (We will never know this if we do not record even a dream that makes no sense to us at the time.)
- Is the dream warning us that we are on a dangerous course that could lead us into serious problems?
- Is the dream simply encouraging us on our present path, urging us on?
- Is the dreamer within providing a drama on the darkened and silent stage of the soul that can give insight into where we have come from, where we are, and where we may be called to go?
- Is the dream trying to show us a part of ourselves that we are not aware of, and that we don't *want* to be aware of? (Most people in our dreams, along with the central action, represent a part of ourselves.)
- Does the dream open a door into a forgotten area of memory, something we are ashamed of?
- How are we to deal with the numinous evil we encounter in our dreams? (In most instances, evil in dreams does not mask itself.)
- Do we find that the dream is presenting us with a symbol that seems to have no connection with our personal lives?
- Is the dream a revelation of the Holy One? Such a dream came to Martin Niemöller. He was confronted in a dream with the Light of God, and he heard the voice of Hitler behind him saying: "Martin, Martin, why didn't you ever tell me?" He then awoke and realized that he had not been faithful to his God or church. He had been face to face with Hitler many times and never mentioned Christ to him. He then spoke out on the faithlessness of his church in Nazi Germany, and he changed the attitude of the church's leaders.

4. Most dream books are useless. They generally try to use dreams as a prediction of the future or as a method of finding direction, without demanding that we use our consciousness and rationality. In fact, though, nearly every message that comes from the unconscious needs to be carefully discerned and weighed. Most dream books also take no account of personal associations to the dream, which are essential for reliable understanding of dreams. Learning the language of dreams is like learning any other language; there are no satisfactory shortcuts.

5. When I can make no sense of a dream that seems significant, I like to tell my dream to a friend who understands symbolic thinking. Even dreams that I thought I understood can give me new insight when I tell them to another person. On occasion, just in telling the dream to another person I see what the dream means before the other person says a word. We do not need to find a trained analyst in order to get help with dreams. Any person that we trust, who understands the language of symbols or parables, can give us objectivity and help us remove our blinders. But since our dreams come from our unconscious—that of which we are not aware or conscious—they are often difficult to decipher, and it is a good idea to find a sensitive friend to help interpret them.

6. One person who believed she did not dream at all received a life-changing dream shortly after she began keeping a journal and pencil by her bedside. She then took the dream into her prayer time before the reserved sacrament, and for more than a year she received increasing insights and transformations as she came to understand her "big" dream.

7. Sometimes reading a dream and imagining that it is the dream of another person enables me to see what the dream is trying to convey. This can be particularly helpful with a repeated dream. When a dream comes again and again, it is usually a sign that I have not yet heard its message.

8. No dream interpretation is correct unless it calls forth in us the "Aha, that's it" response. Sometimes it takes several people giving the same message to get through our resistances so we can hear what is said. (Once it took an analyst, my wife, and my three children to convince me that an autocratic forest ranger with whom I was very angry in a dream was indeed a large and unpleasant part of me.)

9. Dreams are neither good nor bad in themselves. If a dream frightens me and yet warns me of a dangerous course and I take heed, the dream is a very valuable one. If I have a magnificent dream and do nothing to actualize it, the dream experience has been a tragic one: I have failed to bring to reality the opportunity or fulfillment that the dream has suggested could be mine.

10. As I listen to my dreams, I will become more and more aware of dream images and symbols that have little personal meaning. If I am serious about dreams, I will want to learn about some of the common symbols that bubble up out of the depth of me. Although, as I already mentioned, most dream books are useless, in the Selected Bibliography I have listed several that can be helpful in this study.

11. Sometimes dreams can be so ominous and our emotional state so fragile that we need to seek a professional who can steer us through the stormy waters of our inner being. Finding someone who combines a religious framework and a knowledge of the soul and psyche is not always easy. If, however, we continue to seek we can usually find the right person for us. God's hand is not foreshortened. Finding the right person to guide me in listening to the depth of myself was, as I have already described, one of the turning points of my life.

12. One of my most transforming experiences was entering into a dream through imagination, allowing the dream to continue, and discovering months later that I had been led through the very depth of the collective unconscious as well as through my more personal self.

13. Finally, there are those rare times when we meet the Holy in a dream, and this encounter can be a life-changing event. I have given several examples in other books, but let us look at one dream that led the woman who had it to express her experience in poetry and then to take seriously the message of her experience. This led her to years of study, and finally she entered the ordained ministry. Much as C. S. Lewis used the symbol of Aslan the Lion, Nancy DuBois experienced God as a Holy, numinous dog, and she allowed me to share her experience. I know of few more creative pieces of dream work than hers.

Dream—July 13, 1980

I was standing in an opening in the woods. The sun was shining, and I was happy to be among the trees. A stranger came toward me carrying something in his arms. He said to me, "This is the rarest dog in all the world. It is a precious gift for you." He set the puppy on the ground, and I thought he looked like a perfectly ordinary, brown, scruffy, playful puppy. But I wanted him, and I loved him immediately. The stranger left, and the puppy and I played for a long time. Then we lay down together to rest. I slept, and when I awakened there was no puppy. Instead there stood an enormous, elegant, copper-colored dog with beautiful fur waving to the ground. The ends of his fur were all tipped with gold, and there was a golden reflection all around him. I knew he would remain standing there until I really "saw" him with my soul as well as with my eyes. There were no words, but there was total communication between us. After a time, he "was gone." I looked around for him, but suddenly I knew he was gone but not gone. In the moment I "saw" him, he became a part of me forever.

August 30, 1980
The King of Dogs
Written in celebration of dream of July 13, 1980

Beneath the range of human affairs
Lies a darkened place, the quieted land
Where dreams and fancies, hope unfold
Where free and fullest life is lived.

Quickened by sleep, beckoned by love,
I rise, set forth, new voices calling.
Inviolate woods, my dreaming leads
Where spinning sun and shadowed earth
Await the holy kiss of life.

Attendant gods, this moment bless
As leaf and branch are parted now.

I see a man; a stranger, friend
Bearing gift of wriggling joy.
My arms embrace a small, brown dog
A nameless creature, freely given.
My friend, a stranger said it so:
"The rarest dog in all the world,
A precious gift for you this night."
Now, small brown dogs are not so rare
In daily life, where black is black
And what we see is what is seen.
But dreaming hearts know other lands
Where small brown dogs may guard one's soul
From fiercest dragons not yet known.
We meet, we love, small dog and I.
We play, we drink from purest streams.
And then we sleep within the dream.
I waken from this changing rest
But see no creature brown or small.

Before me stands the King of Dogs
Majestic beast of godly strength,
With lovely head and burning eyes.
His copper fur is brushed with gold
Reflecting suns from far off worlds
Where life is love and love is king.
His beauty stuns, my heart grows faint
Till sun and earth fade from my sight.

King dog and I are left alone
Eternal moment, glory shared.
Our spirits touch, bow down, are one
Enjoined forever, destined, crowned.

I do not touch the King of Dogs.
There is no need for word or touch.
For royal blood we share this night
Beyond the grave, beyond last life.

I hear the voices calling him
From holy wood to distant star
To bring the night to ancient dawn,
To lovely darkness show the sun.

My dreaming soul releases me
Returns me now to bounded earth.
Restored, I kneel, refreshed, reborn
Awaiting here the haunting call.[4]

Dreams can be amazing messengers, indeed the dark speech of the Spirit. They can tell us about our forgotten memories or speak in archetypal images. They can reveal parts of our personalities from which we have been hiding. They can show us the true nature of our relationships with other human beings. They can sketch our our journey for us. They can even give us a life-changing experience of the Holy. When I was teaching brilliant, skeptical premedical students at the University of Notre Dame, I found no better way to make them question their materialistic skepticism than having them faithfully keep a dream journal for six months. As the students listened to these nighttime messengers, they found elements and depths in them that simply could not be explained by a mechanical, materialistic worldview. Dreams can reveal another dimension of reality. Keeping track of them can be an important aid in our journey toward wholeness.

Courage

The path toward fulfillment requires courage. Most human beings are attracted and challenged by difficult tasks and problems. In October, for example, people come from all over the world to the Kona coast of the island of Hawaii to watch or participate in the triathalon—the ultimate test of human endurance—beginning with an ocean swim of several miles followed by a one-hundred-twenty-mile stint on a bicycle and ending with a twenty-six mile run. One of the fascinations of such a grand sporting event is that it reveals the training and courage of the participants and enables the watchers to share vicariously their determination. The easy is not always the attractive.

Religions and churches that promise all the goodies of a comfortable life here and hereafter with no effort on our part usually draw only weak or fragile people and produce few results. They provide little more than spiritual tranquilizers. Nearly all the great religious leaders tell us that the journey toward the fulfilled life requires training and courage. Paul, for instance, compares the follower of the Christian way to an athlete preparing to run a race. And in *Pilgrim's Progress*, which has long been one of the most popular religious books in the Western world, John Bunyan described the fortitude and determination required on a spiritual pilgrimage. Thomas à Kempis's *The Imitation of Christ*, a best seller for centuries, offers an exacting discipline, and Dostoyevsky's Father Zossima, concludes that love is only achieved at the end of a long and often discouraging quest. Most serious seekers, in other words, realize that many hurdles and traps are found on the spiritual pilgrimage. The religious journey is not a return to the womb.

The church has prospered more often in times of crisis and persecution than in times of tranquility and wealth. The courage and faith of the early Christian martyrs dying in the arena pierced the souls of the jaded, thrill-seeking spectators. The Greek church, likewise, in its fight to maintain its language and faith against Turkish persecution, inspired the affection of nearly all Greek peole. And the burning Irish Catholic faith was forged as it withstood the violent, vicious determination of the British to stamp it out.

Jesus did not promise an easy, broad, smooth, downhill jaunt for those who wished to follow him to wholeness. Rather, he told them of the narrow gate, the steep, cramped, and rocky path that leads to eternal life. He warned that those who followed him would find that even family and friends might turn against them. He told disciples to pick up their crosses and follow him. If they did not understand these words before his crucifixion and resurrection, after he had risen from an awful death, they began to understand the courage required to follow his way.

Love without strength can be weak and ineffectual. The love that Jesus lived and taught attained its incredible attractiveness and power because it was compounded with another quality as near to the heart and nature of God as love itself. It is strange that we can look at the life of Jesus—his fearless breaking of the law, his radical teaching, his trial and crucifixion—and fail to see the courage of this unique human being. Courage, as well as his closeness to Abba and his love, led Jesus to the cross and resurrection, and courage enabled him to speak only in words of love during those dark last hours of torture. The victory that Jesus won on Golgotha was compounded of many heroic elements: *humanity* (he was willing to become one of us and suffer with us); his deep, continual *communion with Abba*; *love*, through which he expressed by word and deed God's passionate love for lost human beings; and undaunted *courage*. If Jesus indeed revealed the ultimate nature of God, then courage is an essential aspect of the nature of God and of those who would have Abba's spirit moving in and through them.

Jesus was no village fool caught unawares by the vicious forces of evil and destroyed by them. He walked willingly into condemnation and into death in one of its most excruciating forms. He entered into the abyss of human darkness and meaninglessness, and he cried out with courage: "My God, my God, why have you forsaken me?"

Jesus had the courage to live out the deepest level of his being. He had prepared himself for his task, and he went on to affirm his own human-divine destiny. He had the courage to wait until the right moment to start his proclamation of the nearness of the kingdom. He then accepted the accolades of the people, and afterwards accepted exile and rejection. When he knew it was his time to act, he went up to Jerusalem—in spite of the opposition of the authorities; in spite of the fickleness of the crowd that cried out, "Hosanna" and two days later screamed, "Crucify him"; in spite of the cross that stood before him; in spite of fear and death; in spite of the ridicule of the priests; in spite of his human agony and despair. Jesus' story sums up the essential meaning of courage.

Real courage is neither reckless nor foolhardy, and it is far more than a gritty, stoic fortitude that mutely bears physical and psychological pain. It does not seek center stage or admiration. The truly gallant soul is quiet and determined, neither loud nor boasting. Courage is the firm, unyielding resolution to follow our own path to fulfilled life, no matter what the forces of evil and destruction throw against us, no matter how impenetrable the darkness we face, in spite of boredom, tension, fear, anger, hopelessness, and the hell of uncertainty. Courage is more than an emotion. It is not an absence of fear, but the willingness to go on in spite of our human terror.

True light is usually found only on the other side of the darkness of despair and bereavement, of pain and conflict, of anxiety and guilt. But to pass through the dark, dark night we need courage. Rebirth and resurrection lie only on the other side of death. Paul Tillich makes this truth patently clear in his magnificent book *The Courage to Be*. Courage (and no other word has quite the same meaning) enables us to break out of our imprisoning cocoon and continue on the way to wholeness, no matter what the odds against us are. Real courage enables us to bear the conflict of the opposites within us without compromising on a simple solution: The opposites of our androgynous nature, the tension between the beast and angel within us, the tension between our need to care for ourselves and for others. We can pray and love and give alms. We can be humble and thoughtfully eloquent, but until we add courage to our spiritual mix, we may lose our way and miss the pathway to fulfillment. Courageous souls often live hidden lives and are not widely known or praised. They have been true to their deepest intimations of the eternal, and they have taken necessary risks along the way.

I have been unable to discover the author of the following words; they were handed to me at the close of a conference. But these words eloquently express the courage that is necessary if we are to continue growing and maturing, being fulfilled.

> To laugh is to risk appearing the fool.
> To weep is to risk appearing sentimental.
> To reach out for another is to risk involvement.
> To expose feelings is to risk exposing your true self.
> To place your ideas, your dreams, before a crowd is to risk their loss.
> To love is to risk not being loved in return.
> To live is to risk dying.
> To hope is to risk despair.
> To try is to risk failure.
> To prepare is to risk finding nothing.
> But risks must be taken, because the greatest hazard in life is to
>   risk nothing.
> Those who risk nothing do nothing, have nothing, and are nothing.
> They may avoid suffering and sorrow, but they cannot learn, feel,
>   change, grow, love, live.
> Chained by their attitudes, they are slaves; they have forfeited
>   their freedom.
> Only a person who risks, has courage and is free to continue
>   unending growth.

Not only do we need courage to work toward fulfillment, but also to withstand the evil that attacks us and seems bent on keeping us from the fulfilled life. We find evil both in the physical world of reduced awareness and in the domain of expanded awareness. This malignant and destruc-

ive reality appears in sickness, bereavement, depression, discouragement, poverty, and oppression. We need courage and grace if we are not
to be crushed by them.

Many authorities on the spiritual life report that these attacks of
demonic destructiveness often increase as we go further on our journey
toward wholeness. Tertullian wrote with characteristic exaggeration that
only Christians fully know the Evil One. Early Christians were warned:
"Put on the whole armor of God, that you may be able to stand against
the wiles of the devil. For we are not contending against flesh and blood,
but against the principalities, against the powers, against the world rulers
of this present darkness, against spiritual hosts of wickedness in the
heavenly places" (Eph. 6:11–12, RSV). Jesus warned his followers that the
world would not understand them, but would persecute and try to
destroy them as it tried to annihilate their master.

Nearly every great saint has been viewed as heretical. Many of them
have come within a hairbreadth of condemnation by the very church of
Christ. Why should those people who are trying to live out their full
potential have to struggle against evil, which seeks to obstruct them and
keep them from their goal, evil manifested through human beings, or
through outer calamity, or through a spirit of despair and hopelessness
that strikes people in the core of their being? Many on the inner journey
find that they need the same kind of courage that Jesus displayed if they
are to complete their course and come to fulfillment.

In *Under the Eye of the Clock*, Christopher Nolan tells the story of his
own courage and that of his family. They enabled this child, so severely
spastic that he could not talk or move by himself, to graduate from college
and become a widely recognized poet and author—an epic of courage.

We need to look at the nature of evil, that devilry that overwhelms so
many of us and so often confronts those who seek to grow in maturity
and wholeness. I have alluded again and again to the reality of evil, of the
meaninglessness and destructiveness that permeate both our outer and
inner worlds. The time has come to face this problem directly.

CHAPTER 9

Why Evil in a World Created by a God of Love?

Whether they are saints, ordinary decent men and women, people of ambivalent character, or creatures deliberately wreaking vengeance on those around them, many human beings endure tremendous pain and suffering. Although most seekers attest to experiences of transcendent love and light at the core of the universe, at the heart of being, some also describe experiences of malicious destructiveness. How do these fit into the same picture? Trying to answer this question may be foolhardy, but to avoid the problem is to evade the most profound and bitter agony of our human condition.

In order to deal with this extraordinarily complex and difficult human dilemma, we must first look at the reality and universality of the human experience of evil. Then we will look at several of the solutions most often proposed to explain the enigma of evil, and we will look in more detail and at greater depth at the conviction expressed in Ephesians 6. At that point I will describe a view of reality that makes some sense of the baffling experience of the dark agony that I find in myself and in many other human beings as well. Then, in the two chapters that follow, I will present a method of meditation that has helped me and others to survive their inner despair as they are confronted with naked evil. In my conclusion I will describe the vision that Jesus offered as the final destiny of our fragile, noble, tortured, and glorious humanity.

The problem of evil and suffering is far more than theoretical. This became clearer than ever to me as I identified with the pain and helplessness of my dying child. In the Old Testament, the ultimate cruelty a conquering king could perpetrate was to slay the defeated king's son before his eyes, blind the king, and lead him away captive. To such a broken, defeated person, suffering was not a theoretical problem.

Suffering can never be quantified. I remember the agony of one of the finest young men I have known. Sarcoma first cost him his leg, and then spread to his lungs. He held my hand with heartbreaking firmness as I visited him twice a day to pray for him and give him what comfort I could, listening to him gasping for breath.

Is Evil Real?

Many people in North and South America have never known the horror of total modern warfare that has ravaged much of the rest of the world. They have not experienced the devastation that human beings have wrought on one another in the last hundred years, when hundreds of millions have been maimed, killed, or made homeless. Many North Americans live in ghettos of wealth and prosperity, of comfort and protection, and have no conception of the poverty and oppression, the hunger and sickness, the lawlessness and terror under which half of the human race tries to survive. Even worse, many of us do not *want* to know how the others live.

One can go to South Africa as a visitor on a tour and see the grandeur of the great mountains and deserts, the exquisite beauty of the protea, the great cliffs falling into the sea, the inviting beaches, and the great industrial cities, and see little of the tension and pain of that land. Or one can go among the blacks and see and feel a totally different country: one of terror, oppression, almost slavery.

Several nuns in the Philippines write to me regularly. They tell me of the lawless mobs that respect the property of religious communities no more than of secular ones. They tell of the lack of roads and of walking miles through mud to get to their mission stations. One nun from Bangladesh, who works in the Philippines has sent me pictures of human beings hardly living on a human level, and she goes on to tell of the great flood in which millions were made homeless in Bangladesh and during which her father died of hornet stings because there was no way to get him to medical care. And still she works on.

When we are well and those whom we love are well, we may think too seldom about the human misery caused by illness. I was always kept aware of it, though, because ministry to the sick was a large part of my parish work. I tried to help the sick get the best physical medicine and nursing care and found that some were healed through the sacramental healing of the church. I also knew first hand, from my childhood through my teen years, the devastating effects of physical illness. Those who have never known the ravages of sickness have little understanding how often disease destroys human beings far more than it ennobles them. In *Creative Suffering* Paul Tournier notes that for the few hundreds who become creative through suffering, millions are destroyed. In *Awakenings* and *The Man Who Mistook His Wife for a Hat*, Oliver Sacks describes with sensitivity and compassion the struggle of human beings to overcome physical handicaps. And in *Psychology, Medicine and Christian Healing*, I have shown how religion, psychology, and medicine need to work together to alleviate the curse of sickness. We seldom think about the horrors of the recurring bubonic plague that destroyed nearly a third of the population of Europe in the Middle Ages or of the influenza and encephalitis that killed over twenty million following World War I. And even as I write, scarcely a day goes by without mention of AIDS in the daily newspaper — the possible destructiveness of this plague is unknown.

Physical suffering is not the only sort of pain that people endure. Jung has pointed to the inner turmoil, anxiety, and depression that haunt most civilized societies. Once a community's all-encompassing concern to survive is overcome, then collective values can begin to disintegrate and individual men and women are usually troubled from within. Jung notes that he saw only a few practicing Roman Catholics as a therapist; earlier in the century, at least, the Catholic Church supplied those collective values that sustain people. Most neurotics, Jung found, had become so because they were cut off from the reality with which the living religions of humankind keep people in touch.

To dwell only on the anguish and sickness, the oppression and cruelty of the world is one-sided, but to ignore it is to fail to take in the world as it is. Consciously avoiding human suffering is to be callous to the hunger and agony of our brothers and sisters next door and all over the world. In the months of caring for our dying child, I realized how seldom I have deeply felt the extent and agony of human suffering. A certain amount of the ocean of human suffering can be attributed to the evil and ignorance, the greed and violence, the hatred and folly of human beings, but this cannot account for natural calamities and worldwide epidemics. How does all this fit in with the picture of a loving God?

What Is the Source of Evil?

The easiest answer to any question about evil's source is to assert that we live in a purely mechanical and material world which came to exist through pure chance. According to such a theory, the universe has no meaning or value. The words "good" and "evil," "right" and "wrong," have no meaning. Most materialistic scientism of today offers no alternative to this view. All we can do is adjust to the tragic absurdity of a painful and meaningless existence. (Sartre has presented this position with clarity and brilliance.)

Another answer common in Eastern religions is that evil is an illusion, that our experience of evil is the result of our not seeing reality as it really is. When we have the right kind of consciousness, say these religions, then we see that the physical world itself is an illusion and that human suffering dissolves with the dissolution of that world. Christian Science and *A Course in Miracles* provides the West with a similar point of view, maintaining that our sickness is the result of our errors in thinking. From this point of view, human suffering is not *real*. We project it on the world or on ourselves. We make our lives what they are. Some advocates of this view explain human suffering as a retribution for sins committed in a former reincarnation, in a life about which we have little or no memory. But even though there may be some truth in these views of the universe, they do not assuage the deep agony of our common existential pain.

Aristotle and many who follow his thinking argue that God made the world, but in the process there was a *necessary accidental lack of perfection*. Natural disasters and epidemics are simply part of this margin of error. The fact that human beings are so cantankerous, hostile, warlike, and destructive to one another simply means that God did the best God could, but that God's world is flawed. This neo-Aristotelian view has it that God does not intend human suffering, but that suffering is simply a part of the way things are, and it has to be endured. This kind of God, however, fails to attract the unlimited devotion of men and women who have experienced God's love but have also encountered the depths of human suffering.

Still another resolution to the problem of evil is the suggestion that God or the gods are ambivalent. Gods are sometimes kindly and helpful, but then they go on rampages and destroy with earthquakes or diseases or lightning bolts. Such a view demands that we live as carefully as possible, picking a path that will irritate the divinity the least. Many religions portray gods before whom human beings should grovel on their bellies, as they would before a Mogul emperor, and ask no questions. If human sacrifices are required to placate this god, people provide them. In his *Answer to Job*, Jung argues that the Old Testament God, whom his minister father believed in, was just like such a god—and was actually less moral than good human beings. My reaction to such a deity is to rebel—to struggle against such unyielding unreasonableness until I win or until I am struck down. Gods of this kind (and most of the Hindu, Greek, Roman, and Egyptian pantheon share this ambivalence) give us no real consolation in the tragedies of life; they offer no satisfactory salvation from evil.

The Old Testament records the development of the religious consciousness of a whole nation over several thousand years. Within these writings we find many different levels of religious understanding. We are told, for example, that shortly after Moses' ecstatic experience at the burning bush, Yahweh met him on the road to kill him, and Moses was saved only when his wife circumcised his son and touched Moses' genitals with the blood of the severed foreskin (Exod. 4:24–26). Many pepole do find themselves in great danger after a profound religious experience, but I doubt that Moses' attacker was indeed Yahweh.

The Hebrews were struggling so sincerely to avoid the amoral polytheism of the world around them that they could allow themselves to imagine no spiritual reality other than Yahweh operating in Yahweh's universe. Their system had no place for a principle of autonomous evil. Yahweh gave us life and its blessings—as well as death and its horrors. Gradually the theory developed that the righteous received wealth, happiness, many children, and long lives, while God sent sickness, disaster, and misery as a punishment for sin. Much of the later history of Israel was written in final form within the context of this theory, often called the deuteronomic theory. In Deuteronomy 28:27–28, we learn the consequences of breaking any of laws described there; here are these consequences, described in colorful King James language: "The Lord will smite thee with the botch of Egypt, and with emerods, and with the scab, and with the itch, whereof thou canst not be healed. The Lord shall smite thee with madness, and blindness, and astonishment of heart" Such a theory does not encourage the development of the practice of either religious or medical healing, nor does it encourage compassion toward those who suffer.

This theory, I should add, is not the theory of present-day Judaism. Some years ago I was lecturing on the subject of religious and psychological healing, and I stated that Judaism never had a place for medical or religious healing. A rabbi was present, and during the question period he criticized my statement with these words: "You are quite right that there is no place in the Old Testament for healing, but you must remember that no Jew takes the Old Testament *literally*. The Jews always read scripture through the interpretations of the Mishnah, the Talmud, and the Fathers. Only certain Christians read the book in a literal sense."

Even within the Old Testament itself we find violent protests to the theory that sickness is the result of sin. Such protests are recorded most poignantly in the book of Job. We also hear of a healing God in the Psalms, in Hosea, and in the later part of Isaiah. Jesus followed this healing tradition: he was a healer par excellence. His followers continued his healing ministry, and for centuries the church in the West continued Jesus' practices (the Orthodox church never abandoned them). Nonetheless, deep in the unconscious of most nominal Western Christians is the fear that God sends us our sickness and terror, our neurosis and depression as punishment for sin.[1]

Another variation of this theory is that God gives us our tragedies to help us grow and mature. Even some psychologists put forward this idea, stating that all sickness and tragedy have meaning and can prod us into greater consciousness. Once I was talking with the pastoral care staff of a large hospital about the evil of sickness, and many of the staff told me what good results came from sickness. I was shocked, and then I had an inspiration: I asked each of them if any of them had ever been seriously ill. None of them had. It is dangerous, if not immoral, to speak of the value of the suffering that we have not experienced.

Neither of these theories about suffering gives consolation to the sufferer in the midst of what can be irredeemable tragedy and agony. A God that gives cancer, encephalitis, or 80 percent burns to make us grow is vindictive. The God who would place a mother before the cross of an unjustly crucified son to make her more conscious is a monster. A loving God can *use* the afflictions of evil to work good, but a loving God does not *send* evil. As Tournier reminds us, some suffering redeems, but most suffering destroys.

But there is still another answer to our problem: evil is an autonomous reality operating in the spiritual and physical worlds against the design and love of God. A friend, John Whalen, wrote a letter to me in which he stated how absurd it is to try to harmonize good and evil.

I watch Joseph Campbell, whom I respect greatly, talk about having to "harmonize" oneself with the balance of good and evil in the universe! I can't believe that he or anyone who speaks so has experienced the utter destructiveness, the calculating, deliberate, ruthless, uncompromising, unfair negativity, the universe-ending despair of evil. I look forward to reading your chapter on taking advantage of evil's weak spot. I don't know what you had in mind when you wrote that, but what I thought of immediately is that evil simply cannot understand love—love in the sense of caring for another that does not come from self-interest. This had always surprised and amazed me when I have dealt with evil in imagination. The fact of God's love catches it utterly by surprise. It is utterly helpless in the face of this reality. To use your worldview analogy, love is the evil one's red six of spades.

It has no framework for love and therefore cannot see it! This is a delightful thing when you are faced with that horrifying reality. You might even say, worst case, that evil holds all the cards but one, and that one is a red six of spades. But that one card will trump evil every time. Unless evil gets a framework for Love. But then evil's whole reality will crumble! All it has to do is let Love in for a minute and wham! The jig is up.

But until that happens, I don't see any way to harmonize with that reality. Or to harmonize it with the "Good." In fact, that to me seems part of the problem. We talk about the opposite of evil being "good." And that gets us into the philosophical/linguistic/moral issues of "what is good for one person is evil for another." I think the proper pair of opposites is "good" and "bad." The real opposite of evil—as we *experience* it as a psychological/spiritual reality—is Love. Yet how seldom do we see the contrast discussed in these terms? It's a much more instructive comparison.

Love invites; evil invades. Love integrates; evil dis-integrates. Love nurtures, fosters, supports, protects; evil destroys. Love follows truth—truth especially about one's self, one's soul, one's acts, one's relationships; evil thrives on and uses lies, half-truths, distortions, twistings of the truth. Love's weapons are hope, faith, perseverance, trust; evil's fear, despair, hopelessness. Love reveals itself, wants to be known; evil works in concealment—revelation reveals it for what it is and spoils its efforts at destruction. Love wants relationship, in all the myriad meanings hidden behind the abstraction of that word; evil manipulates, subverts, coerces, tortures. Love wants to serve; evil to be served.

This opposition of *experiences*, not philosophical categories or words, is what informs my life. Though on the intellectual level the Jungian/Campbellian "harmony" of the opposites is very attractive to me, it does not work as an explanation of my experience. Evil—as an experience—is as real as the table I am writing on. Thank God Love is just as real. How it will all come out in the end I don't know. But I do know that I need what Andy calls Saving Reality, that in the face of the experience of evil I am a squashed bug without it!

The Reality of Evil

I was brought up in a rigid materialistic worldview with very few cracks in it. The idea that a principle or personality of evil could truly exist was simply beneath contempt intellectually. Likewise the idea that a real spiritual world exists beside and interpenetrates the physical one never occurred to me. I had a vague idea that the world was not purely meaningless and that there was a god-principle (though not one that could be directly experienced—one could only infer such a reality), but relationship with "it" was like having relationship with a complex mathematical formula. As a child I did have a sense of numinous maliciousness, but as I grew older, I was able to repress this experience most of the time. I also had one experience of praying with all my being for the survival of someone crucially important to me. I did seem to meet something, "an other," and the person survived. However, I had no worldview in which to integrate this vivid experience, and it remained suspended in memory and became important only in retrospect. As soon as one becomes convinced that spiritual reality is superstition and nonsense and that material reality alone exists, then God, gods, spirits of good and evil, and the Evil One all seem unreal as well.

In his fascinating and definitive book *Mephistopheles: The Devil in the Modern World*, Jeffrey Burton Russell traces the slow demise of the idea of the devil in Western thought during the last four centuries. Through the influence of Descartes (who ironically received his inspiration for his wholly natural method through an irrational experience, a dream) only those *sense experiences* and *rational ideas* that were clear and objectively verifiable were considered real. The physical world of the five senses was real. The spiritual realm might exist as an idea or theory, but it could not touch or influence us, nor could we relate to it. Only a step or two separated these conclusions from the conviction that the whole idea of a spiritual realm is an illusion, superstitious nonsense, that such a realm is utterly nonexistent. (These skeptics forgot that proving the nonexistence of something is nearly as impossible as it is arrogant. Real proof that something does not exist implies that one has discovered the innermost principle of all reality or has examined *all* significant experience—and both ideas are absurd and vain.) The spiritual realm, both evil and good, was dismissed; it could not have influence on the "real" physical world. Even the *idea* of the demonic or Satan or the devil died. The idea of God as an important organizing principle remained, but not as an Other with whom it was necessary to relate if we human beings were to fulfill our potential.

Nearly all the "enlightened" people bought this view of reality. Pentecostals and Fundamentalists went underground or developed insulated communities in which they would not be contaminated by the godless world. People read books about evil like *Frankenstein* or *Dracula* or went for a thrill to the movies about the supernatural, but spiritual evil was a joke.

C. G. Jung, however, opened me to quite a different idea. I met some of his followers as I sought relief when my unconscious imploded within me. They guided me to find a spiritual realm and an Other to whom I had never before learned to relate. I listened to dreams wiser than I that guided me out of my dead-end street. I also began to read Jung, and I found that his writings confirmed my deepest and most significant experiences and made sense of them. Alone at the ocean during a storm, I read *Memories, Dreams, Reflections*, a book that convincingly verified my own experience of the numinous.

Together with Wolfgang Pauli, the Nobel laureate in physics, Jung devised a theory of "synchronicity," which claims that both ordinary physical causuality and non-causal (nonphysical) influences have an effect on the courses of events in this world of ours. In addition to Jung's works, I read books on modern physics; I found that Werner Heisenberg claimed that physics has become so skeptical that it has become skeptical of its own skepticism; he also noted that all the basic words of classic physics have required redefinition, and he suggested that words of "natural language"—God, soul, and spirit—might be closer to reality than the highly refined words of physics.

In addition, Jung pointed out the eruption of the demonic that occurred in Fascism and most totalitarianism; he saw this movement as the worship of ambivalent Wotan. He also knew the depth of evil within himself, and he stated that none of us can deal with evil *out there* until we deal with the personal and collective (spiritual) evil within each of us. As I began to confront the depth of myself, I knew along with Jung that evil (personal and collective) within us can make us livid with fear and that dealing with that reality can be the most difficult task in life.

The evil that Jung made real to me psychologically and therapeutically was confirmed in the literary writings of Charles Williams, C. S. Lewis, and J. R. R. Tolkien. It became clear to me that the lives of all of us are influenced to some degree by the demonic. As I turned toward the spiritual world, I found a source of love, guidance, and numinosity; but I also came face to face with a spirit that would deceive, ensnare, use, and destroy me, a spirit that brought me to agonizing lostness and hopeless despair. And then I found that the luminous figure of the risen Christ could lift me out of the clutches of this evil reality. I saw for the first time that the great plays of Shakespeare, the great tragedies, are conflicts not just among human beings, but also against the powers of evil (expressed by Shakespeare through images of malicious ghosts and poisoning witches). Jeffrey Burton Russell notes that the last great literary discussion of the reality of the Evil One is Milton's eighteenth-century masterpiece, *Paradise Lost*, and Russell gives a magnificent summary of it. (Incidently, this was one of Freud's favorite poetic works. I think it gives a far more incisive picture of Satan than of God.)

Then I began to read the great fathers of the church: Athanasius, Basil, Gregory of Nazianzus, and Gregory of Nyssa in the East, and Ambrose, Augustine, Jerome, and Gregory the Great in the West. All of them believed that we human beings live in two worlds, and the theory of the atonement that they presented was an attempt to explain our *experience* of being saved from the powers of darkness that try to destroy us. Gustaf Aulén has shown in *Christus Victor* that the death and resurrection of Jesus were understood by the early church as the event during which Jesus faced and defeated the powers of evil and so delivered us from their control. Only later was the satisfaction theory developed, which claimed that Jesus was crucified and rose again to propitiate God's implacable sense of holiness and justice and so make human beings acceptable. (I consider this a downright immoral portrayal of God.)

Many early Christian thinkers identified evil with *death*, which they considered a metaphysical entity, as well as with the painful condition that this entity causes. This uncreative, disintegrating force, they felt, is directly opposed to God, much as Freud's "death wish" is opposed to the life force or libido. This destructive spirit, death, slips into human psyches and turns men and women away from God, the creative, the loving, the Holy Spirit. This power leads human beings spiritually into immorality of all kinds; psychologically it expresses its influence in mental illness; physically it brings bodily disease and finally physical death. Illness, far from being the will of God, is from this viewpoint directly and antagonistically opposed to the creative, loving Spirit.

These first Christians understood well the teaching and practice of Jesus. More is written in the New Testament of Jesus' healing ministry than of his teaching or preaching ministry. Jesus viewed sickness, both physical and mental, as due to demonic, destructive agencies. If we take Jesus' moral teachings seriously, we need to take his theological ideas just as seriously. He knew the reality of evil, and he rejoiced when the seventy returned reporting that many had been healed and that even devils were subject to them. Jesus cried jubilantly: "I saw Satan fall like lightning from heaven" (Luke 10:17, RSV).

The Psalms, the songs of the Hebrews, tell of the Hebrews' faith and their struggles with despair and hopelessness. In the same way Christian hymns speak of the reality of the struggle with death, despair, and evil. The hymns of Christmas speak of Love breaking into the world, and the great songs of Easter rejoice that evil and death have been defeated in a definitive way. The last two stanzas of Luther's great hymn "Ein Feste Burg" tell how the very name of Jesus can defeat the raging powers of evil. And when John Mason Neale was struggling through darkness and he felt that he was wrestling with the forces of evil, he wrote a hymn that he attributed to St. Andrew of Crete, which begins:

> Christian, dost thou see them
> On the holy ground
> How the powers of darkness
> Rage thy steps around?

A full study of the Christian hymnody would show that the reality and defeat of evil runs as a central theme throughout the history of Christian music.

I also realized that Jesus in his unique teaching on prayer told his disciples to pray that God would "deliver us *from the Evil One.*" The Greek version of the Lord's Prayer is patently clear in its personification of evil. Human beings by themselves do not seem to be able to keep out of the clutches of evil. They fall under the power of the Evil One and its minions, and they need divine help if they are to survive the influences of the very real power of *spiritual* evil that permeates both the physical and spiritual levels of reality. In his novel *Shadows of Ecstacy*, Charles Williams awakened me to a crucial truth: in order to be genuinely, recklessly evil, human beings have to be *spiritual*, and just as it takes discipline to be dedicated followers of the Holy One, so does it take discipline to serve evil. In other words, to be really evil we must maintain a close relationship with and tap the powers of spiritual evil. And we must do the same if we wish to serve good: we can continue on the path of fulfillment only by remaining in close contact with God and allowing the power and energy of the Holy to course through us. Only with this help can we overcome the pitfalls evil has placed in our way.

As I studied other religions, I found the same truth. I found the horrible demon statues in Buddhists temples and that a fear of the demonic runs through most popular Chinese thought. The Persian prophet, Zoroaster, was one of the first religious leaders to see and teach clearly that evil and good permeated both physical and spiritual realms; Ahura Mazda, he said, is full of light, hope, and creativity, and Ariman is a power of darkness, disintegration, hatred, annihilation, and death. This religious tradition declares that only if we human beings follow and support the Light can it be victorious and vanquish evil; we have the power to choose.

The Greek religious pantheon also had a little-known goddess of evil, folly, and mischief. She was Até, the eldest daughter of Zeus, and she crept into the minds of gods and mortals to lead them astray. Finally Zeus was so angry at her destructiveness that she was thrown down upon earth where she has been wreaking her havoc ever since. Zeus felt sorry for the mortals who fell under her sway; he sent the Litanies, who tried to help human beings and alleviate their lot. Barbara Tuchman begins her book *The March of Folly*, a history of human stupidity and evil, by telling the story of Até. Tuchman describes Até's power through the ages by detailed accounts of the Trojan War, the Renaissance popes, the British treatment of the American colonies, and the United States' involvement in Vietnam.

One of the finest statements of the reality of evil and its connection with death and sickness is found in Andrew Greeley's *The Mary Myth*. Greeley describes Mary as a symbol of the feminine, caring aspect of God. In describing the pietà aspect of Mary, the mother receiving her dead son, Greeley speaks of that aspect of the eternal that receives us at death for rebirth into a new dimension. He introduces this section of his book with his own poem "The Black-eyed Wife."

Greeley's poem portrays the death of a great man as the battleground where the struggle between the forces of good and evil still rages. The forces of evil were defeated in the resurrection of Jesus and they are defeated once again in this scene he describes:

> Energies and forces fill the air
> Fearsome, primal, ancient
> Spirits, good and evil,
> And something terrible in between.
>
> Here the sizzling electricity of good and evil
> Love and hate, order and chaos invisible.
> Evil has come to conquer a good man's soul
> Chaos to reassert its fearsome hold
> Hatred to open its dread abyss.
>
> It is finished, the day is done
> The demons cackle but they know they're lost
> The powers crackle but their energies are spent
> Strange things yet to happen
> But no matter for the black-eyed woman
> She weeps but she knows that she has won.

Greeley concludes:

> Yet Something tells me as I leave
> "The night there was more at stake
> Than you will ever know"
> And it's nice to think
> As you drive off in the night
> That the side you were on
> Was the side that won.[4]

Overcoming Evil

Greeley's poem echoes one of the central convictions of nearly all vital Christianity. Something happened at Jesus' crucifixion and resurrection that made a decisive difference in the world. Not only did these events show that evil and death do not always have the last word, but also that the nature of the entire universe has been changed and that it is now easier for human beings to break free from the power of the Evil One.

Even if we are slaughtered like the Jews in the Holocaust or like those twenty million snuffed out in the flu epidemic in 1917, we are not just annihilated. There is another dimension into which we emerge in which the opportunities for a full life are infinitely more available. The life we attain will more than make up for the suffering we have experienced and the life we have lost. All this is contained in Jesus' resurrection; the essential message of the teaching, life, death, and resurrection of Jesus is that evil and death have been defeated and that we can share in that victory. Christianity is the only faith that I know that looks squarely at the almost limitless extent of human agony and suffering, takes it seriously, and then offers meaning, reparation, redemption, and victory. Jesus neither ignores human agony nor dismisses it as illusion or as the result of our own choice.

Jesus knew where his path led; he knew that his battle was not just with the religious leaders of his people or the Romans, but with the very powers of Evil. Jesus knew that more was required than a pastoral ministry. He had traveled up and down Palestine, that ancient crossroads of the world, preaching, teaching, and healing. But this was not enough. He had to confront the subtle and naked evil directly, and so he turned his face toward Jerusalem for the last time.

Even his disciples, who had been deaf to his warnings of betrayal, suffering, and death, sensed an enormous difference. Mark, who may have been present, tells the story with stark, breathless simplicity: "And they were on the road, going up to Jerusalem, and Jesus was walking ahead of them; and they were amazed, and those who followed were afraid. And taking the twelve again, he began to tell them what was to happen to him" (Mark 10:32, RSV).

Something in their master sent chills up and down their spines. Their master had a new quality about him—the holy, the numinous. The disciples were awestruck, and they followed in fear and deep foreboding. Their very bodies reacted to what their minds could not fully understand. He was about to grapple with the Evil One, which could be conquered only if he confronted evil's cruelest manifestations: oppressive religious and political authorities, torture, death. Evil had to be met on its own ground and defeated.

The Way of Stories

But where does evil come from? What is its ultimate source? Why does it exist in God's world? I have often asked these questions, and I have come to realize that there is no satisfactory *logical* answer to them. This would lead most of us Westerners to assume that there are no answers at all, wed as we are to the logical, conceptual, rational analysis that is so prized in the Western world. Through its science, this way of thinking has wrung many secrets from the material world, even the potential power to destroy our planet and the human race. But it is value free—it makes no judgments of good or evil—so it is obviously unable to explain the source of good or evil.

There is another kind of thinking that conveys its meaning with images and pictures rather than concepts, with stories rather than analysis. This is the symbolic thinking of the dream and of mythology (myths are really the dreams of a people, a culture, or a tribe). Myths are not the outmoded or the untrue made up to explain what we do not understand. Rather, a myth expresses that which is so true and so near the heart of reality that our concepts and logical thinking cannot do justice to the complexity of this reality. Myths express in images and stories the meaning and nature of both the physical and spiritual worlds in which we live and move and have our being.

One story in particular describes the nature of evil better than any other. This is the story that Jesus believed and acted on; the incredibly courageous and victorious early church accepted it as well. This is the story that makes the most sense to me as I am a companion to others struggling through pain and agony and evil. It is the only story that can carry me through my own encounter with inner and outer evil. It is this story that helped me sit with hope at my son's bedside and wait for him to die.

In the beginning was God, a God of light, love, mercy, peace, and creativity. This creative center was the source of all things; it made both the spiritual world and the physical world. Part of God's creation was a whole hierarchy of spiritual beings with whom the Divine Creator desired fellowship, because Love wants something to love and be loved by. And Love also created human beings.

The trouble began in heaven. One of the finest, most able and magnificent of the angelic host became dissatisfied with the way heaven was run. This numinous androgynous creature came to the conclusion that neither heaven nor earth could be adequately ruled by love. If God's rule by love worked at all, it would surely not work efficiently. This prince of angels (called Lucifer, Satan, or the devil, and many other colorful names) favored power and knowledge over love, and decided that it was morally imperative to throw God out of heaven and take control. Soon a whole group of unhappy and frustrated angels gathered around their glorious leader and agreed that the kind and bungling reign of the loving God should be overthrown. War broke out in heaven, as the book of Revelation describes in the twelfth chapter.

Evil originated when a being created good, wise, and free revolted against the loving, merciful God. As the Evil One separated further and further from the divine, this being became more destructive, merciless, cruel, and malicious. Genuine evil is nearly always a partial good that pretends to be the whole good and acts as it were the whole good; what made Satan so evil was that this angel was so pwerful and good to begin with. And once Satan was thrown to earth (just like the Greek counter-part Até), the earth and the physical realm were infected both physically and spiritually with destructive maliciousness. But the question remains: why did all-powerful God permit this to happen? Why didn't God forsee the horrible consequences of the creation of free creatures? The only answer I can give is that Love is willing to take risks, and Love knows that in the end all will be well.[3]

Evil Defeated

The next chapter in the story of evil occurs on earth. The Creator established the Garden of Eden, where Adam and Eve were blissfully happy. One day, however, in the guise of a snake, Satan approached Eve and suggested that she and her husband eat some fruit from the one tree that was forbidden to them, the tree of the knowledge of good and evil. Eve was afraid, but Satan only laughed. "Why, my dear, if you eat it," the Evil One reasoned, "you will become like gods yourselves!"

Eve tasted the fruit and shared some with Adam. Their eyes were opened; they lost their simplicity and natural goodness. They both dis-covered that they wanted to be like God. They wanted to run their own lives by what *they* wanted rather than listening to the wisdom and love of God. This same attitude has persisted throughout human history. It has become our social inheritance and has been called original sin—the same kind of collective nastiness and ugliness that Jung pointed to in the depth of human beings.

Little more can be said about the origin of evil and how it infected God's world than what is contained in the essential message of this story. Something high and holy, created by God, turned against Divine Love, and this element has contaminated both human beings and their spiritual and physical environments and is corrupting them still.

When God confronted Adam with his action, Adam blamed Eve, and when Eve was confronted, she blamed the snake. They were not willing to accept the blame for their own actions. I wonder what might have happened if they had been willing to take responsibility for what they did.

Mary and Joseph provide an illuminating contrast to their original ancestors. They reversed Adam and Eve's attitude of evading guilt and blaming others. Mary accepted the gift of God's child courageously and with love, knowing full well what people would think and say. Joseph, with some angelic help, trusted Mary and cast no blame on her. From the first couple's pride, guilt, and fear, evil took root in the world; and from a second couple's love, trust, and humility, a savior was born capable of defeating and even destroying the ultimate power of death and evil.

It is difficult for most of us genuinely to believe that the divine, creative Spirit came into our world in a bodily way, that God took on and became part of physical createdness. If we believe that the spiritual world is pure nonsense, then the incarnating of the spiritual is nonsense too. (Incarnation is equally meaningless if the physical world is mere illusion.) Earlier I sketched out a diagram (Figure 3) that best explains all facets of our human knowing and existence; we turn back to it now. The incarnation of the divine makes good sense within this framework, because the framework acknowledges that the divine already has a foothold in every human being, body and soul.

We now provide another diagram (Figure 4) in which the Divine, represented by the parabola, totally overshadows and penetrates the nature of one unique human being, and becomes one with the psyche and body of Jesus of Nazareth. In this human being God becomes flesh and has concrete physical access to the divinely created world. This is the Christian belief in incarnation, God entering as a human being into the nature that God created. The church struggled for centuries with the mystery of the God-human being and finally came to the conclusion that Jesus, the Christ, the Messiah, was fully human and fully God at the same time. God was truly present, and the man Jesus was a real human being, without either divinity or humanity being mixed or mingled or losing the essential qualities unique to each. This paradox became one of the foundation stones on which Christianity was founded.

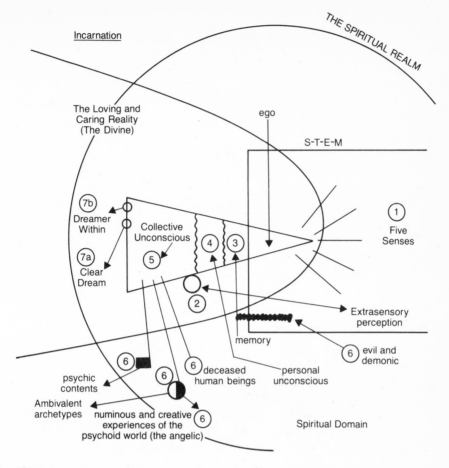

Figure 4

The dynamic presence of divine reality in the person of Jesus of Nazareth effectively prevented evil from infecting his life. Satan thought that the physical world had entirely fallen under Satan's dominion, and the evil angel now realized that this dominion was threatened. God in Jesus Christ was invading the world and completing creation with the birth of Jesus as a baby in Bethlehem. This infuriated the Evil One. The story continues to tell us that the Evil One fought back with fierce power, first through the doubts of Joseph, and then through the fear and viciousness of Herod and the compliance of his soldiers. Later, evil worked through the strange and mixed motives of Judas, the fear of the religious hierarchy, and the indifference of Pilate, through the fickleness of the mob spirit, and through the compliance of the Roman legion.

Throughout the crucifixion, the Evil One sat invisible on a stump, bursting with self-congratulation, gleefully delighting in this magnificent victory. But Jesus did not stay dead; death had no dominion over him. In rising from the dead, Jesus shattered evil's dominion. He established and revealed the ultimate weakness of the powers of evil. No matter how evil rages within and around us, we can enter the empty tomb or meet the Risen One in the garden outside it; then we know that evil's raging is in vain.

In a blaze of glory, Jesus disappeared from the disciples' physical sight, promising that the very spirit of God, the Holy Spirit, would come upon them. They departed in joy, for they had lost nothing, and then Pentecost gave them a sense of special relation and closeness to the Spirit of God and Jesus.

The ascension might better be called the Great Return, a return that made the risen Jesus and the Holy Spirit universally available. In *What Can We Say About the Resurrection*, Gerald O'Collins quotes with approval the statement of the Jesuit scholar, David Stanley: after the return and Pentecost, Jesus became "more dynamically present in the world than ever he was when he walked the hills of Galilee."[4]

A new Spirit and power were poured out on that early Christian fellowship. They endured persecution singing hymns as they faced wild beasts in the arena. They stood together and showed love not only to one another, but even to their persecutors and to the bloodthirsty mob that came to watch them die. The same spirit has empowered heroic Christians throughout the history of the church to withstand persecution.[5]

What we *do* is a better evidence of belief than what we profess with our lips. Few of us continuously manifest the Spirit of Christ in our day-to-day lives. Often we are swept over by feelings of doubt, anger, guilt, fear, anxiety, tension, self-centeredness, selfishness, lust, cowardice, backbiting, gossip, and even outright cruelty, and sometimes we express this attitudes in our actions. In his Letter to the Romans, Paul cries out: "I cannot understand my own behavior. I fail to carry out the things I want to do, and I find myself doing the very things I hate. . . . I act against my own will. . . . What a wretched man I am! Who will rescue me from this body doomed to death?" (Romans 7:15, 16, 24, JB). And so we are sick as a society, and we are also sick as individuals in mind, in body, and in social relationships. We live in an unjust world of poverty, crime, and war, of murder, broken marriages, and abused children. And these things naturally promote hopelessness and despair and doubt.

If we look honestly at the gigantic misery of the world, we may find it hard to believe that Jesus truly rose from the dead and that a God of love has final dominion over the whole universe. But honest doubt and questioning can lead us further into conviction and commitment if we engage them seriously. In his commentary on Matthew in *The Interpreter's Bible*, George Buttrick writes: "Doubt is perhaps not the opposite of faith, but only faith's misgivings. We could hardly doubt what does not exist; if we doubt God, we have perhaps therefore already glimpsed him. We need not fear doubt unless it comes from sin; there is faith in honest doubt." He quotes Philip Bailey's poem "Festus: A Country Town": "Who never doubted never half-believed. / Where doubt there truth is—'tis his shadow." Buttrick's conclusion is one that speaks to me: "the opposite of faith is not doubt, but cynicism."[6] The best healing for doubt is more experience of the Love at the center of the universe, which for me is best embodied in the continuing presence of the luminous, risen Jesus of Nazareth.

Paul endured nearly every indignity possible, from his fellow countrymen, from the Romans, and even from his own petulant nature, and yet a few lines after his cry of despair Paul rises to his greatest power and writes that he thanks God that he can be delivered from his inner and outer conflict through Jesus Christ his Lord. He goes on with these words of ultimate victory:

After saying this, what can we add? With God on our side who can be against us? Since God did not spare his own Son, but gave him up to benefit us all, we may be certain, after such a gift, that he will not refuse anything he can give. Could anyone accuse those that God has chosen? When God acquits, could anyone condemn? Could Christ Jesus? No! He not only died for us—he rose from the dead, and there at God's right hand he stands and pleads for us.

Nothing therefore can come between us and the love of Christ, even if we are troubled or worried, or being persecuted, or lacking food or clothes, or being threatened or even attacked. . . . These are the trials through which we triumph, by the power of him who loved us.

For I am certain of this: neither death nor life, no angel, no prince, nothing that exists, nothing still to come, not any power, or height or depth, nor any created thing, can ever come between us and the love of God made visible in Christ Jesus our Lord (Rom. 8:31–35, 37–39, JB).

I have already outlined many ways in which we can keep in touch with the Easter victory, ways of opening our lives to the spiritual dimension: prayer, sacrament, Eucharist, meditation, and quiet. We have also looked at love, humility, and courage as central to the victorious and fulfilled life. But there is yet another way of encountering this deep truth: through the faculty of imagination. We can make contact with the Risen One through a language that is far older than logical and conceptual language and thinking—the language of images, of poetry, of music, of feeling, of love. It is true that imagination, like logic, *can* lead us toward atom bombs or evil plans; many people, therefore, are afraid of imagination, considering only its evil or escapist uses. But imagination can also open us to the realm of the divine, to the loving, conquering, resurrected Jesus and help us overcome the power of evil.

CHAPTER 10

Taking Advantage of Evil's Weakness

Many of the most capable students at Notre Dame told me that they learned far more theology in their literature classes than in those specifically devoted to theology. Merely rational discussions of God and morality made little impression on them—did not engage them or convince them. God knew that human beings learn more by story and music, by art, symbols, and images than by logical reasoning, theorems, and equations, so God's deepest revelations have always been expressed in images and stories. The divine one also realized that law alone could not bring human beings into acceptance of God's passionate love for them; law merely prepared the nation of Israel, so that when God came into the world in Jesus Christ some of the Hebrews were prepared to understand the meaning of Jesus' stories and could be transformed by the story Jesus lived, the drama we just related.

Amos Wilder, the well-known American author, knew the power of symbols and wrote these words: "Imagination is a necessary component of all profound knowing and celebration. . . . It is at the level of imagination that any full engagement with life takes place."[1] And in her novel *Death Comes for the Archbishop*, Willa Cather tells the poignant story of Bishop Latour, who is saved from his doubt and despair when he ministers to an enslaved Mexican peon and shares in her faith. Reflecting on the depth and power of her faith, he too discovers the value of symbolic images: "He was able to feel, kneeling beside her, the preciousness of the things of the altar to her who was without possessions; the tapers, the image of the Virgin, the figures of the saints, the Cross that took away indignity from suffering and made pain and poverty a means of fellowship with Christ. . . . Ah, he thought, for one who cannot read—or think—the Image, the physical form of Love."[2] Personally, I doubt that many of us are opened to the transforming touch of Love or to the risen Jesus by thinking and logic alone.

In his remarkable study of brain-damaged patients, *Awakenings*, Oliver Sacks describes how these people can be roused out of stupor by music and art when nothing else can reach them. He quotes a passage from Charles Darwin's autobiography, in which Darwin laments that art and music have lost the meaning they used to have for him: "The loss of these tastes, this curious and lamentable loss of the higher aesthetic tastes, is a loss of happiness, and may possibly be injurious to the intellect, and more probably to the moral character, by enfeebling the emotional part of our nature." Darwin attributes this loss to his becoming "a sort of machine for grinding general laws out of large collections of facts."[3] Many psychologists agree that deep emotional crisis is usually necessary before dramatic and profound changes in human personality are possible.

Jung believed that the transforming power of symbols could not be recovered once they were lost. His attitude may well have been the result of a neurotic attitude about Jesus and Christian salvation that he acquired from his sick, confused, and despairing minister father.[4] But I am convinced that through the use of art and imagination, especially through stories, we *can* come through our doubt to a second naïveté in which we attain an even deeper openness to the creative power of symbols, even the transforming symbol of the resurrected Jesus. In his autobiography, the priest-sociologist Andrew Greeley tells why he began to write novels: he came to the conclusion that *only through stories* could he convey what he believes about the passionate love of God for human beings. Whatever one thinks about his novels, Greeley has reached an infinitely larger readership with them than with his numerous sociological books.

Using the Imagination

I was brought up within the materialistic and rationalistic worldview. I had a naïve belief in the literal truth of the New Testament narrative, but when I was faced with an inner crisis, my Christian faith melted away. I regained and immeasurably deepened my faith, however, through a method that I learned from some of Jung's friends, which brought Christian symbols alive for me in a new way. In fact, Jung himself knew well the *Spiritual Exercises* of Ignatius Loyola, and in 1939–40 he gave seminars on them (unfortunately the notes taken during them are not publicly available). When I studied the *Spiritual Exercises* and used them in classes at Notre Dame, I found myself on very familiar ground: through Jung and his followers I had learned a method quite similar to that of Ignatius.

I had learned that sitting in the silence with a journal open in my lap could bring me unexpected insights and new understandings if I stayed there long enough. (Eventually I even realized that I could take my despair, my hopelessness, my inner psychic pain, my doubt into the quietness before God and be healed, though for a long time I feared that these emotions could overwhelm me if I looked directly at them in my solitude.) My Jungian friends taught me that before I could engage any saving power, I had to be quiet and look honestly at what I was feeling and then record these feelings in my journal.

My second step after I record my inner or outer misery is to realize that the feelings that I encounter are not all of me. Many negative statements bubble up: "I am no good; I never will be any good; I am vile and useless; no one could care for me. I am lost and hopeless, and even God would not want anything to do with me." When I see them written down, I realize that these statements do not express all the truth about me. These statements are lies. They overstate the case; I am not that bad. My sense of humor begins to return.

The next step is to hear these statements as judgments *from another* about me. Now I hear them this way: "*You* are no good. *You* are hopeless. No one could ever love *you*. God wouldn't want *you* except burning in hell." As long as I identify with these statements as from me and expressing all of me, there is no way that I can not fight them. But when I look at them written on the page, they seem a bit overstated; even if I am faulty, I'm not *that* bad. Then I can see that they do not come from my essential self; something else is speaking them. And, in any case, I *remember* that Jesus came to save the lost, not the righteous, that the Risen One loves me, with all my flaws, and has lifted me out of my despair before.

Then I call out in the darkness: "Where am I? What can I do? How can I combat these voices of destruction?" Usually I hear a still, small voice whispering: "What does your situation feel like? Get out of your logic. How would you picture the mood that these words portray?" And then I wait in the quiet (and at this point quiet is absolutely essential) until the images begin to emerge and flow: I am in a dungeon, chained to a wall; I am on a battlefield, with people plunging bayonets into each other; I am buffeted and crushed by a mighty storm; I have fallen into a pit. I am chained to a rock as the eagles eat out my liver; I'm stretched on a rack. The images are innumerable. As I enter the appropriate image, the one that feels like my mood, it seems real and hopeless; then after enduring this hell for some time, I suddenly remember that the One who defeated evil has lifted me and others out of this agony before. There is One who wishes to save me, One who died and rose again to deliver me from the very power of evil that is bedeviling me. And I call out to this healing, saving Light to come and lift me out of where I am. When I am persistent enough the Light, the luminous Risen One, does appear, first as a tiny bead of light and then as the glorious Resurrected One surrounded by light. He takes me to the Garden where I am refreshed and renewed. This encounter with evil and rescue from it may take several hours or longer. I write all this down, and usually within an hour or so after finishing this kind of writing, the mood has lost its hold on me, and I am able to function again. The annihilating voices have ceased or are only static in the background.

Just thinking this process through, however, or going through the process in imagination without writing it down does not have the same effectiveness for me, or for most of those who have successfully used this method. It seems that writing incarnates imagination into reality; I actually write something—some thing—down on the page. Furthermore, when I have recorded such a meditation, I can return to it in periods of oppression and see that I have been lifted out of the dungeon of despair before. These facts alone are good reasons for regularly keeping a journal. (For those who cannot read or write, images, as Willa Cather's Archbishop states, can have the same effect.) This kind of written meditation ("active imagination" Jung calls it) allows one to engage and share in the power of the healing, transforming symbol. Some examples will provide a better understanding of what I mean than several dozen pages of exposition would.[5]

The Desolate Valley

I do not remember in what period of tension the following imagery came to me. Perhaps this experience occurred during a time of resolution after conflict, and I was asking why we human beings were so often the victims of evil in one form or another.

I come into the silence and gradually a whole scene appears before my inner eye. On either side of a wide fertile valley are great mountain ranges. One of the massive peaks is higher than any mountain I have ever seen—Himalaya-like and radiating light. Near the top is a jewel-like castle where the hosts of heaven and the Risen One abide. They all stand ready to answer the calls of need of those in the valley below. On the other side of the valley is a dark, cragged peak. The summit is shrouded with black thunderheads, creating a continuous tempest. Lightning flashes streak across the sky, revealing the outlines and battlements of a grim, dark stronghold. Just looking at this place sends shivers down my spine; here the forces of evil make their stand.

On the great plains between these mountains are many million peasant huts where we humans live and struggle to stay alive. Often the forces of evil swoop down from their dark dens and make us their prisoners. They do not need to be invited; they make sorties like Aztec armies to capture victims for their sacrifices. Sometimes they come in the night and move so stealthily that I am captured before I know I am attacked. They are like the army-police force of South Africa, and I cannot stand against them. I am either broken on the spot or dragged away into the dungeons in the caverns beneath the dismal fortress. There the red and stinking volcanic fires burn on and on.

I cannot be delivered by my own power, and these evil forces constantly remind me that no holy God would want anything to do with me. And yet, though I often forget it, I have been in this place before, and I have been rescued again and again. God does rescue me, but only if I face evil and then call for God's help; I cannot be rescued from any situation that I do not face. I cannot even begin to call for help until I know I am in trouble. So in the midst of my terror I begin to call upon the One who conquered evil and death. A speck of light appears, and it grows and grows until the luminous Risen One stands before me with arms outstretched and carries me to a place of restoration and healing where the waters flow and the scent of spring, of roses, and new-mown hay is always in the air. Hope-lessness disappears and I can go about my work and journey once again.

I have discovered that the powers of light and peace, of strength and joy, of courage and love seldom offer their gifts unless we cry out for them continuously and patiently. The Risen One does not mollycoddle us. Again I wish that I were different, but I'm afraid that I seldom seek my risen Lord with persistence until I am lost and the situation seems hope-less. In my experience very few of us seek God's love and power simply because we are pure, devoted, and religious. Generally we seek the Resurrected One because we are forced to—because we realize that we stand against the might of evil within us and around us. It is noteworthy that even the pious Psalmists often cry out for help because they feel that without it they will not survive.

Many tragedies break our ego strength, our self-confidence, and show us how needy we are. The extended illness of a loved one, death and sor-row, betrayal or sickness, political oppression and hunger—all of these show us our own powerlessness. Many men and women in middle life suddenly find that, like Dante, they are lost in a dark wood and can see no way out. The Risen One and the hosts of heaven will come to us when we call out in these situations; we are led to a better place than the deso-late valley or dark forest in which we have been struggling to survive. The Risen One is with us the moment we realize that we cannot help our-selves and ask for the mercy, strength, and love of God. So often it is a matter of knowing how to let the Spirit into our lives.

Before the divine drama of resurrection was played out on the stage of history, we mortals had little sure evidence that we who were so stained with ugliness and darkness had any right to reach out to the Light. Or we doubted that the Light had any understanding or care about our lot, or that God wanted anything to do with creatures such as us. Evil was on a rampage in the world. It still is on a rampage, and it contaminates most of us, but a change has occurred: Jesus came into the world to conquer Evil and to show that God cared and that the powers of Light are available to those who learn to call on them.

Holy Saturday and Easter Morning

Several years ago Barbara and I spent several months of a sabbatical in New Zealand. On the Thursday before Easter, we found ourselves in the little town of Coromandel on a wild peninsula far from civilization. We went into the little Anglican church there and were invited to the paschal supper and service; I was also asked to speak on Good Friday and Easter Sunday. We were far from home and friends, and I felt lonely and depressed; the reality of the crucifixion and the pain and hopelessness of Jesus' disciples and friends struck me, penetrated my inner being. With this came a sense of intolerable oppression—and on top of this I was not feeling well physically.

Saturday morning the inner oppression was still with me. I have learned that this kind of hopelessness and despair does not go away by itself; I knew that I must begin to get some help with it, or I would never be able to give the Easter sermon I had been asked to preach. So I began to meditate, and the first meditation lifted me out of the depth so I could function again, take a walk, and think through a sermon. I slept well that night, but I awoke realizing that some of the oppression was still within me; I had not touched the heart of my problem. I went back to my type-writer and a second meditation flowed forth. When I sent it to my psychologist friend Andrew Canale, he reminded me that I had had a similar experience several years before. I looked back through my journal and there it was. Indeed my friend had been so touched by the first experience that he had used it in an excellent book that he wrote on the religious road to meaning.[6]

Getting in touch with the risen Christ produced the same transformation in New Zealand that it had produced during the earlier experience. (I knew this only because of my journal record, which shows the value of keeping such records.) Following are the meditations that I wrote on that earlier Holy Saturday and Easter Sunday. One of them had raised me from the hopelessness of an anguished Holy Saturday; the second, written very early on Easter morning, gave me back my courage, hope, and joy. I have discovered that when this type of meditation does not bring relief with a first attempt at inward turning, then a second period of deep meditation and appeal for help may be necessary to get me on my feet. (A similar experience occurred to me when I started to write my book, *Resurrection*; it seemed that something was trying to keep me from writing about the defeat of evil at Easter.) Like the importunate widow, I need to keep insistently crying out for the One who has defeated evil to come and lift me out of my misery and despair. But mere survival is not enough; the loving God desires not only to rescue us from grave danger so we can survive, but also to give us the kingdom where we can have life and have it abundantly.

This method does not work for everyone. I do not know the reason for this. My wife, Barbara, tried it for many years, and nothing truly helped her until she found the method that she outlines in Chapter 6. However, many of us in our deepest despair cannot become quiet and come into the presence of Light, Love, and God unless we enter into and are lifted out of hopelessness and despair through image prayer. (I have not edited this meditation, which I wrote some years ago. I wrote it not to publish it, but to survive and get on with life. It was only later that I shared it with Barbara and Dr. Canale.)

Holy Saturday—Everything seems lifeless and useless, no joy, no hope, no certainty about anything, life or meaning. . . . All seems lost and I am alone, alone in the fog. Deep within the voice drums away at me: Hopeless, useless, lost, fraud, deceiver, fool . . . Again and again. Is this me or another? I feel it, whoever it is . . . I would like to lie down and cease the battle . . . no, that is the insidious voice that has seized me.

The fog swirls around me almost as thick as milk. I cannot see my hand in front of my face or my feet that hold me up . . . I hear their voices more clearly. They try to make me believe these words express what I feel and think . . . that I am alone against the world and these are my reflections.

DARK VOICE: Lie down and die; there is no hope. All is lost. Creep into thy narrow bed and breathe your last. . . . Perhaps there will be oblivion, extinction. Give up the battle. It is hopeless and there are only crosses for those not stupid enough to hide and then the bitter end. You are tired; lie down and die.

ME: You touch me at my vulnerable center. Lord, help me believe in your way. This voice allures me.

DARK VOICE: Lord who? There is no Lord, only death and hell and the lucky ones who cease to exist and are blown away like the desert dirt . . .

The fog totally encloses me . . . Ono face, no hands . . . alone, and the voices, seductive, mocking, jeering, taunting.

Dark Voice: Yes, you are alone in hell. Shall we freeze you in ice like our master and then you won't even hear our voices? But we can raise you up and torment you later. You have come to where you belong, home to hell. Welcome to the infinite variety of our subtle and not so subtle torture—or you can join the torturers and have the thrill of seeing others writhe in pain . . . two alternatives.

Me: Lord, how long have I been here? How did I get here?

Then they begin to attack the fortress of my soul. Monstrous claws strike me through the fog, ripping, tearing. I am surrounded on every side. A blow from one direction, a knife twisted in my groin from another . . . and I cannot even see them . . . ghostly attackers whipping, biting, clawing, ripping . . . I feel as though I am in shreds.

Dark Voice: You can still join us. We have infernal means of healing.

Me: My Lord, you died to save us from this. Lord, come. I cannot stand against them. They tear me apart and I feel so alone. I am at this moment so alone.

For awhile the attack continues, and then a haunting melody breaks through the fog and though my eyes are blurred with blood, I begin to see a figure before me, bright and glistening, and around him the fog begins to dissipate. Here is real light and the false, murky opaque fogginess thins out and disappears. I see figures scurrying to the protection of the darkness as the mist rises. I see the Lord there, a figure of living light. Exhausted and torn and bleeding, I fall to the ground at his feet. I am half aware of a figure kneeling beside me and gentle hands touching me, strong arms lifting me, and then I lose consciousness. When I awaken, I am in a room in which a fountain pours water into a large basin. My Lord sits beside me and is smiling at me. I find that the rending pain has diminished. I look at myself. I have been washed and cleaned and I can see that the wounds have healed. I speak.

Me: Lord, you must get sick and tired of rescuing me from one mess after another . . . suddenly lost in the fog and then torn to shreds.

Voice: It is a long time since you have been in trouble like this. My business is rescuing people who get lost, lost sheep, lost children, lost adults. . . . Besides, you have been working too hard and you are frustrated and tired. . . .

Me: And suddenly the bottom dropped out. Lord, sometimes it seems that I have to drop down into the pit before I really know your saving power. Why can't I keep in touch with you and stay out?

Voice: You don't and then there is the attack of the evil one. He is clever, that one.

Me: I live in such a tightrope life. . . . so much on the edge, wondering if I don't do more evil than good. . . . I hope that you have saved me because I have some value or can have. The most insidious thing is that I feel so valueless, so useless.

Voice: The dark voices are still speaking within you and trying to drag you down.

Me: What would you have me do?

Voice: Go slowly. Plan the time for tomorrow. . . . Get a good night's rest. Make your calls tomorrow.

ME: Lord, touch my heart and mind and bring me more belief. I believe, help thou my unbelief. I want to serve you and your people and even me for whom you died and rose again. . . . Help me be what you want me to be . . . even if I have to fight on in darkness.

VOICE: Would you like to go out into the garden or rest another night so that your wounds heal a bit? You really got ripped apart this time, but all this can be healed.

ME: A good night's sleep and then in the morning bring me to the Garden of the Tomb and let the lilies open with the sunrise and the poppies too.

VOICE: Come and rest again. I will sit beside you. The water of life is flowing here and my hand continues to bring healing.

EASTER MORNING—In fact I do sleep, a deep, comfortable, dreamless sleep. I awaken early and realize my contact with the saving Spirit has not been fully restored. I get up and go to my typewriter. I realize I have more work to do. Quietly sitting at the typewriter the images begin to flow. First I realize that it is Easter, but:

I am still in my tomblike room where the water flows. The Lord is still sitting there when I awaken. He smiles at me. Slowly I come to consciousness, dozing off again. Then I fully awaken and look at him and speak:

ME: Lord, I slept well and feel somewhat better, but there is little zip or joy within me. I am still full of doubt and fear, guilt, uncertainty. Is this a meaningful world? Did you rise from the dead? Is it all just one vast meaningless product of blind, stupid chance? Or does goodness, love, mercy emanate from the heart of things? Help me.

VOICE: Come, let us go. Get up and wash in the fountain, anoint yourself.

I get up and wash my hands and face . . . the water is warm. I run my fingers through my hair. He comes to me to embrace me. I return the embrace, but I do not give all of me to it.

VOICE: Why do you hold back?

ME: Because I wonder how you can care for one such as I, one so blemished and imperfect.

VOICE: All humans are imperfect, all have failed. Did I not accept Peter and John and the others who fled in the night? I have ransomed you from your very guilts.

ME: I feel so unclean and contaminated with doubt and fear.

VOICE: So were they all. Receive my grace and love. Part of you has died and needs to rise again. Let us go to a different garden, the Garden of the Tomb.

We take a path out through the heart rock of the earth. We leave the little room in which I slept with the soft music of the fountain and the light provided by the Lord himself. Where he is, there is light. Slowly we walk along a corridor and then take steps. It is a long walk and tiring. I stub my toe on some of the steps and fall against the jagged rock . . . but at last we come to a corner and we see the yellow light of the sun ahead . . . We quicken our steps and break out into the bright sunlight . . . A garden in the full burst of spring, flowers blooming everywhere. A wall of rock on one side with climbing vines and little flowers growing in the ledges. These are blooming too. In the rock cliff a hole has been cut . . . a tomb . . . a great stone has been rolled away . . . As we stand there in the shadows, for the sun has just risen and much of the place is still in the shade and misty, we see women come bearing jars and cloth. They are alarmed when they see the tomb open. They look in and soon come out terrified. They drop their parcels and flee . . . One of them wanders slowly down the hill, the others at a breakneck pace.

ME: Lord, these are your friends. Why do you not let them know that you are alive?

VOICE: They are so certain that I am dead that they could not believe. They are all unstrung. The time is not right. They will know in time.

We watch there quietly as the sun continues its imperious ascent. The one woman returns with two men running on before her . . . Peter and John. They could be no others. They enter the tomb, one dashing in and out, the other enters quietly, meditatively, and as he comes out his whole manner has changed. He walks with a light step. Then Mary comes up to the tomb. She is totally distraught. She just drags herself there. Her head rests upon her chest, her hair disheveled, her whole bearing one of dejection. We move over toward her. She stoops down and looks into the tomb. She is startled into life. We can see the two angelic beings there sitting at the head and foot of the place where Jesus was laid. They speak to her: "Woman, why are you weeping?" In a voice heavy with tears and pain she says: "They have taken my Lord away and I don't know where they have put him." She is so numb that even the bright, awesome holiness of the angels does not reach through to her. As she pauses there with a fresh flood of tears, her body shaken with sobs, my master speaks to me.

VOICE: Only those who die with me can truly rise with me. It is good that you died yesterday and the day before. You need to rise again along with Mary and the others. Then you will know. Real belief comes and goes like the waves of the sea. Only customary dull acceptance continues on undisturbed. You could not stand the full weight of glory all the time; you would be singed like the moth at the flame. The Loving One knows how little humans can bear. You have died to your dullness. Indeed your very darkness, your attack from darkness, is a coming to consciousness, a dying to unconsciousness and dullness, awakening to horror and to life and the absolute necessity of Life, Love, and Resurrection.

ME: But Lord, the darkness could destroy me and has destroyed others.

VOICE: It is the risk that we take. *But remember that you do not know the final destiny of those who appear to be destroyed.* They are not sacrificed for nothing. The Evil One will not keep them. They shall be specially honored in the kingdom that is coming . . . that has come . . . that is now. But enough of this; Mary needs us.

Mary has stood up and turned around. She sees our Lord standing there, her Lord and mine. And Jesus says: "Woman, why are you weeping so?" Another burst of sobs. "Who are you looking for?" Mary can hardly get out the words: "Sir, if you have taken him away, please tell me where you have placed him and I will go and take him away." And then our master, friend, lover, says only one word: "Mary!" Do I hear in that word "Morton" too? Is every name contained within that name? Mary . . .

She knows that voice. It breaks down the wall within her and she comes alive. She throws back her head and straightens up, raises high her hands and then falls to the ground and grasps his legs in her arms and covers his feet with kisses. She is ecstatic with joy. Finally he says to her: "Mary, stop clinging to me. Now I am with you always." Then he turns to me. Yes, I hear "Morton." I too fall to my knees and embrace him. He lifts both of us to our feet and then embraces us. Oh, the joy, the peace, the love, the forgiveness . . . Halleluia . . . the mercy, the mercy at the heart of things . . . and then he is gone in a blaze of glory. I watch Mary running down the hill among the flowers, laughing, joyous, stooping now and then to pick a bright bloom and toss it into the air . . . And then the scene fades, and I am back here in my study looking out over the trees and rooftops that lead down to the bay and the great bridge like a crown with cars coming and going . . . the bridge between two worlds . . . just as the bridge I have crossed and now recrossed.

I get up and stretch. I can breathe with ease and joy. The sense of oppression has lifted. I can see and rejoice in the beautiful Easter day. Although all the doubt and fear, all the guilt and sadness are still there, they no longer own me. I am free. I know the exultant joy of the slaves who on Emancipation Day in Jamaica trouped together up a high mountain in order to greet the new day sooner, crying out over and over again: "Free, free, free, free." Life and hope and joy are mine again; I can return to the desolate valley knowing things are ultimately not as dark or hopeless as they sometimes seem there. I have had a taste of the kingdom, and my courage and caring are restored.

This process took about four hours over two days. But sometimes just remembering that there is One who loves, cares, and saves is enough to enable me to regain my hold on courage and faith. Quite recently, as I have mentioned, I was faced with the imminent death of my son. His body was so ravaged that I knew he wanted to die, that something was trying to release him into new birth. Then old friends came to visit, and we found that one of them was also seriously ill. When I got quiet, I realized that I was overwhelmed with too much death; I had to deal with the Grim Reaper, so I spoke to the dark presence that was dragging me with heavy chains into its darkness. These words flowed out:

Death, you strike again. You laugh at me and speak:

You were frightened when I touched your own blood
And made you the oldest one of all,
The last one to survive. Now you watch

As I crush your son before your eyes.
Remember how they slew his sons as the captured king
Stood by and then they blinded him as well.
That bloody scene was my fine work.
And your good friend eaten away from within,
Like so many that you have known. And now you—
You and all you love, all in my hand
Crushed to sand like rocks standing against
Relentless waves. So ends all life.

We stand glaring at each other. He spits into my face. I wipe away the slime, I do not budge. And then I cry out:

You can strike me down, Death,
But I will not submit to your monstrosity.
Heap corpse upon corpse, and still you will not win.
You cannot kill the spirit, mind, or soul.
That is why you stoop to horror.
You are so afraid. You have lost your power.
I remember now. Strange how I forget.
Death and evil—close kin you are and both
Have been defeated, routed, spoiled.
I need not fear you. I can go on.

The heavy darkness rises and I can see the mountaintops again. Courage and hope return, and I begin a long and busy day with a new attitude and some joy.

This restoration came in less than an hour.

True Healing

For nearly forty years I have been deeply involved with and interested in the healing ministry of the church. As I described earlier, I saw many people healed through the healing ministry of Agnes Sanford. I began to practice this ministry, and I found that many people recovered far more quickly than was expected, and some people were restored to health when all the odds were against any possibility of healing. I began to study the whole subject of healing. It became clear to me that real healing takes place when spirit, mind, and body are healthy and working together. Because most Christian theologians had been so infiltrated with the materialism and rationalism of the Enlightenment and of nineteenth-century scientism, they did not know how to deal with the spiritual dimension of reality. They could not conceive how the intangible spiritual world could have any effect for good or ill upon our bodies or our minds. So the ministry of spiritual healing was lost in most mainline Western Christian churches.

However, more and more members of the medical profession have begun to realize that health is not just the absence of disease but is essentially the harmonious functioning of body, mind, and spirit. Remaining healthy is nearly impossible when an individual lives in a loveless and meaningless environment.[7]

Two problems plague those involved in any kind of healing. Why is it that some people get well while others do not? And why bother healing when eventually all of us die? Phrased in another way, the second question could be: when is it time to die?

I have no satisfactory answer for the first question except that we must never place the blame for not getting well on the patient. All we can say is that the healer, whether spiritual, psychological, or medical, is not able to be an adequate channel of healing power or doesn't have the right magic bullets to fight disease.

I lived with death for four months. Up until about fifteen years ago death was even more unmentionable than sex in polite society. Yet all of us die and most people who have been raised in our materialistic Western civilization take it as one of the givens that human beings cease to exist with the demise of the body, the disintegration of the physical organism. And it is this view, I think, that has made death so unspeakable: total extinction of our loved ones or of ourselves is hard to face. If this life is all we have, then as long as it gives us some pleasure, we would prefer not to be annihilated. We can get sick and be healed and then live on until we get sick again. But at the end of the line, all of us die. The best and wisest and the worst and vilest all go down to the same democratic realm of grave and death; for all of us, the time comes to die.

Love demands that we do all we can for the sick, the disabled, and the broken. However, if there be nothing to hope for beyond this vale of tears, then many of us who think about the implications of this lack of hope will look with utter despair upon our total existence. I am convinced, then, that true health and healing in this world demands that there be something better in store for us. *True and final healing occurs only on the other side of despair, suffering, and death. True healing requires residence in the kingdom of heaven, the kingdom of love.*

No one has stated this conviction better than Pinchas Lapide, a Jewish scholar who lived through the Holocaust, with a view quite different from that of Rabbi Kushner. He believes that life makes no sense without the transformation of life beyond death, and he sees the resurrection of

Jesus as a momentous historical example of the power of God over death. He writes:

All honest theology is a theology of catastrophe, a theology that receives its impulse from the misery and the nobility of our human nature.

- from the fear of death, from the will to live, and from the great hope that not everything is an end when death comes;
- a hope that arises from an anticipation of that incomprehensible infinity and final reality which we call God:
- a hope that cannot acquiesce in the thought that our existence begins with birth pangs and a whimper—only to end with a final rattle of agony;
- a hope that tears, death, and mourning will not have the last word;
- a hope that draws from its confidence "upward" the courage to look "ahead"; courage beyond dying to a life beyond the grave which deprives death of its sting in order to give our life a meaning which cannot perish or decay. . . .

That is the quintessence of the biblical faith in the resurrection, both of Jews and Christians.[8]

Lapide concludes that the founding of the Jewish state gave hope to modern Jews as the resurrection of Jesus empowered the early Christians.

Last year an old friend of mine, Gloria Cushing, died after a heroic battle against cancer. She had kept notes and a journal on her computer; her husband searched through the material on the disks and found these words:

Cancer Is So Limited

They've sentenced you with tiny cells that secrete
   themselves deep in body recesses and multiply.
Lymphonic capture of vital functions.

Can cancer conquer you?
I doubt it, for the strengths I see in you
   have nothing to do with cells, blood, and muscle.

For cancer is so limited.
It cannot cripple love, it cannot shatter hope.
It cannot corrode faith, it cannot eat away peace.
It cannot destroy confidence, it cannot kill friendship.

It cannot shut out memories, it cannot silence courage,
It cannot invade the soul, it cannot reduce eternal life.
It cannot quench the spirit,
It cannot lessen the power of resurrection.

> Can cancer conquer you?
> I doubt it, for the strengths I see in you
> Have nothing to do with cells and blood and muscle.[9]

Cancer, sickness, pain, and oppression are all very limited indeed if the kingdom that Jesus promised is truly waiting for us beyond this realm of space and time. Many of the saints have caught glimpses of it, and nearly all religions give some picture of life beyond death. Only our very limited and (in many ways) tragic Western civilization has as a whole disdained as stupid superstition such belief and experience of another dimension.

Anyone who has read the Gospels knows that this wisdom of which Jesus speaks is not an excuse for our failure to remove oppression, sickness, and evil from the earth. The kingdom is, rather, the model toward which we strive. The religion of Jesus is not an opiate, but a challenge to provide a society of caring and justice, of mercy and love, of health and joy in the here and now. Jesus' stories of Lazarus and the rich man and of the sheep and the goats are as clear as the midday sun: they are about the profound importance of real, earthly justice. A vision of Jesus' kingdom can be an incentive to work at establishing it in this world, not an opiate to help us forget the hell in which so many of us live; the lives of the great saints attest to this truth. But I doubt if anyone can continue to work for justice, peace, and love, can really combat evil, without a solid foundation of faith and hope: a hope for and belief in a great beyond.

CHAPTER 11

Utterly Fulfilled

Just as we lose some of the pleasure of creating a sandcastle when we remember that it will vanish with the next tide, so it is difficult, if not impossible, for most of us to give our best, conscious energy and attention to developing a fulfilled life if we believe that our human existence ends in extinction. Are we just expendable animals in a universe that is slowly winding down to a blackout, to the death of total inertia? If our conscious being ends this way, then what we are and what we do has little ultimate meaning. Indeed, the very word "meaning" makes little sense.

Built into the very structure of both body and psyche is an instinct to survive. Our bodies are so constituted that they respond in time of crisis with spurts of power and vitality. This extra energy enables us to accomplish extraordinary feats—climbing a tree previously impossible for us to scale, lifting a car to save a loved one, running to outdistance an attacker, or finding fortitude during time of persecution. When human beings lose this drive to fight through obstacles, they may die prematurely. And when loss of meaning is completely overwhelming, some people are driven to suicide.

Most people influenced by the Western world live in cultures that have accepted a materialistic view of reality that sees the grave as the final blotting out of human existence. Many of them may profess another view, but their lives and funeral practices betray no hope of any meaningful life beyond the grave. Even among many Christians the subject of death is largely taboo. Most people avoid talking about death because they fear extinction and have no idea or picture of how life can exist without a physical body.

Death—even viewed hopefully—is frightening, and most of us do not want to face that fear. But of course we cannot talk about life after death unless we look squarely at death itself. In *Creative Suffering*, Paul Tournier argues that our culture has a difficult time facing death: "To us the last few centuries appear as a vast and victorious campaign against material deprivation. It is when we come to the trials and tribulations of life, to disease and death, that we see that spiritual deprivation, however, has increased."[1]

And yet as we survey the history of the many cultures that exist and have existed on earth, we discover a nearly universal belief that individual human lives are not annihilated at physical death. There is also increasing evidence that some kind of consciousness does persist after our bodies die and disintegrate.

Interestingly, though, evidence does not come from professionals in religion, but rather from professionals in medicine, psychology, sociology, philosophy, and parapsychology. Indeed, two well-known Christian theologians, Gordon Kaufman and Schubert Ogden, declare that there is no reason to suppose that the lives of individuals continue beyond the grave and that belief in such a life is not an essential article of Christian faith.[2] Few Christian theologians are interested in the data that have emerged about life after death, and some even show hostility toward people interested in such data. Three reasons for this hostility emerge from their writings:

1. The data do not fit their worldview, and so, like people who encounter most data that question their basic point of view, they react with suspicion and anxiety.
2. These experiences are not confined to Christians and so the data cast doubt on the claim that Christians have an exclusive access to God and heaven.
3. Many believe that true faith requires belief without evidence. They are therefore unwilling even to try gathering all the evidence that God has provided so that they can have a more reasonable conviction and substantial faith in a purposeful universe—which will be brought to fruition in a heaven prepared as an end product of evolution by a God of love.

I spent twenty years gathering materials for a book on life after death. I cannot present all the data that I provide there, but I will present a description of the worldview we need if we are to be able even to look at the accumulating evidence that our human personalities continue on after death, and then I will look briefly at the evidence. I will then present the view of Jesus in the New Testament on this critical matter; although it may seem foolhardy, I will attempt to present a picture of heaven provided by the Beatitudes. Afterwards I will briefly discuss how we can prepare for such a numinous state of being. And I will conclude with some suggestions on how to minister to the dying and the bereaved.

Before I go on, I want to share with you one of the most remarkable visions of heaven that I have encountered.

Dear Fox, old friend, thus we have come to the end of the road that we were to go together . . . and so farewell.

But before I go, I have just one more thing to tell you:

Something has spoken to me in the night, burning the tapers of the waning year; something has spoken in the night, and told me I shall die, I know not where. Saying:

"To lose the earth you know, for greater knowing; to lose the life you have, for greater life; to leave the friends you loved, for greater loving; to find a land more kind than home, more large than earth—

—Whereon the pillars of this earth are founded, toward which the conscience of the world is tending—a wind is rising, and the rivers flow."[3]

These were the final words in Thomas Wolfe's last book. They were written by Wolfe before he knew that he had a fatal disease from which he died several months later. He never wrote anything like this before, and he had no connection with formal religion. However, after the experience expressed in the genius of these words, and as he was dying, his final effort at writing was a letter of reconciliation to Maxwell Perkins, the editor who found him and from whom he had been estranged.

The Worldview of Heaven

We have already described three quite different views of the universe. If one opts for the worldview in which the physical and spiritual worlds are both real, there is no reason to believe that the human person should cease to exist with the death of the body. If, however, we are convinced that our world is only material and that human love and faithfulness, art and literature are nothing more than foam on an ocean after a storm, then no amount of data will convince us that human beings are an essential part of our universe and that they can continue to grow in a realm of existence that we can taste now in our finest moments and will know more fully hereafter.

It is difficult for us to observe what we do not believe exists, as the work done in the cognitive learning laboratories at Harvard by Postman and Bruner, demonstrate. An ordinary black six of spades was painted red and inserted into an ordinary deck of cards. When subjects were shown the cards one by one, they did not *see* the red six of spades; they saw an ordinary black six of spades or a six of diamonds or of hearts. And spiritual experiences, which are not objectively verifiable, are even more difficult to observe when we do not believe they are possible.

Nonetheless, many have had such experiences. In 1973, Kalish and Reynolds published an account of their survey funded by the National Institute of Mental Health. They discovered that 44 percent of a carefully selected random sample of Blacks, Hispanics, Japanese, and Caucasians living in a metropolitan area reported that they had experienced the presence of deceased people after the deaths of these people. Only 1 percent of these experiences occurred at seances; the other 43 percent of these contacts with the deceased were spontaneous experiences, about equally divided between dreams and daytime visions. Being good sociologists, these researchers checked their results against all the literature on the subject and discovered that no other careful, scientific study on this subject had been reported up to that time. They then realized that within a materialistic framework (in which most sociologists operated twenty years ago), it was impossible to ask a meaningful question that pertained to nonphysical existence; within the materialistic framework such a query was simply a nonquestion.[4] Other researchers, including Andrew Greeley, subsequently have verified their data. Ordinary human beings in every culture and age do report experiences of the deceased.[5]

But I must reiterate that within a materialistic worldview it is impossible *even to look at* the data about survival beyond death. Indeed, the introduction of such information usually arouses hostility or ridicule. If the fulfilled life requires growth beyond this physical existence, it may require individuals to examine and find a more adequate understanding of the world than that with which most of us have been raised.

A significant body of research data dealing with this issue has been accumulated during the last twenty years as some scientists have become more open to the subject of life after death. The majority of this work has been devoted to three quite different kinds of experiences relating to the continuance of life: (1) near-death experiences, in which people who recovered from apparent death report surprisingly similar series of events, culminating in meeting a being of light; (2) encounters with deceased people by living people who have been close to them; (3) reports of those who minister to the dying of dying people's apparent contact with another realm of reality and with deceased people previously known to them.

Raymond Moody holds a Ph.D. in philosophy; he is also a practicing psychiatrist. He brought the near-death experience out of the closet with his enormously popular and carefully researched book *Life after Life*. After thirteen years of further study, he has given a superb summary of the work done on this subject in *The Light Beyond*. He concludes this book by writing: "I am convinced that NDEers (people who have had near-death experiences) do get a glimpse of the beyond, a brief passage into a whole other reality." And then Moody quotes a letter Jung wrote in 1944 after his own near-death experience: "The dissolution of our timebound form in eternity brings no loss of meaning. Rather, does the little finger know itself a member of the hand."[6]

Any interested or open-minded person can read many accounts of these experiences in Moody's books or in the books to which he refers. A poem by Caryl Porter, a friend and author, gives a better feel for the experience than any single account I have encountered:

Lazarus, Afterward, to His Friends

I slept.
Yes, I remember that,

> But I remember more;
> such peace as I had never known
> and a great, healing light

and then, a voice I knew
calling my name.

> I had to leave the new place
> for that voice

The winding voice
the unwinding cloths,
these I remember
and the long trip back.

> They said it was four days.
> It was an instant.

Everything new . . .
my friend's face,
my sisters' tears,
each leaf, each pebble
shining new.

> But that lost place?

I must take up the old ways
once again;
work in the fields
protect my sisters
from the perils
which surround us all.
Still, one day,
to return?

> Oh let my days go by
> fleet as gazelles
> toward that lost peace
> toward that lost light.[7]

Parapsychology has reported clairvoyant experiences for years, and recent studies show that these experiences often occur in times of crisis. Our paranormal powers of perception are heightened by intense emotional states. We have already referred to Kalish and Reynolds's study of these phenomena. And Andrew Greeley's *The Sociology of the Paranormal: A Reconnaissance* shows that a close relationship exists between those who have mystical experiences and those who have had experiences of the deceased. Greeley reports, furthermore, that such people generally possess a sound, well-developed personality as measured by an emotional maturity test embedded in the questionnaire used to obtain the data. And Christianity has always accepted the reality of these experiences: the phrase in the Apostle's Creed, "the communion of saints," refers to the experience that the living do have communion with the deceased in Christ.

One of the most delightful stories about this kind of communion is told by the biblical scholar J. B. Phillips in his book *Ring of Truth* in which he tells of a visit from the deceased C. S. Lewis, who helped him with a passage in scripture with which he was working. St. Ambrose, similarly, wrote a book telling of the help given to him in running the diocese of Milan by his deceased brother Satyrus. And Sulpicius Severus wrote a letter describing a dream-vision of St. Martin of Tours ascending into heaven—before he knew that St. Martin had indeed died.[8]

Those who minister to the dying report that at the hour of death some of the dying seem to stand between two worlds. They are clearly conscious and can carry on rational conversations with those in their room, and yet at the same time they claim to be in touch with the deceased or the angelic and are carrying on conversations with them. (I first became aware of this kind of experience when a parishioner described the death-bed scene of her clergyman father.) The definitive work on this kind of experience has been done by Dr. Karlis Osis and Dr. Erlendur Haraldsson and is presented in their book *At the Hour of Death*. Their data drew upon cross-cultural surveys in which they found similar experiences among peoples of various religions and nationalities.

I was lecturing in Minneapolis many years ago, and I shared the fact that I believed that such contacts with the deceased are possible. A woman in the group came up to me after the lecture and described the following experience. At my request she later described it again in a letter which she has given me permission to quote. Her narrative presents an experience of contact with the deceased at the time of death, and it also captures some of the quality of the strange events that occur to some people at the hour of death.

It was a pretty predawn morning filled with the fragrance of spring when I was suddenly to find myself wide awake and sitting bolt upright in my bed. The room had taken on a rare atmosphere glistening with a white light tinged with gold. An air of expectancy permeated the room, so much that it made me turn my gaze questioningly to the window at my left, then to those directly across from me, and at that moment, just to the right, this scene appeared.

Two beings of stately yet gentle bearing, almost as tall as the room is high in that area, stood facing each other on either side of a large doorway. They were clothed, each one, in a soft, flowing, opaque garment with a radiance resembling sun-shine on snow tinged with a faint pink. Their arms seemed winglike, reaching from the shoulders almost to the floor. They stood silent and motionless, and yet in a state of expectancy (I seemed to sense) until a feminine figure garbed in a darker hue came into view, with head bent slightly down and forward as if slowly ascending from a lower level. They then moved to enfold her, almost caressingly—and I distinctly saw the smiling face of our mother and heard her familiar voice laughingly say, as if a bit breathlessly, "I've finally made it!" She seemed happy. The smile remained on her face as, still enfolded in their embrace, she and the two beings *glided* by me . . . just inches from the foot of my bed. I reached out to touch her. My heart cried, "Mother! Mother, don't you see me?" Taking no notice of me they glided on by and out of sight.

The room was still scintillating. In fact my whole being seemed charged with a force I had not before known.

The atmosphere in the room was changing now, becoming more normal, although it still remained charged and my body still seemed all aglow. As a matter of fact, this lasted to a degree for several days. Presently the ringing of the tele-phone awakened my husband, and from his response I sensed the message con-veyed by his brother-in-law: "Your mother has just passed away."[9]

These experiences usually have a very positive effect on those who have them; their fear of death is greatly diminished. Both the survivors and the dying frequently describe the beyond as a place or state of love, light, and knowledge. Jung wrote of his own near-death experience in his autobiography, *Memories, Dreams, Reflections*: "I would never have imagined that any such experience was possible. It was not the product of imagination. The visions and experiences were utterly real; there was nothing subjective about them; they all had a quality of absolute objectivity."[10]

In addition to these relatively common experiences of men and women through the ages, there are other more theoretical reasons for expecting some kind of continuance of our personal selves after physical death. In Einstein's theory of relativity, time and space are interrelated. Since there is no absolute time, it is impossible to say when a person has absolutely died, so it is equally impossible to say that we cannot experi-ence that person.

Many of those who spend time in meditation not only find that they have transforming experiences of transcendent love but also often have clairvoyant and telepathic experiences as well as precognitive experi-ences. Frequently these relate to a loved one's death or to the condition of the loved one after death, and some of the circumstances surrounding the person's death, which were experienced telepathically, are often later verified. Poetic gifts, furthermore, appear to bring some people into touch with the realm beyond space and time. And then there is the whole matter of spiritualism and mediumship: undoubtedly some real contact with the deceased does sometimes occur, although the wheat is very difficult to separate from the chaff, as most honest mediums will admit. All these facts fit together to give quite a coherent picture, which is dismissed only by those who are trapped by a materialistic worldview.

Franz Ricklin, a psychiatrist and former director of the Jung Institute in Zürich, wrote an unpublished paper, "Psychotherapy and Death," which discussed the significance of the experiences of the dreams of dying people. In his conclusion he wrote: "But what intrigues me the most is the fact that out of all the dream material I have been able to collect, no evidence is given that death from the point of view of the unconscious means the total end, but is shown as a change, a separation from one's body. . . . The psyche, containing the ego as nucleus of consciousness, seems not to be touched by death as modern man mostly thinks."[11] Ricklin's data supports Jung's similar conclusion in his perceptive paper, "The Soul and Death."[12]

Jesus, the Early Church, and the Kingdom of Heaven

A minister attending one of my seminars at Notre Dame told me that he had been looking back over the last ten years of his sermon file. He had not once preached on the subject of the kingdom of heaven or life after death, and yet he realized that the New Testament is full of references to heaven, eternal life, resurrected life, being raised from the dead, the kingdom of god, immortality, and variations of these expressions. In his *God and the Unconscious*, Victor White makes fun of the polite nineteenth-century liberal attempts to exorcise the demons and devilish passages from the New Testament, and he calls attention to the fact that devils and Satan are found in it from the beginning to the end. And the passages relating to the kingdom are even more common in the New Testament than those referring to evil.

In the Gospel of Mark, after Jesus' baptism and John's imprisonment, Jesus begins his ministry with the message: "The time is fulfilled, the kingdom of God is at hand. Reform and accept the good news" (Mark 1:15, RSV). When Jesus preached to the great crowds telling them that God's kingdom was at hand, what did he mean? What is the relationship between the kingdom of heaven and life after death?

This is not the place to discuss this matter at length. The finest short discussion of this subject is by John Sanford; it was written as an introductory chapter for his popular book *The Kingdom Within*. Sanford's conclusion is based on a careful reading of today's major writers on the subject and of the best minds of the early church, thinkers who knew their Greek very well. John Sanford claims that both Jesus' view and that of the early church was that in light of the fact of Jesus' birth, life, death, resurrection, and the gift of the Holy Spirit, *the spiritual domain was radically more accessible to human beings*. The kingdom is within *and* among those of us who love, and it needs to be expressed in the here and now, but its *final* consummation will occur only in the dimension beyond space and time in the age to come. The kingdom is both present and future, partially realized now and yet fully realized only in the glorious life after death, a dimension of reality "more kind than home, more large than earth" or than the entire physical universe.[13]

The references in Figure 5 that were gathered together for *Afterlife* describe a state of being in which we can participate that is quite different from our ordinary daily existence – particularly in that it does not come to an end, that it shares God's eternity, and that it is characterized by love and never-ending growth. Removing all of these more than six hundred references (which occur in every part of the New Testament) or ignoring them means that we are trying to read our Western materialism into the New Testament narrative; we are not listening to the proclamation of Jesus, to the real meaning of the resurrection, nor to the witness of the persecuted and victorious early church.[14]

Before we go on to describe this kingdom as indeed our utter fulfillment, let us face the problem of hell, purgatory, and limbo, which were so much a part of the picture given by the institutional church for so many years. To begin with, Love never forces itself on anyone; if human beings seriously wish to remain forever in the torment of their own rebellion, God is not going to force them into the kingdom of love. But I am more optimistic than C. S. Lewis in *The Great Divorce* and *The Last Battle*; Lewis sees many people as eternally resistant to God's love. Human beings can be stubborn and ornery, but when they are wooed for eternity by Love itself, I believe that most of them will eventually capitulate. Along with Charles Williams, who eloquently presented his optimistic belief in his novel *Descent into Hell*, I cannot but believe that the love that comes to me in the depth of my despair, will continue to seek out the lost and broken even if they continue on past death in the misery of their self-absorption. St. Catherine of Genoa said that the flames of hell are only the rejected, misunderstood flames of divine love. If the nonphysical realm is as real as this one and we retain any of our free will, there is every reason to believe that God will continue through eternity to

References to Eternal Life, Resurrection, and the Kingdom of God or of Heaven in the New Testament			
	Gospels	Other New Testament Writings	Total
Eternal or everlasting life ——— *zōè aíōnios**	25	18	43
Life (in the sense of eternal, everlasting, or heavenly) ——— *zōé*	20	30	50
To live (in the sense of being resurrected, finding eternal life) ——— *záō*	9	9	18
To give life (in the sense of resurrection or eternal life) ——— *zopóieō*	1	5	6
Resurrection ——— *anástasis*	14	26	40
To rise or be raised from the dead ——— *anístemi ek nekrōn***	23	12	35
——— *egeírō ek nekrōn***	32	42	74
To bring back from the dead ——— *anágō ek nekrōn*	–	2	2
The kingdom of God ——— *basileíatoû theoû*	60	24	84
The kingdom of heaven ——— *basileía tōn oúranōn*	32	–	32
The kingdom (eternal or of heaven or God) ——— *basileía*	15	5	20
Heaven or heavenly (in the sense of God's kingdom) ——— *oúranós*	97	135	232
Immortality ——— *athanasía****	–	2	2
	328	310	638

* There are also five references in the Gospels and fifteen in the other writings to eternal habitation or house, eternal glory, salvation, inheritance, punishment, judgment, fire, destruction, etc.

** In a few instances the words "from the dead" are omitted, but are clearly implied.

*** Paul also speaks of immortality as "incorruptibility" *(aphtharsía)* in six places in his letters, but these references also contain certain of the other words listed above and are included under those headings.

encourage us to escape from the hopelessness of our own tragic, finite being and to enter into the spaciousness of divine light and love.

The New Testament has little if anything to say about purgatory. Again St. Catherine said that people are not thrown into purgatory, but that they want so much to know more of the joy and love of God that they wish to be cleansed of any stains or blemishes that keep them from full participation in that reality. To say that purgatory exists is merely to admit that even the best of us have a lot of growing and unlearning to accomplish. It is also to admit that unless most of us change radically, heaven will be boring to everyone including God.

What Is Heaven Like?

Several years ago I was meditating on what to share with my congregation on All Saints Day. As I listened, the words of the Beatitudes came alive to me; they took on a new life and meaning. I realized that in addition to presenting Jesus' view of the fulfilled life, they are giving us a picture of heaven. Jesus was telling us what heaven is like. This passage is so rich and full that I quote it in its entirety in the majestic and familiar words of the King James Version of the Bible.

Blessed are the poor in spirit; for theirs is the kingdom of heaven.
Blessed are they that mourn: for they shall be comforted.
Blessed are the meek: for they shall inherit the earth.
Blessed are they which do hunger and thirst after righteousness: for they shall be filled.
Blessed are the merciful: for they shall obtain mercy. Blessed are the pure in heart: for they shall see God.
Blessed are the peacemakers: for they shall be called the children of God.
Blessed are they which are persecuted for righteousness' sake: for theirs is the kingdom of heaven. (Matt. 5:3–10, KJV)

Jesus was preaching and teaching on a hill at the end of the Sea of Galilee telling the crowd about the human qualities that are dear to the heart of God, the qualities that will bring about our greatest fulfillment in the dimension where Divine Love dwells. Indeed, as I meditated on these powerful words, all at once I noticed that the last half of each beatitude describes what each of these qualities becomes in the fellowship of heaven.

I noticed that the conclusions to the first and the eighth of these resulting states of being are the same: "Blessed are the poor [in Greek, beggars] in spirit: for their is the *the kingdom of heaven*"; and "blessed are they who are persecuted for righteousness sake: for theirs is *the kingdom of heaven."* These two phrases form, in a sense, parentheses around six other heavenly states of being. It occurred to me, and has made sense to many people with whom I have shared this insight, that these six other statements are descriptions of the kingdom of heaven. Jesus was using these statements to describe as precisely as he could what heaven is like.

Certainly these six results given in the Beatitudes don't always, or even very frequently, occur on earth. Mourners do not always find comfort in the here and now; some die in despair. The meek do not inherit the earth. Those who hunger and thirst for food and drink often die of starvation, and those who seek righteousness sometimes end up on crosses or are thrown out of the church. And the merciful often lose their shirts, and receive rejection rather than mercy. The next two descriptions tell us that the pure in heart (or the single-minded) and the peacemakers behold God and will be called the children of God; Jesus is saying directly here—indirectly in the other beatitudes—what goes on in heaven. And from a Christian viewpoint I know of no one better equipped than Jesus to describe the nature of the beyond—in fact, people of nearly all cultures and religions agree that when it comes to matters of the spirit, Jesus stands supreme.

Let us look at each of these descriptions, these various facets of the state of being (I cannot call heaven a place without being misunderstood) known as heaven in which we can be utterly fulfilled.

There are very few of us who have not experienced sadness, sorrow, bereavement, tears, and pain. How hopeful, then, is the first promise! *Those who mourn will be comforted.* First of all, we will no longer be plagued with these frail bodies that often become more and more of a hindrance as we grow older or sicker. We will no longer have to sit beside loved ones who are sick, broken, dying. And if physical pain is terrible, it seldom compares with mental and spiritual anguish. Few people take their lives because of physical illness or pain; it is emotional torment that usually drives people to suicide. (Remember that the most painful cry from the cross was an expression of spiritual anguish: "My god, my god, why have you forsaken me?") And the first meaning of this promise-gift is that not only will our physical pain and limitations be taken away, but our fears, frustrations, and sorrows will be wiped away as well. (In Revelation, those in heaven are described as those whose tears have been wiped away.)

So this second beatitude allows us to look at the totality of human failures and successes and *know*, along with Mother Julian of Norwich that all will be well; the wounds that made us mourn will be healed, we will be given a new and richer fellowship with our beloved who have died and a joy that far outbalances any sorrow that we have had.

In the Greek in which the New Testament was written, the word for comfort is *parakaleo*. From it comes the word *paraclete*, which means comforter, a word often used to describe the Holy Spirit. People who are comforted are not just soothed and relieved of misery; they are strengthened, reconstituted, and reestablished. (The English verb "to comfort" carries some of this Greek meaning, for it means to strengthen and to give hope to another person.) The promise of the kingdom is that those who have come to the end of life and are tired and have lost their vision and courage, and even their desire to go on, are made new, refreshed, and ready to sally forth reborn, filled with the Spirit. In heaven all our grief will be assuaged; we will be recharged with a vigor that will never wear out as we step into a fantastic new reality prancing like a high spirited horse. We shall be comforted.

Although some early texts do not contain the next beatitude, it certainly expresses the spirit of Jesus of Nazareth and of the God who was willing to become a human being. The first to be commended by Jesus are the beggars in the spirit, those who know that they are not full enough yet. And these may also be the mourners of the second beatitude, since those who realize their spiritual beggarliness will surely mourn. The third beatitude gives hope to the gentle spirited, the modest, the unpretentious,, the *meek*—those who recognize their poverty in spiritual things and who mourn for themselves and for their world. They don't cast stones at others. They are not aggressive; they don't try to impose their ideas or plans on other people. They wish to serve, to minister, to love. And it is they, Jesus says, who are the earth's great heirs.

The heirs of an estate are the ones who will ultimately control and enjoy that estate; they do not have it now, but the time will come when it will be theirs. And it is the meek, Jesus said, who will inherit the earth. Heaven is very much interested in what earth becomes, and this beatitude reflects that interest. Much of the good on earth is due to those meek ones who have entered heaven and exert a gentle, hardly perceptible, but infinitely powerful, influence upon the earth. They are gradually inspiring those on earth so that more will be well. Sometimes when we look only at the misery still present in our world, we fail to see how much better conditions are than they have been—how much less slavery and oppression exist now, how much more concern for children and the hungry and sick there is now than even a hundred years ago. It is the gentle-spirited, I think, who are bringing heaven's bounty closer to realization on the earth. They help to create, and then they enjoy, human fineness.

Jesus went on to say that in the kingdom the hungry and thirsty will be filled. Heaven, then, is a state of being where seekers find what they are searching for, where they find themselves more and more *fulfilled*. Heaven is where the unsatisfied are continually being satisfied, the empty more and more filled. For many of us, our greatest human sickness is that we haven't the vaguest idea what could satisfy us; the great philosopher John Stuart Mill, when asked what would satisfy him, replied he could not imagine what would be able to meet his deepest desires. But Augustine wrote that God made us to be receivers of Divine Love, and *nothing else* can fill our need. In fact, heaven meets needs we didn't even know we had, as well as those for which we are quite consciously hungering and thirsting.

Jesus used concrete pictures to describe heaven: it is like a treasure that exceeds our wildest imagination, like a pearl so magnificent that we would sell everything we owned to possess it, like a king's banquet where every known delight is served. (Remember that Jesus was talking to people who often were continuously hungry.) But the best part of heaven goes beyond such physical images; it is a state in which we will no longer be frustrated by the pettiness, failure, guilt, alienation, loneliness, and feeling of peculiarity that are so much a part of the lives of most of us. During our lifetimes we are never able to shake these frustrations no matter how hard we try; in heaven, though, we will at last begin to become the people we always longed to be. Our self-hatred, self-condemnation, self-castigation will gradually disappear. We will be able to hit the mark at which we aim and become what we desire to be. Neither defects of personality, of mind, or of ability, nor weariness of soul or body, will get in the way of our fulfillment.

Not only will the heavenly counterpart of our physical needs to filled, but our intellectual, moral, creative, and artistic aspirations will be met as well. We will be able to see clearly into the heart and center of reality— and we will understand. To use a poet's image, we will stand before a ten-league canvas and paint with brushes of comet's hair. We will be able to convey with superb accuracy the ineffable visions of our hearts. We will be able to love and forgive, to understand, to minister to the needs of others as we longed to on earth and never quite succeeded. We will be able to slough off our pride, vanity, and resentments, our hates and dislikes, our bitterness and scornfulness. Perhaps we will even be able to enter into the divine playfulness of heaven with better games than we have ever played on earth.

The goal of heaven is infinitely increasing fulfillment. We are unable to endure all of God's grace and love at once. We will be slowly transformed until we become the kind of people we have always wanted to be. At that stage we will be given visions of new possibilities, and we will gradually move toward these and then be given new visions and new ways of fulfillment. We will be filled, satisfied, utterly and continuously, eternally, and with each new fullness we will come closer to the wholeness that is our destiny.

Christianity is the only major religion in human history that promises free forgiveness to all those who have the courage and humility to ask for it sincerely. Few of us have ever been accepted and given mercy as completely as the prodigal son is in Jesus' story. Seldom have we been so received as we came home after breaking all the rules and standards of our families, but it will be so in heaven. The justice of God finds its completion and fruition in *mercy* and *love*: these are the magic ambrosia that work miracles of transformation in normal human beings. Our psyches can be so messed up that we are unable to respond to mercy, but in heaven even these flaws will be healed. One of my most helpful prayers is the Jesus Prayer, the simple repetition of the words: "Jesus Christ, Son of God, have mercy on me, a sinner." Sometimes I simplify this prayer to: Jesus, mercy.

The Greek word most often used for mercy-compassion-forgiveness in the New Testament is *'éleos*. This word indicates feelings that produce action and bring help and healing to a pitiful situation. (The Greeks worshipped a divine being, Eleos, who embodied these qualities.) It is this Greek word that is used in the fifth beatitude: "Blessed are the merciful, for they shall obtain mercy." When we consider all the passages in the New Testament, the meaning of the word "mercy" is clear. The person to whom mercy is shown is rescued and restored, and this beatitude could be translated: blessed are the merciful, for they shall be *restored*. The truly merciful are those who can give this kind of mercy without asking anything in return.

St. John of the Cross speaks of the utter love and mercy that he received in his encounter with the Christ. Austin Farrer speaks of a similar encounter in less familiar words: "God forgives me, for he takes my head between his hands and turns my face to his to make me smile at him. And though I struggle and hurt those hands—for they are human, though divine, human and scarred with nails—though I hurt them, they do not let me go until he has smiled me into smiling; and that is the forgiveness of God."[15]

To be given mercy and to be fully loved has this joyful quality. Sometimes in our deepest meditation we can have experiences of this kind; they give us a foretaste of the life that stretches beyond death. Jesus promised that as the merciful pass through the dark night of death, they will meet just such restoring and healing mercy.

Few of us have ever been fully listened to, let alone truly loved in the fullness of mercy. Those who have been given this kind of compassion by other human beings know what it is to be reborn in this life. And we will experience such rebirth again and again in the life beyond death as new levels within our inexhaustible psyches keep opening and being transformed by mercy. Mercy is eternal, forever ongoing.

One by one these descriptions of heaven touch the depth of us like waves eroding away a granite cliff. The next beatitude praises "the pure of heart." This phrase might better be translated "the single-minded," the ones set upon a definite course with conscious determination. These are the great lovers, for who is more single-minded than the lover, the one who loves? We travel to meet our beloved, and our hearts beat faster. And finally, as we see her or him standing waiting to be greeted, our joy for the moment is complete. This beatitude promises that if we love with all our hearts, we will at last come face to face with the Love, who has created love.

In the New Testament, we are told again and again that we cannot love God if we do not love our brothers and sisters — not only our friends and our beloved, but strangers and even our enemies. The capacity to love is given us in order to draw us to God. Those who have never been head over heels in love simply can't imagine the joy and utter fulfillment that is ours when we actually know the embrace of the source of love. Many have criticized Andrew Greeley for his erotic novels, but his theology is right: passionate human love and desire are symbols to open our hearts and minds to God's infinite love for us, and God's passionate love for human beings far surpasses any human passion and desire.

The spiritual life is rhythmic in nature. We need moments of quiet ecstasy and quiet adoration, and we need times of work, action, and reaching out to others. Mercy implies action as well as feeling. The peacemakers, the subject of Jesus' next beatitude, express the *activity* needed in the spiritual life more clearly than the other qualities called blessed in the Beatitudes. And what do these peacemakers achieve in heaven? They will be called the children of God, part of the intimate family of God. (Knowing Jesus' attitude toward women and children, there can be no doubt that Jesus was referring to "children" in an intimate, familiar way.)

Children who are truly loved, love to be with their parents both in work and at play. Children who have not been ruined by our sick society are insatiable learners and doers, workers and players. Our industrial society does not give many children the opportunity to go haying with their fathers—or even to help women keepers of the home, let alone women in the marketplace or office. As children of God, however, we are God's helpers; we work on with God without weariness or fatigue. We become instruments of Divine Love. We learn the meaning of the phrase: "whose service is perfect freedom." In heaven, as children of God, our work is pure play, full of joy and fulfillment, and so we continue to grow and develop and learn and serve. And if our work is pure play, then our play is pure ecstasy. We think too seldom of the playfulness and humor of God, but religions do celebrate these aspects of the kingdom. Song, dance, and music are part of most religions. Eucharist is divine psychodrama. Jesus said that we need to be little children to enter the kingdom; children are symbols of the fulfilled life because, among other things, they share God's playfulness. As children of God we share in the spirit of John Masefield's poem:

> Laugh and be merry, remember, better the world with a song,
> Better the world with a blow in the teeth of a wrong.
> Laugh, for the time is brief, a thread the length of a span.
> Laugh and be proud to belong to the old proud pageant of man.
>
> Laugh and be merry; remember, in olden time
> God made Heaven and Earth for joy He took in a rhyme,
> Made them, and filled them full with the strong red wine of His mirth
> The splendid joy of the stars: the joy of the earth.
>
> So we must laugh and drink from the deep blue cup of the sky,
> Join the jubilant song of the great stars sweeping by,
> Laugh, and battle, and work, and drink of the wine outpoured
> In the dear green earth, the sign of the joy of the Lord.
>
> Laugh and be merry together, like brothers akin,
> Guesting awhile in the rooms of a beautiful inn.
> Glad till the dancing stops, and the lilt of the music ends.
> Laugh till the game is played; and be you merry, my friends.[16]

What is the fulfillment of heaven? It is that eternal state of being where we will be comforted, made heirs of all earth's real treasure, and have our deepest longings filled and transformed into greater longings. We shall receive pardon and mercy and love, and then know the joy of being part of the family of Love, working and playing divine games. Boethius wrote: "Heaven is the simultaneous fruition of life without bounds." It is like a bud bursting into eternal bloom, like a bloom ripening into eternal fruit, like a train emerging from a dark tunnel into the full light of day and then on to a superb alpine valley.

We can tell much about a house by the furniture in it. We can tell much about a public place by the people who frequent it. We can learn much about a country by the people from it. And we can tell much about heaven by the people whom we know are there. Heaven is the reality in which we find the kindly, humble, fine, noble, courageous, understanding, forgiving, striving, childlike, caring spirits we have loved on earth. This is their home, in which they find fulfillment and consummation.

Farewell

Death is birth into a new dimension of reality. For those who wish the transformation and fulfillment of heaven, death can be an entrance into greater joy than we can imagine. But dying is another matter; it can be painful, grim, and heart-rending for the dying and for those who watch with them. As I wrote these words, my wife and I had been watching for four months the slow physical and finally mental disintegration of a handsome and sensitive young man, our son. Paul Tournier has written that the conscious descent toward death is the supreme deprivation from an earthy point of view; the dying, therefore, need fellowship and companionship and love more than any other people.

Loneliness, aloneness, is one of the most difficult burdens that human beings can bear, and we die alone—we take the final journey all by ourselves. The importance of being with the dying can hardly be exaggerated. It prepares them for the last stage of their earthly journey. And for those who minister to them, it can be a time of self-giving that is infinitely rewarding. These four months brought us closer to each other than the three of us had ever been. It was a painful privilege, a great release, and a great loss, a grief-filled victory that leaves a deep emptiness and yet a sense of fulfillment in the two of us who are left.

One of the tasks of the shaman in many religions is to accompany the dying to the other side. Indeed, one important aspect of any religious calling has been ministering to the dying, listening to them, being willing to talk about their doubts and fears, being with them. Everything I have written about love applies particularly to our treatment of the dying: they especially need to be loved. Elisabeth Kübler-Ross awakened the medical and religious community to the fact that many of us are afraid of the dying, and we tend to shun them.

If we have not dealt with our own fear of death, we will find it difficult, if not impossible, to minister to the dying. If we basically believe that death is the end and that there is nothing beyond, it will be virtually impossible to sustain the dying with hope. Our unconscious attitude will seep through any of our efforts at being upbeat. True caring, sensitivity

to their needs, never forcing our belief systems upon them, and faithfulness are essential for ministering to the dying. And we must not mini-
mize the pain that death inflicts: even though the church's picture of the
communion of saints conveys a real truth, we on this side of death do lose
the touch and intimate physical caring that our beloved gave us when
they were alive. And we lose the closeness that touch and smile and
words gave to our beloved and to us. Death is a great divide, one through
which the dying pass alone and one that causes us deep sorrow. Is there
any greater pain than losing a partner with whom we have lived for many
years, or a child whom we have nurtured, cared for, let go and then
received back as a close friend?

And yet we must let our beloved go. I received a letter from a woman
whose son had been killed under tragic circumstances. In an early-morning
vision, the dead son returned to the women to let her know that he was
all right and that her holding on to him was stifling him. We need to strike
a balance between hanging on too tightly to the dead whom we have loved
and forgetting them, having them slip from our hearts altogether.

While I was sitting by our son's bed, the following words came to me;
I call them, "My Son at the Door of Death."

> Fear not for me. I'm not afraid.
> A new adventure awaits me,
> A new more brilliant being
> Is about to birth
> Into a different space and time.
> The garden of heaven and those abiding there
> Are calling me insistently. They want me soon.
> They sing of my courage and frustration,
> Of years of seeking, relentless searching . . .
> So many roads that petered out
> In scorching desert and burning sand
> And still I kept on, was guided.
> These voices promise
> To answer all my questions
> With love unbounded, limitless.
> They offer intimacy, closeness, far richer
> Than I had dared to hope for, and wisdom, too,
> And living water drawn from the deepest well
> That holds the secret mysteries safe
> From vain and curious wanderers.
> The voices also sing of love and loving,
> Of giving all I had and only at this moment
> Knowing that my arrow struck its mark.

Do not hold me back. I'll be with you still
In fuller measure than I've ever given.
The sun is rising from the sea
As one by one the stars are lost in light.
The broken has been mended.
I can be loved and love.
It is time to go.
Pushed beyond the limits
Of death and pain and hope,
I find the real
Eternal Love.

I read these words to him. Later he asked me for a copy of them. He shared them with a friend, saying to her: "Father understands how I feel."

When John died we had eucharist and the burial office at his bedside with the roaring of the waves as accompaniment to our words. When I watched his body leave his home by the sea, the words that Horatio spoke at Hamlet's death rose from the well of memory:

Now cracks a noble heart. Good-night, sweet prince,
And flights of angels sing thee to thy rest![17]

I spoke them to our other son who stood beside me. John was entering a new adventure. How much his faith sustained us.

Alan Paton was one of the most magnificent human beings we ever met. He combined deep religious conviction with a passion for justice and political action. He lived the message of his book *Cry, the Beloved Country*. His wife was his editor and stood with him in his political struggles in South Africa. When she died, he was devastated. He wrote out his remembrances of her as if he were talking to her. When he finished, his paralyzing grief and depression had lifted. He published this writing as a tribute to her in a book, *For You, Departed*.

In the months that have passed since our son's death, we have found that writing down our memories of our life together has given us a sense of John's presence. This writing is also bringing to completion the fellowship and intimacy that we experienced in four months of daily interaction and personal care taking. The finality and mystery of death remain, but this sharing of memories and love has not fallen unnoticed into the void. This sharing seems to be received and acknowledged by one now on the other side of the communion of saints.

We conclude these reflections on the journey with our own prayer for John's fulfillment and for our own. These words are a response to the feelings that we articulated for him and which he endorsed as his very own. A prayer that a friend sent to Paton helped him greatly. This prayer opened our hearts to a new way of praying for our beloved departed. This is our prayer for our beloved John:

O Mother-Father God, ever loving and ever living, the final reality in which all souls find their completion, rest and fulfillment, we pray for him whom you know and love far more deeply than we can even imagine. Give him your light and love for which he sought so fervently. In your mercy heal, strengthen, enlighten, and guide him as he enters the unbounded and mysterious vistas of eternity. May his immortal being reveal more and more the infinite potential of wisdom, joy, and compassion with which you endow the human soul. May he know the intimate fellowship of the children of God and become an ambassador of your caring and peace to all dimensions of your universe.

O Gracious One, let him know how much we love and miss his physical presence and long to be with him. Grant that he may be allowed to guide and guard our journey until we meet in that condition where partings cease. Until then give us a sense of his loving presence. Heal all his wounds inflicted by an insensitive and unconscious society. Let us minister in any way we can to his growth, peace, and joy. Let us do nothing that keeps us from fellowship together in the communion of saints. We ask this of you, a loving God who created us, saw our misery, came among us, suffered with us, suffered for us, and by rising again opened to us the portals of eternal life. Amen.

Notes

Chapter 2

1. Laurens van der Post, *The Face Beside the Fire* (New York: William Morrow, 1953), 79.
2. *The Comedy of Dante Alighieri: Cantica III, Paradise*, trans. Dorothy L. Sayers and Barbara Reynolds (Baltimore: Penguin Books, 1963), 347. Reprinted by permission of the translators and Penguin Books.
3. Johann Wolfgang von Goethe, *Faust*, second part, act 5, line 11935.

Chapter 4

1. Those interested in this unique program can write Don McClanen, Ministry of Money, 2 Professional Drive, Suite 220, Gaithersburg, MD 20879.

Chapter 5

1. Ronald J. Glasser, M. D., *The Body Is the Hero* (New York: Random House, 1976), 280. In *Fearfully and Wonderfully Made* (Grand Rapids, MI: Vondervan, 1980), Dr. Paul Brand and Philip Yancey describe with great sensitivity the wisdom and interrelationship of these myriad cells within the body.
2. Aldous Huxley, *The Doors of Perception* (New York: Harper & Row, 1970), 22–24.
3. Greeley, Andrew. *The Sociology of the Paranormal: A Reconnaissance* (Beverly Hills, CA: Sage Publications, 1975).
4. I am deeply grateful to Mr. Finney, who was present at my Finch Lecture at Fuller Seminary, for sharing his dissertation research on this subject. The most important resources are the many studies of R. W. Hood, Jr., in *Journal for the Scientific Study of Religion* (abbreviated below as *JSSR*), as well as the work of N. G. Holm, G. Lea, and Orlo Strunk, Jr. See Hood, *JSSR* 9:285–91; *JSSR* 13:65–71; *JSSR* 14:29–41; *JSSR* 17:279–87; Psychological Reports (1973) 33:549–50; 39:1127–2236; 44:804–6; *Review for Religious Research* 17:179 - 88; 18:264–70. See also Holm, *JSSR* 21:268–76; Lea, *Journal of Religion and Health* (1982): 336–51; and Strunk, *Mature Religion: A Psychological Study* (New York: Abingdon, 1965).
5. Robert F. Jahn, "The Persistent Paradox of Psychic Phenomena: An Engineering Perspective," *Proceedings of the Institute of Electrical and Electronic Engineers* 70, No. 2 (February 1982): 136–70.
6. I have discussed this material and the sources of it more fully in *The Christian and the Supernatural* (Minneapolis: Augsburg, 1976), *Christianity as Psychology* (Minneapolis: Augsburg, 1986), *The Encyclopedia of Religion*, s.v. "Miracles: Modern Perspectives," and *Companions on the Inner Way* (New York: Crossroad, 1984), chaps. 5 and 6.
7. In *Dreams: A Way to Listen to God* (Ramsey, NJ: Paulist, 1978), *The Other Side of Silence* (Ramsey, NJ: Paulist, 1976), and *Adventure Inward* (Minneapolis: Augsburg, 1980), I have discussed the meaning of some of these dream symbols. John Sanford gives an excellent discussion of dream symbolism in *Dreams and Healing* (Mahwah, NJ: Paulist Press, 1978)

and *Dreams: God's Forgotten Language* (San Francisco: Harper & Row, 1989). Ad de Vries provides an excellent guide to the meaning of symbols in his *Dictionary of Symbols and Imagery* (New York: Elsevier Science Publishing Co., 1984). Jung's writings on dreams have been gathered together in *Dreams* (Princteon, NJ: Princteon University Press, 1974). Many dream interpreters have no place for a relationship to the Holy and so fail to give a balanced view of dreams.

8. I have dealt with this material in *Encounter with God* (Mahwah, NJ: Paulist Press, 1988), *Christianity as Psychology*, and *Companions*, chap. 5.

9. *C. G. Jung Letters*, ed. Gerhard Adler and Aniela Jaffe (Princeton, NJ: Princteon Univ. Press, 1973), 377.

Chapter 6

1. Morton Kelsey, *Companions*, 114.

2. Barbara Kelsey has written a similar statement in Morton and Barbara Kelsey, *Sacrament of Sexuality* (Warwick, NY: Amity House, 1986), 255–65.

3. George Herbert, "Love," in *The Home Book of Verse*, ed. Burton Egbert Stevenson (New York: Henry Holt & Co., 1918), 3718.

4. Karl Jaspers, "Karl Jaspers, Existential Philosopher," in *Death to Life* (Chicago: Argus Communications, 1968), 34, 37.

5. *Complete Poems of Emily Dickenson*, ed. Thomas H. Johnson (Boston: Little, Brown and Co., 1960), 432.

Chapter 7

1. James Baldwin, quoted in Richard Coan in *Hero, Artist, Sage or Saint* (New York: Columbia University Press, 1977), 301.

2. Aldous Huxley, *Tomorrow and Tomorrow and Tomorrow, and Other Essays* (New York: Harper & Brothers, 1956), 68.

3. Robert Evans and Thomas Parker, *Christian Theology: A Case Study Approach* (New York: Harper & Row, 1976), 91.

4. There are some exceptions to this rule. Psychotics, alcoholics, and some drug abusers need to be confronted, restrained, and controlled before they can be open to the healing power of love. These controls can only be used with the greatest care. I am very suspicious of the phrase "tough love."

5. *The Comedy of Dante Alighieri: Paradise*, Canto 33, lines 143–45.

6. Nikos Kazantzakis, *Report to Greco* (New York: Simon and Schuster, 1965), 24–25.

7. Barbara has developed an expertise in the understanding and use of type theory. She describes the use of types in *Christo-Psychology* (New York: Crossroad, 1982), chap. 7.

8. I have related this story in *Caring: How Can We Love One Another?* (Ramsey, NJ: Paulist, 1981), 142 - 47.

9. This point of view is expressed well by Luciano L'Abate in her article "Intimacy Is Sharing Hurt Feelings: A Reply to David Mace," *Journal of Marriage and Family Counseling* (April 1977): 13–16.

10. Charles Whitaker, "Gatherings," *The Family Therapy Networker* 6, no. 2 (March-April 1920): 15.

11. See my book *Caring* 151-4.

12. Feodor Dostoyevsky, *Brothers Karamazov*, trans. Constance Garnett (New York: Grosset and Dunlap, n.d.), 58.

Chapter 8

1. T. S. Eliot, *The Complete Poems and Plays* (New York: Harcourt, Brace and World, 1952), 145.

2. I have addressed in depth the subject of personal journal keeping in *Adventure Inward*.

3. An excellent blank-page journal entitled *Journaliing to Recovery* created in 1989 by Barbara S. Reznicek with forward by Morton Kelsey, is produced by Abbey Press.

4. Used by permission of author, Nancy DuBois.

Chapter 9

1. I have discussed this matter in depth in *Psychology, Medicine and Christian Healing* (New York: Harper & Row, 1988).
2. Andrew M. Greeley, *The Mary Myth* (New York: Seabury Press, 1977), 183–84.
3. The best modern statements of this story are found in the C. S. Lewis trilogy of *Out of the Silent Planet, Perelandra,* and *That Hideous Strength;* in the seven novels of Charles Williams; and in J. R. R. Tolkien's *The Hobbit* and *The Lord of the Rings.* Some of them have been runaway best-sellers.
4. Quoted in Gerald O'Collins, *What Can We Say About the Ressurection?* (Ramsey, NJ: Paulist Press, 1978), 104. O'Collins goes on to summarize the Stanley method.
5. This simple sketch of the drama of evil's defeat through the death and resurrection of Jesus is the central message of Jesus and vital Christianity. I have described this story as a seven-act drama in my book *Resurrection: Release from Oppression* (Ramsey, NJ: Paulist, 1985).
6. George Buttrick, "Matthew," in *The Interpreter's Bible* (Nashville: Abingdon, 1956), 7:621.

Chapter 10

1. Amos Wilder, quoted in O'Collins, *What Can We Say About the Resurrection?,* 70.
2. Willa Cather, *Death Comes for the Archbishop* (New York: Vintage Books, 1971), 217–19.
3. Charles Darwin, quoted in Oliver Sacks, *Awakenings* (New York: E. P. Dutton, 1983), 254.
4. I have discussed this matter and provided the data for this conclusion in *Christianity as Psychology,* 42- 45.
5. I have described this process at length in *The Other Side of Silence, Adventure Inward,* and *Companions on the Inner Way.* In *The Other Side of Silence,* I have given many examples of this process in the last chapter, "Windows Inward."
6. In an unpublished manuscript, *The Road to Meaning,* Dr. Canale has given the finest description of how this kind of meditation can be used and how this practice relates to other more popular methods of dealing with depression and meaningless. He appreciates other approaches but gives evidence that continued healing seldom occurs where the religious aspect is ignored.
7. I have discussed this whole matter in detail in my book *Psychology, Medicine and Christian Healing,* and I have pointed out some of the leading medical and psychological studies supporting this view. Since then two more important books relevant to the subject have come to my attention: Andrew Weil, *Health and Healing* (Boston: Houghton Mifflin, 1988) and Oliver Sacks, *Awakenings.* Medicine and psychology that do not take into account the emotional and spiritual aspects of healing are defrauding their patients.
8. Pinchas Lapide, *The Resurrection of Jesus: A Jewish Perspective* (Minneapolis: Augsburg Publishing House, 1984), 148–49.
9. These words were given to a friend, Gloria Cushing, who was dying of cancer. The author was unknown to the one who sent them and to my knowledge they have never been published or copyrighted. Gloria's husband, Richard Cushing, sent them on to me. The original sender has since died.

Chapter 11

1. Paul Tournier, *Creative Suffering* (New York: Harper & Row, 1982), 26.
2. Gordon Kaufman, *Systematic Theology: An Historical Perspective* (New York: Charles Scribner's Sons, 1968), 464; Schubert Ogden, *The Reality of God* (London: SCM Press, 1977), 230.
3. Thomas Wolfe, *You Can't Go Home Again* (New York: Harper & Brothers, 1940), 743.
4. Richard A. Kalish and David K. Reynolds, "Phenomenological Reality and Post-Death Contact," *Journal for the Scientific Study of Religion* 12 (June 1973): 209–21.
5. In *Afterlife: The Other Side of Dying* (New York: Crossroad, 1982), I have shown the critical importance of our worldview and presented in detail the evidence for survival beyond death. And in an article entitled "Otherworlds," I have summarized the data

relating to the universality of belief in life beyond death. See *The Encyclopedia of Religion*, s.v. "Otherworlds."

6. Raymond Moody, *The Light Beyond* (New York: Bantam Books, 1988), 154 -55.

7. Caryl Porter, "Lazarus, Afterward, to His Friends," *Christian Herald*, 1 April 1977. This poem was on an unnumbered page along with table of contents.

8. J. B. Phillips, *Ring of Truth* (New York: Macmillan, 1967), 119; Ambrose, *On the Decease of Satyrus*, bk. 1, sec. 72, in *The Letters of Sulpicius Severus*, Letter 2 to the Deacon Aurelius.

9. Quoted in Morton Kelsey, *Afterlife*, 101 - 2.

10. C. G. Jung, *Memories, Dreams, Reflections* (New York: Random House, 1965), 272–73.

11. Morton Kelsey, *Afterlife*, 117.

12. *The Structure and Dynamics of the Psyche*, Collected Works, vol. 8 (Princeton, Princeton University Press, 1960), 404–14. Jung's important discussion of synchronicity follows his discussion of death. He views death not as the end of the psyche but an entrance into another dimension of reality.

13. The original editors thought that Mr. Sanford's introduction was too scholarly. It was never published until I placed it in my book *Afterlife*, 274–89.

14. My analysis of these references to the more than human life available now and hereafter is taken from *Afterlife*, 160.

15. Austin Farrer, *A Faith of Our Own* (Cleveland: World Publishing Co., 1960), 68.

16. John Masefield, *Poems* (New York: Macmillan, 1953), 51–52.

17. William Shakespeare, *Hamlet*, act V, scene 2, lines 259–60.

Selected Bibliography

The text of this book does not give support for many of the views expressed. The following books will provide evidence for those who want more information.

PSYCHOLOGY AND FULFILLMENT

GENERAL SURVEY

Coan, Richard. *Hero, Artist, Sage or Saint?: A Survey on Views on What Is Variously Called Mental Health, Normality, Maturity, Self-Actualization, and Human Fulfillment*. New York: Columbia University Press, 1977.
> An excellent survey of modern psychological theory with special reference to the optimal personality, including the religious orientation of each point of view.

CLASSIC STUDIES

Freud, Sigmund. *The Future of an Illusion*. New York: Norton, 1975.
James, William. *The Varieties of Religious Experience*. New York: Macmillan, 1961.
Jung, Carl. *Psychology and Religion: West and East*. 2d ed. of this volume of the CW, Vol. 2, *Collected Works*. Princeton, NJ: Princeton University Press, 1969. (This will be more understandable if Jung's books listed in the next section are read prior to this volume.)
> These three works are classic studies of the relationship of fulfillment and psychology.

JUNGIAN THOUGHT, CHRISTIANITY, AND THE FULFILLED LIFE

Kelsey, Morton. *Christianity as Psychology*. Minneapolis: Augsburg, 1986.
_____. *Christo-Psychology*. New York: Crossroad, 1982.
_____. *Companions on the Inner Way*. New York: Crossroad, 1984.
_____. *Prophetic Ministry*. New York: Crossroad, 1982.
_____. *Reaching for the Real*. Pecos, NM: Dove Publications, 1981.
> A simple presentation of the relationship between Jungian thought, Christianity, and the fulfilled life.

Sanford, John. *Dreams and Healing*. New York: Paulist Press, 1978.
———. *The Invisible Partners*. New York: Paulist Press, 1980.
———. *The Kingdom Within*. San Francisco: Harper & Row, 1989.
———. *The Strange Trial of Mr. Hyde*. San Francisco, Harper & Row, 1987.

MEDICINE, PSYCHOLOGY, AND MEANING

Lynch, James. *The Broken Heart*. New York: Basic Books, 1977.
———. *The Language of the Heart*. New York: Basic Books, 1986.

PSYCHOLOGICAL THOUGHT

GENERAL SURVEY

Coan, Richard. *Hero Artist, Sage or Saint?: A Survey of Views on What Is Variously Called Mental Health, Normality, Maturity, Self-Actualization, and Human Fulfillment*. New York: Columbia University Press, 1977.
    An excellent survey of the main lines of psychological thought.

SCHOOLS OF PSYCHOLOGICAL THOUGHT

Freud, Sigmund. *The Interpretation of Dreams*. New York: Avon, 1967.
———. *Introductory Lectures on Psychoanalysis*. New York: Liveright, Norton, 1977.
    These books present Freud's basic theory.
Janet Malcolm. "Trouble in the Archives." *The New Yorker*, December 5 & 12, 1983, 59–152, 60–119.
    A violent controversy has raged over the Freud Archives and is thoroughly discussed in this article.
Jung, C. G. *Memories, Dreams, Reflections*. New York: Random House, 1965.
———. *Man and His Symbols*. New York: Dell, 1968.
———. *The Tavistock Lectures, On the Theory and Practice of Analytical Psychology*. Vol. 18, *Collected Works*. Princeton, NJ: Princeton, Univ. Press, 1976.
———. *Modern Man in Search of a Soul*. New York: Harcourt Brace & World Inc., 1955.
———. *Two Essays on Analytical Psychology*. Vol. 7, *Collected Works*. Princeton, NJ: Princeton Univ. Press, 1972.
    The thought of Jung is complex. His books should be read in the above order if he is to be understood. Once these books have been read, the reader can go on to:
———. *Psychology and Religion: West and East*. 2d ed. Vol. 2, *Collected Works*. Princeton, NJ: Princeton Univ. Press, 1969.
———. *Civilization in Transition*, Vol. 10, *Collected Works*. Princeton, NJ: Princeton Univ. Press, 1964.
    Once these books have been read, the reader can go on to Jung's other works.
Konner, Melvin. *The Tangled Wing: Biological Constraints on the Human Spirit*. New York: Holt, Rinehart and Winston, 1982.
    An up-to-date presentation of the biomedical view of human beings.
Skinner, B. F. *Walden Two*. New York: Macmillan, 1948. (Out of print.)
    Behaviorism in the form of a best-selling novel.

_____. *Beyond Freedom and Dignity*. New York: Bantam, 1972.
>Presents Skinner's behavioristic theory of value.

Tageson, C. William. *Humanistic Psychology: A Synthesis*. Homewood, IL: Dorsey, 1982.
>An excellent summary of the many hues of humanistic psychology.

JUNGIAN THOUGHT AND FULFILLMENT

Clift, Wallace. *Jung and Christianity: The Challenge of Reconciliation*. New York: Crossroad, 1982.

Schaer, Hans. *Psychotherapy and the Cure of Souls in the Psychology of Jung*. New York: Pantheon, 1950. (Out of print.)

Stein, Murray. *Jung's Treatment of Christianity*. Evanston, IL: Chiron Publications, 1985.

Welch, John L. *Spiritual Pilgrims: Carl Jung and Teresa of Avila*. New York: Paulist, 1982.
>These four books are excellent studies of Jung's thought and its implications for the fulfilled life.

TOWARD A NEW WORLDVIEW

PHYSICS AND NEUROLOGY

Davies, Paul. *God and the New Physics*. New York: Simon and Schuster, 1983.
>An exploration of the latest thinking in physics.

Heisenberg, Werner. *Physics and Philosophy: The Revolution in Modern Science*. World Perspectives Series. New York: Harper & Row, 1958.
>One of the greatest physicists of all time, Heisenberg details how changes came about in physics and how this understanding can open up a new view of reality.

Kuhn, Thomas S. *The Structure of Scientific Revolutions*, 2d ed. Chicago: Univ. of Chicago press, 1970.
>By mapping the process of scientific change, Kuhn shows how new facts are revealed and thus how a new worldview emerges.

Sacks, Oliver. *Awakenings*. New York: E. P. Dutton, 1983.

_____. *A Leg to Stand On*. New York: Harper & Row, 1987.

_____. *A Man Who Mistook His Wife for a Hat*. Harper & Row, 1987.
>Sacks reaches his conclusions concerning the development of a new worldview through the study of neurology.

Toben, Bob, and Fred A. Wolfe. *Space-Time and Beyond*. New York. Bantam, 1975.
>Toben provides cartoons to make the insights of new physics comprehensible.

LANGUAGE AND LOGIC

Ayer, Alfred Jules. *Language, Truth and Logic*. 2d ed. New York: Dover, 1936.

Johnson, Kenneth G. *General Semantics: An Outline Survey*. San Francisco: International Society of General Semantics, 1972.
>Two indispensable works that delineate the uses and limitations of language and logic in our search for knowledge.

CHRISTIANITY AND A NEW WORLDVIEW

In the books below I have sketched out a new worldview; the data I present in them would not be meaningful except in terms of an open worldview.

Kelsey, Morton. *Afterlife: The Other Side of Dying* (New York: Crossroad, 1982).

_____. *Christo-Psychology*. New York: Crossroad, 1982.

_____. *Companions on the Inner Way*. (New York: Crossroad, 1984.

_____. *Encounter with God*. Mahwah, NJ: Paulist Press, 1988.

Includes a survey of the history of thought showing how we fell into the materialistic worldview. Also includes a theory of perception based in part on the work of Huxley, Lovejoy, Weil, and Whyte (see next section for bibliographic information on these works).

_____. *Psychology, Medicine and Christian Healing*. San Francisco: Harper & Row, 1988.

_____. *Prophetic Ministry: Psychology and Spirituality of Pastoral Care*. New York: Crossroad, 1982.

Küng, Hans. *Theology for the Third Millennium, An Ecumenical View*. New York: Doubleday, 1988.

A brilliant theologian attempts to construct an ecumenical theology without considering worldview and therefore has no place for religious experience as one important criterion of theology. He ignores the work of von Hügel.

PERCEPTION

The following books are excellent studies of perception:

Huxley, Aldous. *Door of Perception*. New York: Harper & Row, 1970.

Lovejoy, Arthur O. *The Revolt Against Dualism*. 2d ed. New York: Open Court, 1960.

A brilliant study of human knowing that broadens the view of how knowledge is acquired beyond what is usually recognized by our culture.

Weil, Andrew. *The Natural Mind: A New Way of Looking at Drugs and the Higher Consciousness*. Boston: Houghton Mifflin, 1972.

Suggests that we will not begin to solve the growing drug problem until we are ready to deal with the need for altered states of consciousness.

_____. *Healing and Health*. Boston: Houghton Mifflin, 1988.

States that medicine that does not deal with the human psyche and meaning is not adequate.

Whyte, Lancelot. *The Unconscious before Freud*. Classics in Psychology and Psychiatry Series. Dover, NH: Frances Pinter, 1978.

A survey of the twisting path toward recognition of a realm of largely unconscious experience and the questions raised by that recognition.

GIFTS OF THE SPIRIT AND RELIGIOUS EXPERIENCE

MANIFESTATIONS OF THE DIVINE IN THE WORLD

Almost all major religious groups have maintained that divine influences are manifested in the ordinary physical world. The following works explore this belief:

Dodds, E. R. *The Greeks and the Irrational*. Sather Classical Lectures, no. 25. Berkeley: University of California Press, 1951.

Shows that the Greeks, usually considered the paragons of rationality, were as irrational as the Hebrews and other people.

The Encyclopedia of Religion, s.v. "Miracle in the Western World."

Here I have presented a theoretical base for manifestation of divine influences in the physical world.

Kelsey, Morton. *Resurrection: Release from Oppression*. Ramsey, NJ: Paulist, 1985.

Presents a more fully developed worldview in which the resurrection of Jesus and the gifts of the Spirit are meaningful.

GIFTS OF THE SPIRIT: STUDIES

For the last twenty years, I have presented studies of the various gifts of the Spirit because no careful studies have been done within a framework that made sense in our modern world. These studies, as well as related ones, follow:

Caring, Love, and Pastoral Care

Kelsey, Morton. *Caring: How Can We Love One Another?* Ramsey, NJ: Paulist, 1981.

Explores how we can allow God's love to flow through us and make us true followers of Christ.

_____. *Prophetic Ministry: The Psychology and Spirituality of Pastoral Care*. New York: Crossroad, 1982.

Discernment of Spirits and the Subject of Evil

Kelsey, Morton. *Discernment: A Study in Ecstasy and Evil*. Ramsey, NJ: Paulist, 1978.

Healing

Kelsey, Morton. *Psychology, Medicine and Christian Healing*. New York: Harper & Row, 1988.

This book is the result of forty years of study and research.

Sacks, Oliver. *Awakenings*. New York: E. P. Dutton, 1983.

Weil, Andrew. *Health and Healing*. Boston: Houghton Mifflin, 1988.

Knowledge and Wisdom

Kelsey, Morton. *The Chritian and the Supernatural*. Minneapolis: Augsburg, 1976.

Prophecy, Tongue Speaking, and Interpretation of Tongues

Kelsey, Morton. *Tongue Speaking: The History and Meaning of Charismatic Experience*. New York: Crossroad, 1981.

Revelation

Kelsey, Morton. *Adventure Inward*. Minneapolis: Augsburg, 1980.
> Suggestions on the use of a personal journal to facilitate the experience of God.
_____. *Companions on the Inner Way*. New York: Crossroad, 1983.
> Suggestions on how to lead others to valid religious experiences.
_____. *Dreams: A Way to Listen to God*. Ramsey, NJ: Paulist, 1978.
_____. *God, Dreams and Revelation*. Minneapolis: Augsburg, 1974.
> The original edition of this book was titled *Dreams: The Dark Speech of the Spirit* (Garden City, NY: Doubleday: 1968. It contains an appendix of early Christian statements about dreams and revelation in general.
_____. *The Other Side of Silence*. Ramsey, NJ: Paulist, 1976.
> The theory and practice of how we can be open to an experience of God.

DREAMS

De Vries, A., *Dictionary of Symbols & Imagery*. 2d ed. New York: Elsevier, 1976.
> The best dictionary of dream symbols.
Jung, C. G., *Collected Works*. Princeton: Princeton Univ. Press, various dates.
> Vol. 20 of the *Collected Works* contains an index of all the dream symbols that Jung interpreted in the entire *Collected Works* and is helpful to those wishing to understand archetypal dream symbols.

An Overview of the Depth and Meaning of the Christian Faith

Greeley, Andrew. *The Mary Myth*. New York: Seabury Press, 1977.
> A fine study of the love of God for human beings.
Kelsey, Morton. *Companions on the Inner Way*. New York: Crossroad, 1982.
> The nature of mature Christianity and how we can achieve it.
_____. *Myth, History and Faith*. Ramsey, NJ: Paulist, 1974.
> The meaning and importance of myth as revelation.
_____. *Resurrection: Release from Oppression*. Ramsey, NJ: Paulist, 1985.
> Shows that the resurrection of Jesus is only meaningful in terms of the total cosmic Christian drama and then gives suggestions as to how we can enter into the fullness of resurrected life.
_____. *Transcend*. New York: Crossroad, 1981.
> A popular overview of the meaning of Christian life and experience.
Von Hügel, Friedrich. *Essays and Addresses on the Philosophy of Religion*. 2 vols. Greenwood, SC: Attic Press, 1974.
_____. *The Mystical Elements of Religion as Studied in St. Catherine of Genoa and Her Friends*. 2 vols. Greenwood, SC: Attic Press, 1961.
> Von Hügel provides one of the most sophisticated analyses of the nature, depth, and relevance of the Christian faith for modern people.

Life after Death

Greeley, Andrew. *Sociology of the Paranormal: A Reconnaissance*. Beverly Hills, CA: Sage Publications, 1975.
> Supports the data of Kalish and Reynolds' study cited below.

Kalish, Richard, and David Reynolds. "Phenomenological Reality and Post-Death Contact." *Journal for the Scientific Study of Religion* 12 (June 1973): 209–21.
> A fine study of life after death.

Kelsey, Morton. *Afterlife: The Other Side of Dying*. New York: Crossroad, 1982.
> A full study of the experimental, theological, and theoretical aspects of this mysterious subject.

Moody, Raymond, Jr. *The Light Beyond*. New York: Bantam, 1988.
> A definitive study of the near-death experience (NDE).

Osis, Karlis, and Erlendur Haraldsson. *At the Hour of Death*. New York: Avon, 1977.
> Provides a careful study of experiences of the beyond reported at the time of death.

SUFFERING, CREATIVITY, AND EVIL

Kelsey, Morton. *The Cross*. New York: Paulist, 1980.

Nolan, Christopher. *Under the Eye of the Clock: The Life Story of Christopher Nolan*. New York: St. Martin's Press, 1987.
> One of the finest accounts of overcoming suffering. Through the love and help of his family and school, this brain-damaged young man was enabled to manifest his creative genius.

Russell, Jeffrey Burton. *The Devil: Perceptions of Evil from Antiquity to Primitive Christianity*. Ithaca, N.Y.: Cornell Univ. Press, 1977.

_____. *Satan: The Early Christian Tradition*. Ithaca, N.Y.: Cornell Univ. Press, 1981.

_____. *Lucifer: The Devil in the Middle Ages*. Ithaca, N.Y.: Cornell Univ. Press, 1984.

_____. *Mephistopheles: The Devil in the Modern World*. Ithaca, N.Y.: Cornell Univ. Press, 1986.

_____. *The Prince of Darkness: Radical Evil and the Power of Good in History*. Ithaca, N.Y.: Cornell Univ. Press, 1988.
> Russell's first four listed books are the authoritative history of the idea of evil and the devil in the Western world. *The Prince of Darkness* is a summary of his findings and his conclusions regarding the reality of evil and how we can deal with it.

Tournier, Paul. *Creative Suffering*. New York: Harper & Row, 1982.
> Treats the subject of suffering with depth and understanding.